Learn To Read English With Directions In Korean
Answer Key
Classwork
Color Edition

Classwork

ISBN 978-1-945738-67-8
© 2022 – Wendy A. Charles & Alexander J. Charles
All Rights Reserved
Baldwin, New York
www.intellastic.com

All rights reserved. No portion of this book may be reproduced, stored in a retrieval system, or transmitted in any form or by any means – electronic, mechanical, photocopy, recording, video presentation, private instruction, scanning or other – except for brief quotations in critical reviews or articles, without the prior written permission of the writers.

All Rights Reserved. Printed in the USA.

Table of Contents

Unit A

Lesson 1.1	Reading Words with the Letter A/a	1
Lesson 1.2	Reading Words with the Short Vowel "a" Sound	2
Lesson 1.2	Reading & Writing Words with the Short Vowel "a" Sound	3
Lesson 1.3	Reading Words with the Long Vowel "a" Sound	4
Lesson 1.3	Reading & Writing Words with the Long Vowel "a" Sound	5
Lessons 1.2 & 1.3	Reading Short Vowel and Long Vowel Words	6
Lesson 1.4	Reading Words with the "age" Letter Combination	7
Lesson 1.5	Reading Words with the "ai" Vowel Pair	8
Lesson 1.6	Reading Letter "a" Words with the Schwa Sound	9
Lesson 1.7	Reading Words with the "ar" Letter Combination	10
Lesson 1.7	Reading Words with the "ar" Letter Combination	11
Lesson 1.8	Reading Words with a Silent Letter "a"	12
Unit Review	Reading Words with Vowel "a" Sounds: /ă/,/ā/,/ə/ & Silent	13
Lesson 1.9	Reading Multisyllable Words	14
Lesson 1.9	Reading Multisyllable Words	15
Lesson 1.10	Proper and Common Nouns and Adjectives	16

Unit B

Lesson 2.1	Reading Words with the Letter B/b	17
Lesson 2.2	Reading Words with the "br" Letter Combination	18
Lesson 2.3	Reading Words with the "bl" Letter Combination	19
Lesson 2.3	Reading Words with the "ble" Letter Combination	20
Lesson 2.4	Reading Words with the "mb" Letter Combination	21
Lesson 2.4	Reading Words with the "bt" Letter Combination	22
Lesson 2.5	Reading Words with a Silent Letter "b"	23
Lesson 2.6	Reading Multisyllable Words	24
Lesson 2.6	Reading Multisyllable Words	25
Lesson 2.7	Proper and Common Nouns and Adjectives	26

Classwork

Unit C

Lesson 3.1	Reading Words with the Letter C/c	27
Lesson 3.1	Reading Words with the Hard Letter "c"	28
Lesson 3.2	Reading Words with the Soft Letter "c"	29
Lessons 3.1 & 3.2	Reading Hard Letter "c" and Soft Letter "c" Words	30
Lesson 3.3	Reading Words with the "cr" Letter Combination	31
Lesson 3.4	Reading Words with the "cl" Letter Combination	32
Lesson 3.4	Reading Words with the "cle" Letter Combination	33
Lesson 3.5	Reading Words with the "ct" Letter Combination	34
Lesson 3.6	Reading Soft Letter "c" Words	35
Lesson 3.6	Reading Soft Letter "c" Words	36
Lesson 3.7	Reading Words with the "ch" Letter Combination	37
Lesson 3.8	Reading Words with the "cc" Letter Combination	38
Lesson 3.9	Reading Words with a Silent Letter "c"	39
Lesson 3.10	Reading Multisyllable Words	40
Lesson 3.10	Reading Multisyllable Words	41
Lesson 3.11	Proper and Common Nouns and Adjectives	42

Unit D

Lesson 4.1	Reading Words with the Letter D/d	43
Lesson 4.2	Reading Letter "d" Words with the /d/ Sound & /j/ Sound	44
Lesson 4.2	Reading Words with the "dr" Letter Combination	45
Lesson 4.3	Reading Words with the "ed" Suffix/ Past Tense Verbs	46
Lesson 4.4	Reading Words with a Silent Letter "d"	47
Lesson 4.5	Reading Multisyllable Words	48
Lesson 4.5	Reading Multisyllable Words	49
Lesson 4.6	Proper and Common Nouns and Adjectives	50

Unit E

Lesson 5.1	Reading Words with the Letter E/e	51
Lesson 5.2	Reading Words with the Short Vowel "e" Sound	52
Lesson 5.2	Reading & Writing Words with the Short Vowel "e" Sound	53

Lesson 5.3	Reading Words with the Long Vowel "e" Sound	54
Lesson 5.3	Reading & Writing Words with the Long Vowel "e" Sound	55
Lessons 5.2 & 5.3	Reading Short Vowel and Long Vowel Words	56
Lesson 5.4	Reading Words with Letter "e" Vowel Pairs	57
Lesson 5.5	Reading Words with the Final Letter "e"	58
Lesson 5.6	Reading Letter "e" Words with the Schwa Vowel Sound	59
Lesson 5.7	Reading Words with the "er" Letter Combination	60
Lesson 5.8	Reading Words with the "eu" and "ew" Letter Combinations	61
Lesson 5.9	Reading Words with the "ey" Letter Combination	62
Lesson 5.10	Reading Words with a Silent Letter "e"	63
Unit Review	Reading Words with Vowel "e" Sounds: /ĕ/, /ē/, /ə/ & Silent	64
Lesson 5.11	Reading Multisyllable Words	65
Lesson 5.11	Reading Multisyllable Words	66
Lesson 5.12	Proper and Common Nouns and Adjectives	67

Unit F

Lesson 6.1	Reading Words with the Letter F/f	68
Lesson 6.2	Reading Words with the "fr" Letter Combination	69
Lesson 6.3	Reading Words with the "fl" Letter Combination	70
Lesson 6.3	Reading Words with the "fle" Letter Combination	71
Lesson 6.4	Reading Words with the "ft," "lf" and "ff" Letter Combinations	72
Lesson 6.5	Reading Words with a Silent Letter "f"	73
Lesson 6.6	Reading Singular and Plural forms of Words Ending in "-f" & "-fe"	74
Lesson 6.7	Reading Multisyllable Words	75
Lesson 6.7	Reading Multisyllable Words	76
Lesson 6.8	Proper and Common Nouns and Adjectives	77

Unit G

Lesson 7.1	Reading Words with the Letter G/g	78
Lesson 7.1	Reading Words with the Hard Letter "g"	79
Lesson 7.2	Reading Words with the Soft Letter G/g	80
Lessons 7.1 & 7.2	Reading Hard Letter "g" and Soft Letter "g" Words	81

Classwork

Lessons 7.1 & 7.2	Reading Hard Letter "g" and Soft Letter "g" Words	82
Lesson 7.3	Reading Words with the "gr" Letter Combination	83
Lesson 7.4	Reading Words with the "gl" Letter Combination	84
Lesson 7.4	Reading Words with the "gle" Letter Combination	85
Lesson 7.5	Reading Words with the "gh" Letter Combination	86
Lesson 7.6	Reading Words with the "gn" Letter Combination	87
Lesson 7.7	Reading Words with a Silent Letter "g"	88
Lesson 7.8	Reading Multisyllable Words	89
Lesson 7.8	Reading Multisyllable Words	90
Lesson 7.9	Proper and Common Nouns and Adjectives	91

Unit H

Lesson 8.1	Reading Words with the Letter H/h	92
Lesson 8.2	Reading Words with the Letter "h" Combinations: "sh," "wh," "ch," "th," "rh," "ph" and "gh"	93
Lesson 8.2	Reading Words with the Letter "h" Combinations: "sh," "wh," "ch," "th," "rh," "ph," "gh" and "sch"	94
Lesson 8.3	Reading Words with a Silent Letter "h"	95
Lesson 8.4	Reading Multisyllable Words	96
Lesson 8.4	Reading Multisyllable Words	97
Lesson 8.5	Proper and Common Nouns and Adjectives	98

Unit I

Lesson 9.1	Reading Words with the Letter I/i	99
Lesson 9.2	Reading Words with the Short Vowel "i" Sound	100
Lesson 9.2	Reading & Writing Words with the Short Vowel "i" Sound	101
Lesson 9.3	Reading Words with the Long Vowel "i" Sound	102
Lesson 9.3	Reading & Writing Words with the Long Vowel "i" Sound	103
Lessons 9.2 & 9.3	Reading Short Vowel and Long Vowel Words	104
Lesson 9.4	Reading Words with Letter "i" Vowel Pairs	105
Lesson 9.5	Reading Words with the Final Letter "i"	106
Lesson 9.6	Reading Letter "i" Words with the Schwa Vowel Sound	107

Lesson 9.7	Reading Words with the "ir" Letter Combination	108
Lesson 9.8	Reading Letter "i" Words with the Long Vowel "e" Sound	109
Lesson 9.9	Reading Words with a Silent Letter "i"	110
Unit Review	Reading Words with Vowel "i" Sounds: /ĭ/, /ī/, /ə/ & Silent	111
Lesson 9.10	Reading Multisyllable Words	112
Lesson 9.10	Reading Multisyllable Words	113
Lesson 9.11	Proper and Common Nouns and Adjectives	114

Unit J

Lesson 10.1	Reading Words with the Letter J/j	115
Lesson 10.2	Reading Multisyllable Words	116
Lesson 10.2	Reading Multisyllable Words	117
Lesson 10.3	Proper and Common Nouns and Adjectives	118

Unit K

Lesson 11.1	Reading Words with the Letter K/k	119
Lesson 11.2	Reading Words with the Letter "k" and "ck" Letter Combination	120
Lesson 11.3	Reading Words with the "kle" Letter Combination	121
Lesson 11.4	Reading Words with a Silent Letter "k"	122
Lesson 11.5	Reading Multisyllable Words	123
Lesson 11.5	Reading Multisyllable Words	124
Lesson 11.6	Proper and Common Nouns and Adjectives	125

Unit L

Lesson 12.1	Reading Words with the Letter L/l	126
Lesson 12.2	Reading Words with the Letter "l" Combinations: "fl," "pl" & "sl"	127
Lesson 12.3	Reading Words with a Silent Letter "l"	128
Lesson 12.4	Reading Multisyllable Words	129
Lesson 12.4	Reading Multisyllable Words	130
Lesson 12.5	Proper and Common Nouns and Adjectives	131

Classwork

Unit M

Lesson 13.1	Reading Words with the Letter M/m	132
Lesson 13.2	Reading Words with a Silent Letter "m"	133
Lesson 13.3	Reading Multisyllable Words	134
Lesson 13.3	Reading Multisyllable Words	135
Lesson 13.4	Proper and Common Nouns and Adjectives	136

Unit N

Lesson 14.1	Reading Words with the Letter N/n	137
Lesson 14.2	Reading Words with the "ng" Letter Combination	138
Lesson 14.3	Reading Words with a Silent Letter "n"	139
Lesson 14.4	Reading Multisyllable Words	140
Lesson 14.4	Reading Multisyllable Words	141
Lesson 14.5	Proper and Common Nouns and Adjectives	142

Unit O

Lesson 15.1	Reading Words with the Letter O/o	143
Lesson 15.2	Reading Words with the Short Vowel "o" Sound	144
Lesson 15.2	Reading & Writing Words with the Short Vowel "o" Sound	145
Lesson 15.3	Reading Words with the Long Vowel "o" Sound	146
Lesson 15.3	Reading & Writing Words with the Long Vowel "o" Sound	147
Lessons 15.2 & 15.3	Reading Short Vowel and Long Vowel Words	148
Lesson 15.4	Reading Words with Letter "o" Vowel Pairs	149
Lesson 15.5	Reading Words with the Final Letter "o"	150
Lesson 15.6	Reading Letter "o" Words with the Schwa Vowel Sound	151
Lesson 15.7	Reading Words with Vowel "o" Sounds: /ŏ/, /ō/ & /$\overline{oo}$/	152
Lesson 15.8	Reading Words with the "or" Letter Combination	153
Lesson 15.8	Reading Words with the "or" Letter Combination	154
Lesson 15.9	Reading Words with a Silent Letter "o"	155
Unit Review	Reading Words with Vowel "o" Sounds: /ŏ/, /ō/, /ə/ & Silent	156
Lesson 15.10	Reading Multisyllable Words	157
Lesson 15.10	Reading Multisyllable Words	158

| Lesson 15.11 | Proper and Common Nouns and Adjectives | 159 |

Unit P

Lesson 16.1	Reading Words with the Letter P/p	160
Lesson 16.2	Reading Words with the "ph" Letter Combination	161
Lesson 16.3	Reading Words with the "pr" Letter Combination	162
Lesson 16.4	Reading Words with the "pl" Letter Combination	163
Lesson 16.4	Reading Words with the "ple" Letter Combination	164
Lesson 16.5	Reading Words with a Silent Letter "p"	165
Lesson 16.6	Reading Multisyllable Words	166
Lesson 16.6	Reading Multisyllable Words	167
Lesson 16.7	Proper and Common Nouns and Adjectives	168

Unit Q

Lesson 17.1	Reading Words with the Letter Q/q	169
Lesson 17.2	Reading Words with the Letter "q" and "qu" Letter Combination	170
Lesson 17.2	Reading Words with the "qu" Letter Combination	171
Lesson 17.3	Reading Multisyllable Words	172
Lesson 17.3	Reading Multisyllable Words	173
Lesson 17.4	Proper and Common Nouns and Adjectives	174

Unit R

Lesson 18.1	Reading Words with the Letter R/r	175
Lesson 18.2	Reading Words with the Letter "r" Combinations: "br," "cr," "dr," "fr," "gr," "pr" and "tr"	176
Lesson 18.3	Reading Multisyllable Words	177
Lesson 18.3	Reading Multisyllable Words	178
Lesson 18.4	Proper and Common Nouns and Adjectives	179

Unit S

| Lesson 19.1 | Reading Words with the Letter S/s | 180 |
| Lesson 19.1 | Reading Words with the Letter S/s | 181 |

Classwork

Lesson 19.2	Reading Words with the "sion," "sial" & "scious" Suffixes	182
Lesson 19.3	Reading Words with the "sch" Letter Combination	183
Lesson 19.4	Reading Words with the "scr," "shr," "spr" & "str" Letter Combinations	184
Lesson 19.5	Reading Words with the "sl" & "sle" Letter Combinations	185
Lesson 19.5	Reading Words with the "sle" Letter Combination	186
Lesson 19.6	Reading Words with the "sm" Letter Combination	187
Lesson 19.7	Reading Words with the "ss" Letter Combination	188
Lesson 19.8	Reading Words with a Silent Letter "s"	189
Lesson 19.9	Reading Multisyllable Words	190
Lesson 19.9	Reading Multisyllable Words	191
Lesson 19.10	Proper and Common Nouns and Adjectives	192

Unit T

Lesson 20.1	Reading Words with the Letter T/t	193
Lesson 20.2	Reading Words with the "thm" Letter Combination	194
Lesson 20.3	Reading Words with the "tion," "tial" & "tious" Suffixes	195
Lesson 20.4	Reading Words with the "tr" Letter Combination	196
Lesson 20.5	Reading Words with the "tle" Letter Combination	197
Lesson 20.6	Reading Words with the Letter "t" Sounds	198
Lesson 20.7	Reading Words with a Silent Letter "t"	199
Lesson 20.8	Reading Multisyllable Words	200
Lesson 20.8	Reading Multisyllable Words	201
Lesson 20.9	Proper and Common Nouns and Adjectives	202

Unit U

Lesson 21.1	Reading Words with the Letter U/u	203
Lesson 21.2	Reading Words with the Short Vowel "u" Sound	204
Lesson 21.2	Reading & Writing Words with the Short Vowel "u" Sound	205
Lesson 21.3	Reading Words with the Long Vowel "u" Sound	206
Lesson 21.3	Reading & Writing Words with the Long Vowel "u" Sound	207
Lessons 21.2 & 21.3	Reading Short Vowel and Long Vowel Words	208
Lesson 21.4	Reading Words with Letter "u" Vowel Pairs	209

Lesson 21.5	Reading Words with the Final Letter "u"	210
Lesson 21.6	Reading Letter "u" Words with the Schwa Vowel Sound	211
Lesson 21.7	Reading Words with the "ur" Letter Combination	212
Lesson 21.8	Reading Words with a Silent Letter "u"	213
Unit Review	Reading Words with Vowel "u" Sounds: /ŭ/, /o͞o/, /ə/ & Silent	214
Lesson 21.9	Reading Multisyllable Words	215
Lesson 21.9	Reading Multisyllable Words	216
Lesson 21.10	Proper and Common Nouns and Adjectives	217

Unit V

Lesson 22.1	Reading Words with the Letter V/v	218
Lesson 22.2	Reading Multisyllable Words	219
Lesson 22.2	Reading Multisyllable Words	220
Lesson 22.3	Proper and Common Nouns and Adjectives	221

Unit W

Lesson 23.1	Reading Words with the Letter W/w	222
Lesson 23.2	Reading Words with a Vowel before the Letter "w"	223
Lesson 23.3	Reading Words with a Silent "w" and "wr" Letter Combination	224
Lesson 23.3	Reading Words with a Silent Letter "w"	225
Lesson 23.4	Reading Multisyllable Words	226
Lesson 23.4	Reading Multisyllable Words	227
Lesson 23.5	Proper and Common Nouns and Adjectives	228

Unit X

Lesson 24.1	Reading Words with the Letter X/x	229
Lesson 24.1	Reading Words with the Letter X/x	230
Lesson 24.2	Reading Multisyllable Words	231
Lesson 24.2	Reading Multisyllable Words	232
Lesson 24.3	Proper and Common Nouns and Adjectives	233

Classwork

Unit Y

Lesson 25.1	Reading Words with the Letter Y/y	234
Lesson 25.1	Reading Words with the Letter Y/y	235
Lesson 25.2	Reading Words with a Vowel before the Letter "y"	236
Lesson 25.3	Reading Words with the "cy" Letter Combination	237
Lesson 25.4	Reading Words with the Final Letter "y"	238
Lesson 25.5	Reading Words with the "yr" Letter Combination	239
Lesson 25.6	Reading Letter "y" Words with the Schwa Sound	240
Lesson 25.7	Reading Words with a Silent Letter "y"	241
Lesson 25.8	Reading Multisyllable Words	242
Lesson 25.8	Reading Multisyllable Words	243
Lesson 25.9	Proper and Common Nouns and Adjectives	244

Unit Z

Lesson 26.1	Reading Words with the Letter Z/z	245
Lesson 26.1	Reading Words with the Letter Z/z	246
Lesson 26.2	Reading Words with a Silent Letter "z"	247
Lesson 26.3	Reading Multisyllable Words	248
Lesson 26.3	Reading Multisyllable Words	249
Lesson 26.4	Proper and Common Nouns and Adjectives	250

Appendix

Appendix 1.0	Introduction of the Letter A/a	251
Appendix 2.0	Introduction of the Letter B/b	252
Appendix 2.0	Letter Recognition B/b	253
Appendix 3.0	Introduction of the Letter C/c	254
Appendix 3.0	Letter Recognition C/c	255
Appendix 4.0	Introduction of the Letter D/d	256
Appendix 4.0	Letter Recognition D/d	257
Appendix 5.0	Introduction of the Letter E/e	258
Appendix 6.0	Introduction of the Letter F/f	259
Appendix 6.0	Letter Recognition F/f	260

Appendix 7.0	Introduction of the Letter G/g	261
Appendix 7.0	Letter Recognition G/g	262
Appendix 8.0	Introduction of the Letter H/h	263
Appendix 8.0	Letter Recognition H/h	264
Appendix 9.0	Introduction of the Letter I/i	265
Appendix 10.0	Introduction of the Letter J/j	266
Appendix 10.0	Letter Recognition J/j	267
Appendix 11.0	Introduction of the Letter K/k	268
Appendix 11.0	Letter Recognition K/k	269
Appendix 12.0	Introduction of the Letter L/l	270
Appendix 12.0	Letter Recognition L/l	271
Appendix 13.0	Introduction of the Letter M/m	272
Appendix 13.0	Letter Recognition M/m	273
Appendix 14.0	Introduction of the Letter N/n	274
Appendix 14.0	Letter Recognition N/n	275
Appendix 15.0	Introduction of the Letter O/o	276
Appendix 16.0	Introduction of the Letter P/p	277
Appendix 16.0	Letter Recognition P/p	278
Appendix 17.0	Introduction of the Letter Q/q	279
Appendix 17.0	Letter Recognition Q/q	280
Appendix 18.0	Introduction of the Letter R/r	281
Appendix 18.0	Letter Recognition R/r	282
Appendix 19.0	Introduction of the Letter S/s	283
Appendix 19.0	Letter Recognition S/s	284
Appendix 20.0	Introduction of the Letter T/t	285
Appendix 20.0	Letter Recognition T/t	286
Appendix 21.0	Introduction of the Letter U/u	287
Appendix 22.0	Introduction of the Letter V/v	288
Appendix 22.0	Letter Recognition V/v	289
Appendix 23.0	Introduction of the Letter W/w	290
Appendix 23.0	Letter Recognition W/w	291

Classwork

Appendix 24.0	Introduction of the Letter X/x	292
Appendix 24.0	Letter Recognition X/x	293
Appendix 25.0	Introduction of the Letter Y/y	294
Appendix 25.0	Letter Recognition Y/y	295
Appendix 26.0	Introduction of the Letter Z/z	296
Appendix 26.0	Letter Recognition Z/z	297

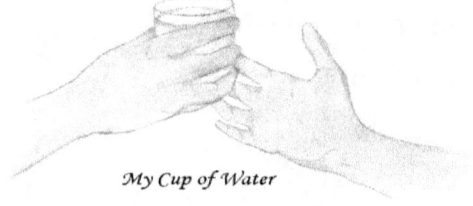

My Cup of Water

Name: _____ Date: ___/___/_____ Score: _____

Lesson 1.1

Reading Words with the Letter A/a

✓ **Lesson Check Point**

Directions: Read each target word. Find the letter "a" and put a check (✓) in the column that identifies its position: beginning, within or end.
지도: 각 대상 단어를 읽으십시오. 문자 "a"를 찾아 해당 위치를 나타내는 열에 확인 표시(✓)를 하십시오: 시작, 내부 또는 끝.

Target Words	Beginning (First Letter)	Within	End (Last Letter)
1. taxicab		✓	
2. black		✓	
3. anklet	✓		
4. opera			✓
5. above	✓		

Directions: Read each target word. Read the words in the row and circle the word that has a different vowel "a" sound.
지도: 각 대상 단어를 읽으십시오. 행에 있는 단어를 읽고 모음 "a" 소리가 다른 단어에 동그라미를 치십시오.

Target Words				
6. am	cat	sand	(pail)	bank
7. apple	cab	(sofa)	back	sad
8. happy	band	ant	sank	(cake)
9. pants	(zebra)	sat	cap	man
10. thanks	cash	(bake)	map	pan

Classwork

 Name: _____ Date:___/___/_____ Score:_____

Lesson 1.2

Reading Words with the Short Vowel "a" Sound

✓ **Lesson Check Point**

 **Directions:** Read the words in the four boxes. Circle two words with the short vowel /ă/ sound. The anchor word for the short vowel /ă/ sound is <u>apple</u>.

지도: 네 개의 상자에 있는 단어를 읽으십시오. 짧은 모음 /ă/ 소리로 두 단어에 동그라미를 치십시오. 단모음 /ă/ 소리의 앵커 워드는 apple입니다.

day	(hat)	(grass)	(nap)	agree	(yam)
(cap)	sofa	tuna	lake	(sand)	paint

Asia	(pad)	walk	father	(flag)	(man)
ago	(back)	(flap)	(map)	grape	bake

Directions: Read the words in the four boxes. Circle two words that rhyme. Rhyming words have the same ending sound, such as <u>tap</u> and <u>map</u>.

지도: 네 개의 상자에 있는 단어를 읽으십시오. 운이 맞는 두 단어에 동그라미를 치십시오. 운율이 있는 단어는 tap 및 map과 같이 끝 소리가 같습니다.

(had)	tax	(nap)	cake	(camp)	(lamp)
(dad)	zap	cape	(map)	spa	alike

away	plane	game	(cat)	take	(tan)
(ran)	(man)	(sat)	lane	ate	(ran)

Learn To Read English With Directions In Korean

Name: _____ Date: ___/___/_____ Score: _____

Lesson 1.2

Reading & Writing Words with the Short Vowel "a" Sound

✓ **Lesson Check Point**

Directions: Read each sentence and underline three words with the short vowel /ă/ sound. Then, write the underlined words on the lines below. The anchor word for the short vowel /ă/ sound is apple.

지도: 각 문장을 읽고 세 단어에 짧은 모음 /ă/ 소리에 밑줄을 긋습니다. 그런 다음 밑줄 친 단어를 아래 줄에 쓰십시오. 단모음 /ă/ 소리의 기준어는 appple입니다.

Model

Ann raised her hand in class.

Ann	hand	class

1. Pam's tan hat is faded.

| Pam's | tan | hat |

2. My father asked for apples and grapes.

| asked | apples | and |

3. Sam and Dan walked by the lake.

| Sam | and | Dan |

4. David planted the flag in the sand.

| planted | flag | sand |

5. My music teacher plays the sax in a large jazz band.

| sax | jazz | band |

Learn To Read English With Directions In Korean

Classwork

Name: _____ Date:___/___/_____ Score: _____

Lesson 1.3

Reading Words with the Long Vowel "a" Sound

✓ Lesson Check Point

Directions: Read the words in the four boxes. Circle two words with the long vowel /ā/ sound. The anchor word for the long vowel /ā/ sound is <u>ape</u>.

지도: 네 개의 상자에 있는 단어를 읽으십시오. 장모음 /ā/ 소리로두단어에 동그라미를 치십시오. 장모음 /ā/ 소리의 기준어는 ape입니다.

cap	(sale)		alike	cat		(ate)	sofa
talk	(nail)		(gain)	(pace)		(wave)	tap

rat	(lake)		(page)	(mate)		(stay)	above
(male)	ago		pan	about		alone	(sail)

Directions: Read the words in the four boxes. Circle two words that rhyme. Rhyming words have the same ending sound, such as <u>wait</u> and <u>date</u>.

지도: 네 개의 상자에 있는 단어를 읽으십시오. 운이 맞는 두 단어에 동그라미를 치십시오. 운율이 있는 단어는 wait 및 date와 같이 끝 소리가 같습니다.

mama	(wake)		tuna	(lane)		land	puma
(take)	ban		dad	(cane)		(rate)	(late)

(came)	man		(tale)	Asia		(pave)	(gave)
(same)	panda		bran	(mail)		villa	have

Learn To Read English With Directions In Korean

Name: _____ Date: ___/___/_____ Score: _____

Lesson 1.3

Reading & Writing Words with the Long Vowel "a" Sound

✓ Lesson Check Point

Directions: Read each sentence and underline three words with the long vowel /ā/ sound. Then, write the underlined words on the lines below. The anchor word for the long vowel /ā/ sound is ape.

지도: 각 문장을 읽고 장모음 /ā/ 소리로 세 단어에 밑줄을 긋습니다. 그런 다음 밑줄 친 단어를 아래 줄에 쓰십시오. 장모음 /ā/ 소리의 기준어는 ape입니다.

Model

Ann has grapes and cake on her plate.

grapes   cake   plate
_____   _____   _____

1. Dain can't wait to paint the chair.

   Dain   wait   paint
   _____   _____   _____

2. The skates and sails are packed in the basement.

   skates   sails   basement
   _____   _____   _____

3. Alvin did not take the large slice of cake from the plate.

   take   cake   plate
   _____   _____   _____

4. Dale Anderson said, "Beware of garter snakes by the lake."

   Dale   snakes   lake
   _____   _____   _____

5. Jackson and Andrew sold chocolate cupcakes at Annie's bake sale.

   cupcakes   bake   sale
   _____   _____   _____

Learn To Read English With Directions In Korean   5

Classwork

Name: _____ Date: ___/___/_____ Score: _____

Review Lessons 1.2 & 1.3

Reading Short Vowel and Long Vowel Words

Directions: Read the target words in the word box. In the first column, write the words that have the short vowel /ă/ sound, as in the word apple. In the second column, write the words that have the long vowel /ā/ sound, as in the word ape.

지도: 단어 상자에 있는 대상 단어를 읽습니다. 첫 번째 열에는 apple이라는 단어에서와 같이 단모음 /ă/ 소리가 나는 단어를 씁니다. 두 번째 열에는 장모음이 포함된 단어를 쓰십시오 /ā/ 소리, 단어 ape에서와 같이.

Target Word Box				
bagel	grass	glad	clan	basic
trap	came	taken	grapes	hat
fame	maps	sand	stay	gain
slaps	bake	train	flag	brand

Letter "a" has the /ă/ sound as in the word apple

- hat
- glad
- clan
- trap
- flag
- grass
- sand
- slaps
- maps
- brand

Letter "a" has the /ā/ sound as in the word ape

- gain
- stay
- came
- bake
- train
- fame
- basic
- bagel
- taken
- grapes

 Name: _____ Date: ___/___/_____ Score: _____

Lesson 1.4

Reading Words with the "age" Letter Combination

✓ Lesson Check Point

 **Directions:** Read each target word. Find the "age" letter combination and put a check (✓) in the column that correctly identifies its sounds.
지도: 각 대상 단어를 읽으십시오. "age" 문자 조합을 찾아 해당 소리를 올바르게 식별하는 열에 체크(✓)를 하십시오.

Target Words	"age" has the /ā/ + /j/ sounds as in the word stage	"age" has the /ĭ/ + /j/ sounds as in the word package	"age" has the /ä/ + /j/ or /ä/ + /zh/ sounds as in the word massage
1. camouflage			✓
2. Anchorage		✓	
3. enrage	✓		
4. baggage		✓	
5. teenagers	✓		

 **Directions:** Read each sentence and underline the word that has an "age" letter combination that has the /ĭ/ + /j/ sounds, as in the word package.
지도: 각 문장을 읽고 단어 package에서와 같이 /ĭ/ + /j/ 소리가 나는 "age" 문자 조합이 있는 단어에 밑줄을 긋습니다.

6. The teenager's albums and books are in the <u>cottage</u>.

7. The teenager's <u>luggage</u> set was stolen from the airport.

8. My large boxes from <u>Anchorage</u>, Alaska are on the stage.

9. The backstage <u>manager</u> ate apple pie and drank lemonade.

10. Everyone in the entourage had massages after their long <u>voyage</u>.

Classwork

 Name: _____ Date:___/___/_____ Score:_____

Lesson 1.5

Reading Words with the "ai" Vowel Pair

✓ Lesson Check Point

 Directions: Read each target word. Circle the word in the column that has the same "ai" sound as the target word.
지도: 각 대상 단어를 읽으십시오. 목표 단어와 같은 "ai" 소리가 나는 열의 단어에 동그라미를 치십시오.

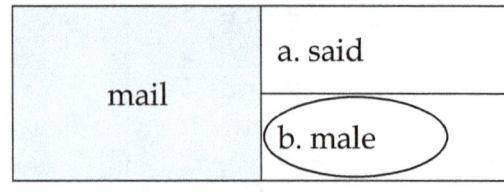

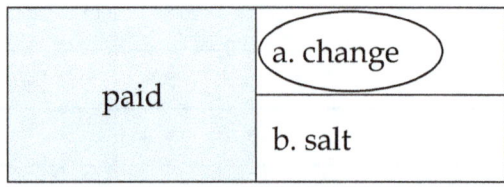

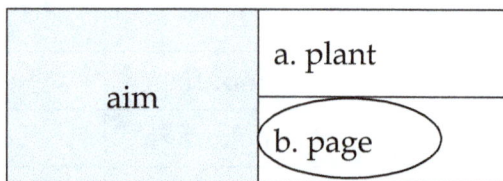

 Directions: Read each target word. Put a check (✓) under the correct column heading.
지도: 각 대상 단어를 읽으십시오. 올바른 열제목 아래에 체크(✓)를 하십시오.

Target Words	Words have the long "a" sound as in the word <u>sail</u>	Words do not have the long "a" sound
1. tail	✓	
2. trait	✓	
3. plaid		✓
4. pain	✓	

Name: _____ Date:___/___/_____ Score:_____

Lesson 1.6

Reading Letter "a" Words with the Schwa Vowel Sound

✓ Lesson Check Point

 Directions: Read each target word. Circle the word in the column that has the same "a" sound as the target word.
지도: 각 대상 단어를 읽으십시오. 대상 단어와 동일한"a"소리가 나는 열의 단어에 동그라미를 치십시오.

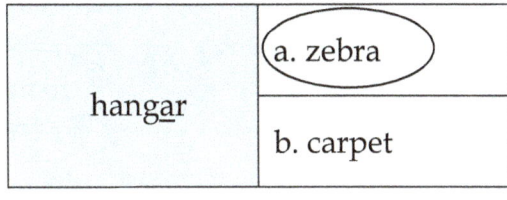
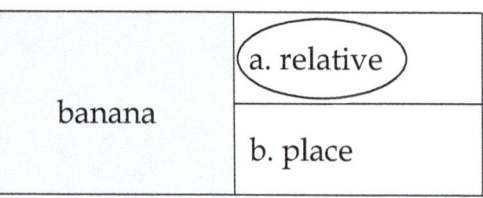
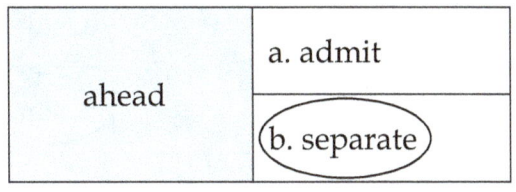
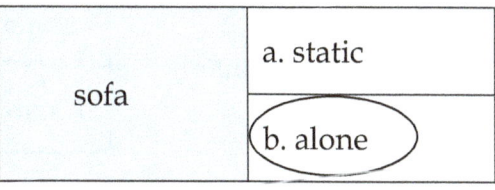

 Directions: Read each sentence and underline the letter "a" word that has the schwa vowel /ə/ sound. The anchor word for the letter "a" schwa vowel sound is sofa.
지도: 각 문장을 읽고 슈와 모음 /ə/ 소리가 있는 문자"a" 단어에 밑줄을 긋습니다. 문자"a" 슈와 모음 소리의 앵커 단어는 sofa입니다.

1. The class is going to the <u>opera</u>.

2. The Erie <u>Canal</u> is an awesome place.

3. On Saturday, Ann ate two large <u>bananas</u>.

4. This year, I have an <u>amazing</u> math teacher.

5. Dr. Anderson paid the cab driver three <u>dollars</u>.

6. Andrew ate whole wheat <u>spaghetti</u> with white sauce.

Classwork

 Name: _____ Date: ___/___/_____ Score: _____

Lesson 1.7

Reading Words with the "ar" Letter Combination

✓ Lesson Check Point

 **Directions:** Read each target word. Circle the word in the column that has the same "a" + "r" sounds as the target word.
지도: 각 대상 단어를 읽으십시오. 해당 열에 있는 단어에 동그라미를치십시오. 대상 단어와 동일한 "a" + "r" 소리가 있습니다.

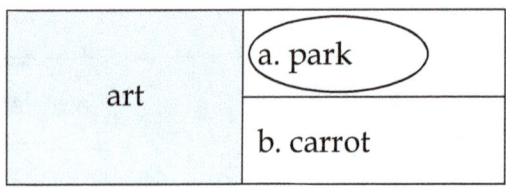

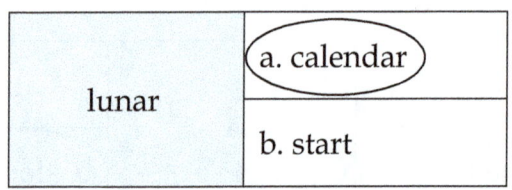

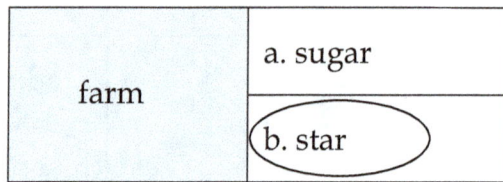

 **Directions:** Read each target word. Put a check (✓) under the correct column heading.
지도: 각 대상 단어를 읽으십시오. 올바른 열 제목 아래에 체크(✓)를하십시오.

Target Words	"ar" has the /ă/ + /r/ sounds as in the word <u>baron</u>	"ar" has the /ə/ + /r/ sounds as in the word <u>dollar</u>	"ar" has the /ä/ + /r/ sounds as in the word <u>car</u>	"ar" has the /ô/ + /r/ sounds as in the word <u>war</u>
1. art			✓	
2. marry	✓			
3. lunar		✓		
4. farm			✓	

 Name: _____ Date: ___/___/_____ Score: _____

Lesson 1.7

Reading Words with the "ar" Letter Combination

Dictionary Skills/ Vocabulary

✓ **Lesson Check Point**

 Directions: Read each target word and its definition. Write the target word on the line in front of its meaning. Use a dictionary or the Internet to check your answers.
지도: 각 대상 단어와 그 정의를 읽으십시오. 의미 앞 줄에 대상단어 를 쓰십시오. 사전이나 인터넷을 사용하여 답을 확인하십시오.

Target Word Box				
Oscar	narrator	party	paramedics	garlic

1. _party_   a fun gathering where people socialize
2. _paramedics_   medical professionals
3. _Oscar_   a boy or man's name
4. _garlic_   an edible plant that looks like a bulb
5. _narrator_   a person who tells the events of the story

 Directions: Read each sentence and write the target word that correctly completes the sentence.
지도: 각 문장을 읽고 다음과 같은 목표 단어를 쓰십시오. 장을 올바르게 완성합니다.

6. Baroness invited all her friends to the ___party___.

7. _Oscar_ registered for classes at the registrar's office.

8. The dynamic ___narrator___ dramatically read the play's stage directions.

9. I enhanced the flavor of the soup by adding vinegar and ___garlic___.

10. The skilled ___paramedics___ saved Arty's life by administering CPR.

Classwork

 Name: _____ Date:___/___/_____ Score:_____

Lesson 1.8

Reading Words with a Silent Letter "a"

✓ Lesson Check Point

 Directions: Read the target words in the word box. Write the words that have a silent letter "a" in the first column. Write the words that do not have a silent letter "a" in the second column.

지도: 단어 상자에 있는 대상 단어를 읽습니다. 첫 번째 열에 묵음 문자"a"가 있는 단어를 쓰십시오. 두 번째 열에 묵음 문자"a"가 없는 단어를 쓰십시오.

Target Word Box				
floats	pain	dragon	aisle	goats
games	broad	oasis	sandy	anthills
beauty	oats	days	raining	crash
central	gloating	bread	bureau	boating

Letter "a" is silent

- oats
- aisle
- goats
- broad
- beauty
- floats
- bread
- bureau
- boating
- gloating

Letter "a" has a letter "a" sound

- pain
- crash
- days
- oasis
- sandy
- games
- anthills
- raining
- dragon
- central

Learn To Read English With Directions In Korean

 Name: _____ Date: ___/___/_____ Score: _____

Unit Review - A/a

Reading Words with Vowel "a" Sounds: /ă/, /ā/, /ə/ & Silent

✓ **Lesson Check Point**

 Directions: Read each target word. Circle the word in the column that has the same "a" sound as the target word.

지도: 각 대상 단어를 읽으십시오. 대상 단어와 동일한 "a" 소리가 나는 열의 단어에 동그라미를 치십시오.

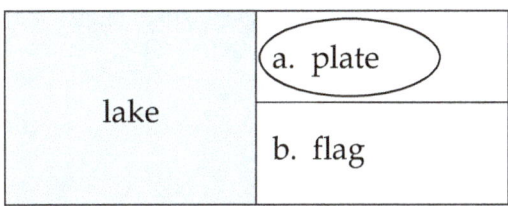

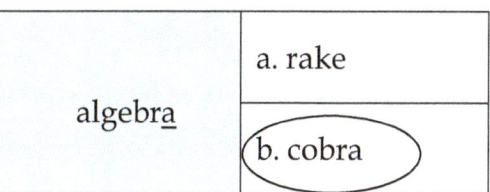

 Directions: Read each target word. Put a check (✓) under the correct column heading.

지도: 각 대상 단어를 읽으십시오. 올바른 열 제목 아래에 체크(✓)를 하십시오.

Target Words	"a" has the /ă/ sound as in the word <u>apple</u>	"a" has the /ā/ sound as in the word <u>ate</u>	"a" has the /ə/ sound as in the word <u>sofa</u>	"a" is silent as in the word <u>boat</u>
1. lake		✓		
2. plant	✓			
3. past<u>a</u>			✓	
4. algebr<u>a</u>			✓	

Classwork

Name: _____ Date: ___/___/_____ Score: _____

The Reading Challenge

Lesson 1.9

Reading Multisyllable Words

 Lesson Check Point

 Directions: Read and divide each target word into syllables. Write each word and place a hyphen (-) between the syllables in the second column. Write the number of syllables in the third column. Use a dictionary or the Internet to check your answers.

지도: 각 대상 단어를 읽고 음절로 나눕니다. 각 단어를 쓰고 두 번째 열의 음절 사이에 하이픈(-)을 넣습니다. 세 번째 열에 음절 수를 쓰십시오. 사전이나 인터넷을 사용하여 답을 확인하십시오.

Target Words	Words Divided into Syllables	Number of Syllables
1. payback	pay-back	2
2. slogan	slo-gan	2
3. turban	tur-ban	2
4. abdomen	ab-do-men	3
5. batman	bat-man	2
6. husband	hus-band	2
7. Alaskan	A-las-kan	3
8. Scotland	Scot-land	2
9. embanking	em-bank-ing	3
10. migrated	mi-grat-ed	3

 Name: _____ Date:___/___/_____ Score:_____

The Reading Challenge

Lesson 1.9

Reading Multisyllable Words

✓ **Lesson Check Point**

 **Directions:** Read each target word. Circle the word in the row that is divided correctly into syllables. Use a dictionary or the Internet to check your answers.
지도: 각 대상 단어를 읽으십시오. 음절로 올바르게 나누어진 행에 있는 단어에 동그라미를 치십시오. 사전이나 인터넷을 사용하여 답을 확인하십시오.

Model

| important | (a. im-por-tant) | b. im-port-ant | c. im-porta-nt |

| 1. diploma | (a. di-plo-ma) | b. di-plom-a | c. dip-lom-a |

| 2. absolute | a. a-bso-lute | b. a-bsol-ute | (c. ab-so-lute) |

| 3. admonish | a. adm-o-nish | b. a-dmon-ish | (c. ad-mon-ish) |

| 4. magistrate | (a. mag-is-trate) | b. mag-i-strate | c. ma-gis-trate |

| 5. kilogram | a. ki-lo-gram | b. ki-log-ram | (c. kil-o-gram) |

| 6. caravan | a. ca-rav-an | (b. car-a-van) | c. car-av-an |

| 7. admiral | a. ad-mir-al | (b. ad-mi-ral) | c. a-dmir-al |

| 8. monogram | a. mo-no-gram | b. mo-nog-ram | (c. mon-o-gram) |

Learn To Read English With Directions In Korean   15

Classwork

 Name: _____ Date: ___/___/_____ Score: _____

Lesson 1.10

Reading and Writing

Proper and Common Nouns and Adjectives

✓ Lesson Check Point

 **Directions:** Read the words in the word box. Put an (X) on the line next to each word that is written incorrectly. Remember that all proper nouns and proper adjectives are capitalized. Use a dictionary or the Internet to check your answers.

지도: 단어 상자에 있는 단어를 읽으십시오. 잘못 쓰여진 각 단어 옆의 줄에 (X)를 표시하십시오. 모든 고유 명사와 고유 형용사는 대문자임을 기억하십시오. 사전이나 인터넷을 사용하여 답을 확인하십시오.

Word Box					
__	August	__	Argentina	X	Author
X	Achievers	__	advanced	__	adventure
X	apollo	X	athens	__	America
__	airmail	X	alaska	X	ArubA

 **Directions:** Read each unedited sentence and underline the word that is written incorrectly. Write each sentence correctly on the line.

지도: 편집되지 않은 각 문장을 읽고 잘못 쓰여진 단어에 밑줄을긋습 니다. 각 문장을 줄에 올바르게 쓰십시오.

Model

Andrew has a view of the <u>atlantic</u> Ocean from his apartment.
<u>Andrew has a view of the Atlantic Ocean from his apartment.</u>

1. Anne and <u>alex</u> are from Australia.
<u>Anne and Alex are from Australia.</u>

2. The <u>Author's</u> article, "Awaken," is amazing.
<u>The author's article, "Awaken," is amazing.</u>

3. Mr. <u>aaron</u> got a lot of cash from the ATM.
<u>Mr. Aaron got a lot of cash from the ATM.</u>

4. In <u>august</u>, Ashley will attend Ace Academy.
<u>In August, Ashley will attend Ace Academy.</u>

Name: _____ Date: ___/___/_____ Score: _____

Lesson 2.1

Reading Words with the Letter B/b

✓ **Lesson Check Point**

 Directions: Read each target word. Find the letter "b" and put a check (✓) in the column that identifies its position: beginning, within or end.
지도: 각 대상 단어를 읽으십시오. 문자"b"를 찾아 위치를 나타내는열: 시작, 내부 또는 끝에 체크(✓)를 하십시오.

Target Words	Beginning (First Letter)	Within	End (Last Letter)
1. cab			✓
2. bit	✓		
3. table		✓	
4. tab			✓
5. bottom	✓		

 Directions: Read each sentence and underline the words that begin with the letter "b." Write all the underlined words in alphabetical order on the lines below.
지도: 각 문장을 읽고"b"로 시작하는 단어에 밑줄을 긋습니다. 밑줄친모든단어를 아래 줄에 알파벳 순서로 쓰십시오.

6. Andy's <u>bat</u> is <u>black</u>.

7. He has a <u>belt</u> and a <u>billfold</u>.

8. There is a cat on the <u>baby's</u> <u>bib</u>.

9. Abe and Andy are in the <u>big</u> <u>band</u>.

10. Annie and Aaron have the <u>best</u> <u>books</u>.

baby's _____   band _____   bat _____
belt _____   best _____   bib _____
big _____   billfold _____   black _____
                   books _____

Classwork

Name: _____ Date: ___/___/_____ Score: _____

Lesson 2.2

Reading Words with the "br" Letter Combination

Dictionary Skills/ Vocabulary

✓ **Lesson Check Point**

Directions: Read each target word and its definition. Write the letter of the definition on the line of each target word. Use a dictionary or the Internet to check your answers.

지도: 각 대상 단어와 그 정의를 읽으십시오. 각 대상 단어의 행에 정의의 문자를 씁니다. 사전이나 인터넷을 사용하여 답을 확인하십시오.

Target Words	Definitions
1. _c_ brags	a. a large country on the South American continent
2. _a_ Brazil	b. a physical injury without an open cut
3. _d_ broccoli	c. to say something in a boastful way
4. _e_ bridal	d. a green vegetable with densely clustered flower buds
5. _b_ bruise	e. something or someone pertaining to a wedding

Directions: Read each sentence. Underline the word in the parentheses that correctly completes each sentence. Then, write the underlined word on the line.

지도: 각 문장을 읽으십시오. 각 문장을 올바르게 완성하는 괄호 안에 있는 단어에 밑줄을 긋습니다. 그런 다음 밑줄 친 단어를 줄에 쓰십시오.

6. The bride has a nice _____bridal_____ dress. (<u>bridal</u>, brags)

7. The _____bruise_____ on Betsy's back is black. (Brazil, <u>bruise</u>)

8. I ate _____broccoli_____ and bread for breakfast. (bruise, <u>broccoli</u>)

9. Brenda _____brags_____ about her brand new boat. (<u>brags</u>, broccoli)

10. Do you know that _____Brazil_____ is a big country? (bruise, <u>Brazil</u>)

Name: _____ Date: ___/___/_____ Score: _____

Lesson 2.3

Reading Words with the "bl" Letter Combination

Dictionary Skills/ Vocabulary

✓ Lesson Check Point

 Directions: Read each target word and its definition. Write the target word on the line in front of its meaning. Use a dictionary or the Internet to check your answers.

지도: 각 대상 단어와 그 정의를 읽으십시오. 의미 앞 줄에 대상단어 를 쓰십시오. 사전이나 인터넷을 사용하여 답을 확인하십시오.

Target Word Box				
blanket	blasted	bleed	blender	blinks

1. <u>bleed</u>   the flow of blood out of a blood vessel
2. <u>blender</u>   a machine that mixes things together
3. <u>blinks</u>   the quick closing and opening movement of eyes
4. <u>blasted</u>   to have shot something out with great force
5. <u>blanket</u>   a large cloth covering used to cover a bed

 Directions: Read each sentence. Underline the word in the parentheses that correctly completes each sentence. Then, write the underlined word on the line.

지도: 각 문장을 읽으십시오. 각 문장을 올바르게 완성하는 괄호 안에 있는 단어에 밑줄을 긋습니다. 그런 다음 밑줄 친 단어를 줄에 쓰십시오.

6. My big rocket <u> blasted </u> off. (blinks, <u>blasted</u>)

7. Bill blends bananas in his <u> blender </u>. (blanket, <u>blender</u>)

8. Bethany <u> blinks </u> her big, brown eyes. (bleed, <u>blinks</u>)

9. Betty puts a big, blue <u> blanket </u> on her bed. (<u>blanket</u>, blender)

10. The big blade cut Bill and made him <u> bleed </u>. (<u>bleed</u>, blasted)

Classwork

 Name: _____ Date: ___/___/_____ Score: _____

Lesson 2.3

Reading Words with the "ble" Letter Combination

✓ Lesson Check Point

 Directions: Read each target word. Find the "ble" letter combination and put a check (✓) in the column that identifies its position: beginning, within or end.

지도: 각 대상 단어를 읽으십시오. "ble" 문자 조합을 찾아 위치를 식별하는 열에 체크(✓)를 하십시오: 시작, 내부 또는 끝.

Target Words	Beginning (First 3 Letters)	Within	End (Last 3 Letters)
1. table			✓
2. problem		✓	
3. bleach	✓		
4. adorable			✓
5. scribbler		✓	

 Directions: Read each target word. Put a check (✓) in the "yes" column if the "ble" letter combination has the /b/ + /ə/ + /l/ sounds. Put a check (✓) in the "no" column if the "ble" letter combination does not have the /b/ + /ə/ + /l/ sounds.

지도: 각 대상 단어를 읽으십시오. "ble" 문자 조합에/b/ + /ə/ + /l/ 소리가 있는 경우 "yes" 열에 체크(✓)를 하십시오. "ble" 문자 조합에/b/ + /ə/ + /l/ 소리가 없으면 "no"열에 체크(✓)를 하십시오.

Target Words	Yes	No
6. bleed		✓
7. bleach		✓
8. babble	✓	
9. agreeable	✓	
10. collectible	✓	

 Name: _____ Date: ___/___/_____ Score: _____

Lesson 2.4

Reading Words with the "mb" Letter Combination

✓ **Lesson Check Point**

 Directions: Read each target word. Circle the word in the column that has the same "mb" sound(s) as the target word.
지도: 각 대상 단어를 읽으십시오. 대상 단어와 동일한 "mb" 소리가 있는 열의 단어에 동그라미를 치십시오.

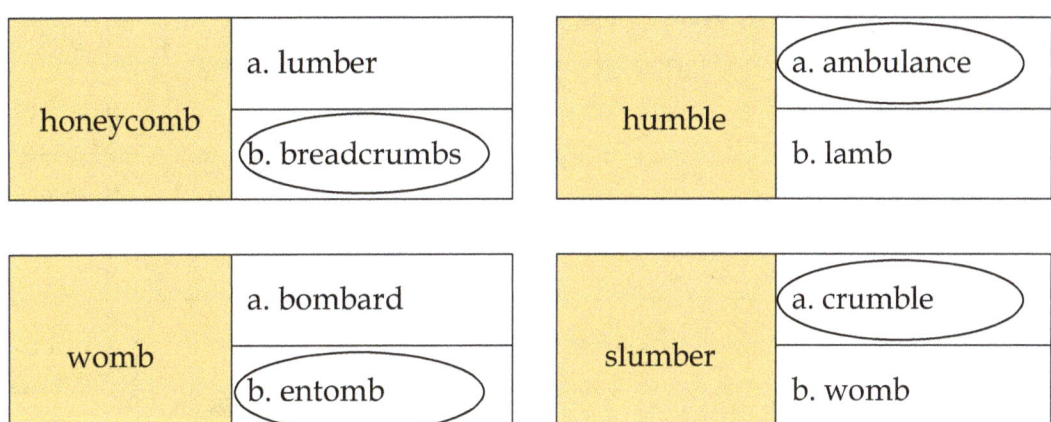

 Directions: Read each target word. In the second column, write the number of letters in the word. In the third column, write the number of letters heard in the word.
지도: 각 대상 단어를 읽으십시오. 두 번째 열에는 단어의 글자 수를 씁니다. 세 번째 열에는 단어에서 들리는 글자 수를 쓰십시오.

Target Words	Number of letters in the word	Number of letters heard
1. combat	6	6
2. climber	7	6
3. limbs	5	4
4. lumber	6	6

Classwork

 Name: _____ Date:___/___/_____ Score:_____

Lesson 2.4

Reading Words with the "bt" Letter Combination

✓ **Lesson Check Point**

 Directions: Read each target word. Circle the word in the column that has the same "bt" sound(s) as the target word.

지도: 각 대상 단어를 읽으십시오. 대상 단어와 동일한 "bt" 소리가 있는 열의 단어에 동그라미를 치십시오.

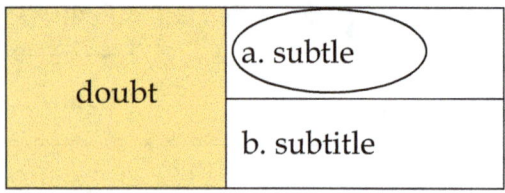

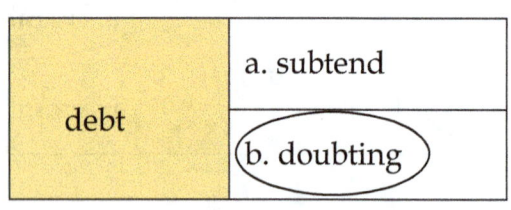
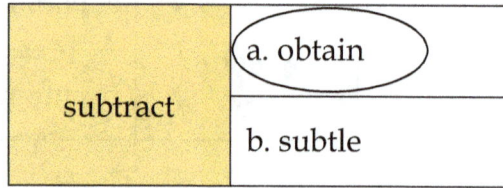

 Directions: Read each target word. In the second column, write the number of letters in the word. In the third column, write the number of letters heard in the word.

지도: 각 대상 단어를 읽으십시오. 두 번째 열에는 단어의 글자 수를 씁니다. 세 번째 열에는 단어에서 들리는 글자 수를 쓰십시오.

Target Words	Number of letters in the word	Number of letters heard
1. doubt	5	4
2. subtext	7	7
3. debt	4	3
4. subtract	8	8

Name: _____   Date: ___/___/_____   Score: _____

Lesson 2.5

Reading Words with a Silent "b"

✓ **Lesson Check Point**

 Directions: Read the target words in the word box. Write the words that have a silent letter "b" in the first column. Write the words that do not have a silent letter "b" in the second column.

지도: 단어 상자에 있는 대상 단어를 읽습니다. 첫 번째 열에 묵음 문자 "b"가 있는 단어를 쓰십시오. 두 번째 열에 묵음 문자 "b"가 없는 단어를 쓰십시오.

Target Word Box				
labels	climbing	bread	zebra	subpoena
thumbs	bugs	debt	crumb	lamb
abandon	plumbers	basement	ability	bedroom
combs	brother	entomb	books	limbs

Letter "b" is silent	Letter "b" has the /b/ sound
debt	labels
crumb	books
limbs	bugs
lamb	ability
thumbs	bread
entomb	zebra
combs	brother
climbing	abandon
plumbers	basement
subpoena	bedroom

Learn To Read English With Directions In Korean

Classwork

 Name: _____ Date: ___/___/_____ Score: _____

The Reading Challenge

Lesson 2.6

Reading Multisyllable Words

✓ **Lesson Check Point**

 Directions: Read and divide each target word into syllables. Write each word and place a hyphen (-) between the syllables in the second column. Write the number of syllables in the third column. Use a dictionary or the Internet to check your answers.

지도: 각 대상 단어를 읽고 음절로 나눕니다. 각 단어를 쓰고 두 번째 열의 음절 사이에 하이픈(-)을 넣습니다. 세 번째 열에 음절 수를 쓰십시오. 사전이나 인터넷을 사용하여 답을 확인하십시오.

Target Words	Words Divided into Syllables	Number of Syllables
1. balance	bal-ance	2
2. submit	sub-mit	2
3. sublet	sub-let	2
4. bigwig	big-wig	2
5. banana	ba-nan-a	3
6. obstacle	ob-sta-cle	3
7. biceps	bi-ceps	2
8. tablet	tab-let	2
9. beckon	beck-on	2
10. blanket	blan-ket	2

 Name: _____ Date:___/___/_____ Score:_____

The Reading Challenge

Lesson 2.6

Reading Multisyllable Words

✓ **Lesson Check Point**

 Directions: Read each target word. Circle the word in the row that is divided correctly into syllables. Use a dictionary or the Internet to check your answers.

지도: 각 대상 단어를 읽으십시오. 음절로 올바르게 나누어진 행에 있는 단어에 동그라미를 치십시오. 사전이나 인터넷을 사용하여 답을 확인하십시오.

Model

| because | (a. be-cause) | b. beca-use | c. b-ecause |

| 1. bachelor | a. bac-he-lor | (b. bach-e-lor) | c. ba-ch-elor |

| 2. backpack | (a. back-pack) | b. ba-ckpa-ck | c. ba-ckp-ack |

| 3. bellboy | a. be-llboy | b. bellb-oy | (c. bell-boy) |

| 4. blackout | a. bla-ckout | (b. black-out) | c. bl-ackout |

| 5. bicycle | a. bi-cycle | (b. bi-cy-cle) | c. bicy-cle |

| 6. baritone | a. ba-ri-tone | b. ba-rit-one | (c. bar-i-tone) |

| 7. bracelet | a. bracel-et | b. bra-celet | (c. brace-let) |

| 8. bumblebee | (a. bum-ble-bee) | b. bumb-le-bee | c. bu-mbleb-ee |

Classwork

Name: _____ Date: ___/___/_____ Score: _____

Lesson 2.7

Reading and Writing

Proper and Common Nouns and Adjectives

✓ **Lesson Check Point**

Directions: Read the words in the word box. Put an (X) on the line next to each word that is written incorrectly. Remember that all proper nouns and proper adjectives are capitalized. Use a dictionary or the Internet to check your answers.

지도: 단어 상자에 있는 단어를 읽으십시오. 잘못 쓰여진 각 단어 옆의 줄에 (X)를 표시하십시오. 모든 고유 명사와 고유 형용사는 대문자임을 기억하십시오. 사전이나 인터넷을 사용하여 답을 확인하십시오.

Word Box					
__	Bolivia	X	BuBBle	__	absent
__	barber	__	bottom	X	BarBados
X	Bread	__	bread	__	bridges
X	buckingham	X	bulB	X	bahamas

Directions: Read each unedited sentence and underline the word that is written incorrectly. Write each sentence correctly on the line.

지도: 편집되지 않은 각 문장을 읽고 잘못 쓰여진 단어에 밑줄을긋습 니다. 각 문장을 줄에 올바르게 쓰십시오.

Model
<u>brandon's</u> books are about big boats.
<u>Brandon's books are about big boats.</u>

1. The black <u>Bat</u> is really big.
<u>The black bat is really big.</u>

2. <u>bob</u> has a brown bag.
<u>Bob has a brown bag.</u>

3. The blue <u>taBle</u> is too big.
<u>The blue table is too big.</u>

4. <u>benjamin's</u> baked bread is in his bag.
<u>Benjamin's baked bread is in his bag.</u>

Name: _____ Date: ___/___/_____ Score: _____

Lesson 3.1

Reading Words with the Letter C/c

✓ Lesson Check Point

Directions: Read each target word. Find the letter "c" and put a check (✓) in the column that identifies its position: beginning, within or end.
지도: 각 대상 단어를 읽으십시오. 문자 "c"를 찾아 위치를 나타내는 열: 시작, 내부 또는 끝에 체크(✓)를 하십시오.

Target Words	Beginning (First Letter)	Within	End (Last Letter)
1. clog	✓		
2. toxic			✓
3. tackle		✓	
4. basic			✓
5. picture		✓	

Directions: Read each sentence and underline the words that begin with the letter "c." Write all the underlined words in alphabetical order on the lines below.
지도: 각 문장을 읽고 "c"로 시작하는 단어에 밑줄을 긋습니다. 밑줄 친 모든 단어를 아래 줄에 알파벳 순서로 쓰십시오.

6. The big <u>cows</u> are <u>cute</u>.

7. The black <u>car</u> is very <u>clean</u>.

8. The <u>child</u> is in the blue <u>crib</u>.

9. Bobby has a <u>cap</u> and a big <u>coat</u>.

10. The boys are <u>chasing</u> the <u>chicken</u>.

cap _____   car _____   chasing _____
chicken _____ child _____   clean _____
coat _____   cows _____   crib _____
                     cute _____

Learn To Read English With Directions In Korean

Unit C
Lesson 3.1

Classwork

Name: _____ Date: ___/___/_____ Score: _____

Lesson 3.1

Reading Words with the Hard Letter "c"

✓ **Lesson Check Point**

Directions: Read each target word. Put a check (✓) under the correct column heading.

지도: 각 대상 단어를 읽으십시오. 올바른 열 제목 아래에 체크(✓)를 하십시오.

Target Words	Hard "c" has the /k/ sound as in the word <u>cat</u>	Soft "c" has the /s/ sound as in the word <u>cell</u>
1. school	✓	
2. cleaning	✓	
3. cement		✓
4. civilized		✓
5. character	✓	

Directions: Read each sentence and underline the words that have the hard "c" sound, as in the word <u>cat</u>. Write all the underlined words in alphabetical order on the lines below.

지도: 각 문장을 읽고 단어 cat에서와 같이 단단한"c" 소리가 나는 단어에 밑줄을 긋습니다. 아래 줄에 밑줄 친 단어를 알파벳 순서로 모두 쓰십시오.

6. Ms. <u>Clarke's</u> big chips are <u>crunchy</u>.

7. The <u>cake</u> has a <u>caramel</u> apple center.

8. Andrew is chewing <u>cranberry</u> <u>candy</u>.

9. Cindy is <u>counting</u> the <u>crabs</u> in the bowl.

10. Everyone in my <u>class</u> had a bowl of ice <u>cream</u>.

cake_____	candy_____	caramel_____
Clarke's_____	class_____	counting_____
crabs_____	cranberry_____	cream_____
	crunchy_____	

Unit C Lesson 3.1

Learn To Read English With Directions In Korean

Name: _____ Date: ___/___/_____ Score: _____

Lesson 3.2

Reading Words with the Soft Letter "c"

Directions: Read each target word. Put a check (✓) under the correct column heading.

지도: 각 대상 단어를 읽으십시오. 올바른 열 제목 아래에 체크(✓)를 하십시오.

Target Words	Hard "c" has the /k/ sound as in the word <u>cat</u>	Soft "c" has the /s/ sound as in the word <u>cell</u>
1. face		✓
2. curl	✓	
3. cast	✓	
4. city		✓
5. clue	✓	

Directions: Read each sentence and underline the words that have the soft "c" sound, as in the word <u>cell</u>. Write all the underlined words in alphabetical order on the lines below.

지도: 각 문장을 읽고 cell이라는 단어에서처럼 부드러운 "c" 소리가 나는 단어에 밑줄을 긋습니다. 아래 줄에 밑줄 친 단어를 알파벳 순서로 모두 쓰십시오.

6. <u>City</u> Hall is in the <u>center</u> of Clarkston.

7. <u>Lucy</u> said, "The comedian is a <u>cynic</u>."

8. Caleb said, "We live in a <u>civilized</u> <u>society</u>."

9. The baby in the crib ate cranberry and <u>cinnamon</u> <u>cereal</u>.

10. I stored my <u>bicycles</u> and <u>ceramic</u> casserole dishes in the den.

<u>bicycles</u>   <u>center</u>   <u>ceramic</u>
<u>cereal</u>   <u>cinnamon</u>   <u>City</u>
<u>civilized</u>   <u>cynic</u>   <u>Lucy</u>
                     <u>society</u>

Classwork

Name: _____ Date: ___/___/_____ Score: _____

Review Lessons 3.1 & 3.2

Reading Hard Letter "c" and Soft Letter "c" Words

 Directions: Read the target words in the word box. In the first column, write the words with the letter "c" that have the /k/ sound, as in the word <u>cat</u>. In the second column, write the words with the letter "c" that have the /s/ sound, as in the word <u>cell</u>.

지도: 단어 상자에 있는 대상 단어를 읽으십시오. 첫 번째 열에는 cat라는 단어에서와 같이 /k/ 소리가 나는 문자"c"가 있는 단어를 씁니다. 두 번째 열에는 cell이라는 단어에서와 같이 /s/ 소리가 나는 문자"c"가 있는 단어를 씁니다.

Target Word Box				
cause	cook	citizen	city	curb
curve	mice	cute	code	citrus
cedar	cube	cake	call	spicy
coil	cysts	place	cease	cent

Hard letter "c" has the /k/ sound as in the word <u>cat</u>

- call
- coil
- code
- cook
- cube
- cute
- curb
- cake
- curve
- cause

Soft letter "c" has the /s/ sound as in the word <u>cell</u>

- cent
- city
- mice
- cysts
- cedar
- place
- cease
- citrus
- spicy
- citizen

 Name: _____ Date: ___/___/_____ Score: _____

Lesson 3.3

Reading Words with the "cr" Letter Combination

Dictionary Skills/ Vocabulary

✓ Lesson Check Point

 Directions: Read each target word and its definition. Write the letter of the definition on the line of each target word. Use a dictionary or the Internet to check your answers.
지도: 각 대상 단어와 그 정의를 읽으십시오. 각 대상 단어의 행에 정의의 문자를 씁니다. 사전이나 인터넷을 사용하여 답을 확인하십시오.

Target Words	Definitions
1. _d_ cranberry	a. to really want something, such as food
2. _a_ craving	b. to move along the ground on hands and knees
3. _b_ crawls	c. a thick dairy product made from milk
4. _c_ cream	d. a small, tart, red berry-like fruit
5. _e_ crumbs	e. small pieces of bread or other baked goods

 Directions: Read each sentence. Underline the word in the parentheses that correctly completes each sentence. Then, write the underlined word on the line.
지도: 각 문장을 읽으십시오. 각 문장을 올바르게 완성하는 괄호 안에 있는 단어에 밑줄을 긋습니다. 그런 다음 밑줄 친 단어를 줄에 쓰십시오.

6. The cats ate the cookie __crumbs__. (crawls, <u>crumbs</u>)

7. Cindy's ice __cream__ is very cold. (<u>cream</u>, craving)

8. The baby __crawls__ on the carpet. (<u>crawls</u>, cream)

9. I have a __craving__ for cotton candy. (<u>craving</u>, cranberry)

10. Chad likes to drink __cranberry__ juice. (crumbs, <u>cranberry</u>)

Classwork

L Name: _____ Date: ___/___/_____ Score: _____

Lesson 3.4

Reading Words with the "cl" Letter Combination

Dictionary Skills/ Vocabulary

✓ **Lesson Check Point**

Directions: Read each target word and its definition. Write the target word on the line in front of its meaning. Use a dictionary or the Internet to check your answers.

지도: 각 대상 단어와 그 정의를 읽으십시오. 의미 앞 줄에 대상단어 를 쓰십시오. 사전이나 인터넷을 사용하여 답을 확인하십시오.

Target Word Box				
cleared	cliff	clipped	clock	closet

1. __cliff__ the overhanging of a mountain
2. __clock__ a device used to display time
3. __closet__ a small inner room used for clothing and storage
4. __cleared__ to have moved something out of the way
5. __clipped__ to fasten or grip with a firm metal or plastic clamp

Directions: Read each sentence. Underline the word in the parentheses that correctly completes each sentence. Then, write the underlined word on the line.

지도: 각 문장을 읽으십시오. 각 문장을 올바르게 완성하는 괄호 안에 있는 단어에 밑줄을 긋습니다. 그런 다음 밑줄 친 단어를 줄에 쓰십시오.

6. Chad cleaned out his bedroom ___closet___. (<u>closet</u>, cliff)

7. Charles ___cleared___ the clogged drain. (<u>cleared</u>, closet)

8. Yesterday, we climbed up the steep ___cliff___. (clipped, <u>cliff</u>)

9. I ___clipped___ my index cards on the clipboard. (<u>clipped</u>, clock)

10. This morning, my alarm ___clock___ woke me up. (<u>clock</u>, cleared)

Name:  Date:___/___/_____ Score:_____

Lesson 3.4

Reading Words with the "cle" Letter Combination

✓ Lesson Check Point

Directions: Read each target word. Find the "cle" letter combination and put a check (✓) in the column that identifies its position: beginning, within or end.

지도: 각 대상 단어를 읽으십시오. "cle" 문자 조합을 찾아 위치를 식별 하는열에 체크(✓)를 하십시오: 시작, 내부 또는 끝.

Target Words	Beginning (First 3 Letters)	Within	End (Last 3 Letters)
1. article			✓
2. cleaning	✓		
3. inclement		✓	
4. particle			✓
5. cleverly	✓		

Directions: Read each target word. Put a check (✓) in the "yes" column if the "cle" letter combination has the /k/ + /ə/ + /l/ sounds. Put a check (✓) in the "no" column if the "cle" letter combination does not have the /k/ + /ə/ + /l/ sounds.

지도: 각 대상 단어를 읽으십시오. "cle" 문자 조합에/k/ + /ə/ + /l/ 소리가있으 면"yes" 열에 체크(✓)를 하십시오. "cle" 문자 조합에/k/ + /ə/ + /l/소리가없으 면"no" 열에 체크(✓)를 하십시오.

Target Words	Yes	No
6. article	✓	
7. cleaning		✓
8. inclement		✓
9. particle	✓	
10. cleverly		✓

Classwork

Name: _____ Date: ___/___/_____ Score: _____

Lesson 3.5

Reading Words with the "ct" Letter Combination

✓ Lesson Check Point

Directions: Read each target word. Circle the word in the column that has the same "ct" sound(s) as the target word.
지도: 각 대상 단어를 읽으십시오. 대상 단어와 동일한 "ct" 소리가 있는 열의 단어에 동그라미를 치십시오.

| conflict | (a. impact) |
| | b. benediction |

| predict | (a. viaduct) |
| | b. prediction |

| electric | (a. inject) |
| | b. victual |

| Connecticut | a. connection |
| | (b. indict) |

Directions: Read each target word. Put a check (✓) under the correct column heading.
지도: 각 대상 단어를 읽으십시오. 올바른 열 제목 아래에 체크(✓)를 하십시오.

Target Words	"ct" has the /k/ + /t/ sounds as in the word <u>fact</u>	"ct" has the silent "c" + /t/ sound as in the word <u>indict</u>
1. conflict	✓	
2. predict	✓	
3. electric	✓	
4. Connecticut		✓

 Name: _____   Date: ___/___/_____   Score: _____

Lesson 3.6

Reading Soft Letter "c" Words

✓ Lesson Check Point

 Directions: Read each target word. Circle the word in the column that has the same "cean," "cian," "cial," "cious," or "cient" sound as the target word.
지도: 각 대상 단어를 읽으십시오. 대상 단어와 동일한 "cean," "cian," "cial," "cious" 또는 "cient" 소리가 나는 열의 단어에 동그라미를 치십시오.

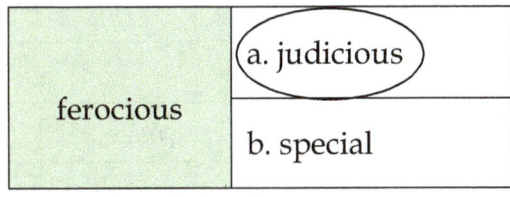
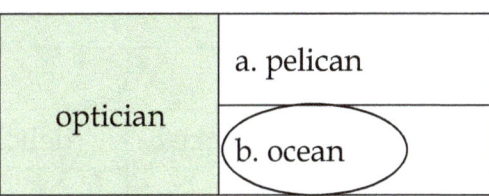
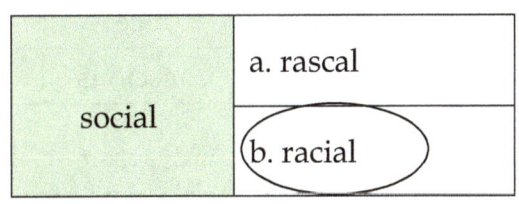
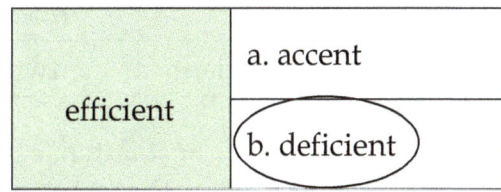

 Directions: Read each target word. Put a check (✓) in the column that identifies the same "cean," "cian," "cial," "cious," or "cient" sound within the target word.
지도: 각 대상 단어를 읽으십시오. 대상 단어 내에서 동일한 "cean," "cian," "cial," "cious" 또는 "cient" 소리를 식별하는 열에 체크(✓)를 하십시오.

Target Words	"cean" has the /sh/+/ə/+/n/ sounds as in the word <u>ocean</u>	"cial" has the /sh/+/ə/+/l/ sounds as in the word <u>special</u>	"cious" has the /sh/+/ə/+/s/ sounds as in the word <u>delicious</u>	"cient" has the /sh/+/ə/+/n/+/t/ sounds as in the word <u>ancient</u>
1. ferocious			✓	
2. optician	✓			
3. social		✓		
4. efficient				✓

Classwork

Name: _____ Date: ___/___/_____ Score: _____

Lesson 3.6

Reading Soft Letter "c" Words

Directions: Read the target words in the word box. In the first column, write the words with the letter "c" that have the /s/ sound, as in the word <u>cell</u>. In the second column, write the words with the letter "c" that have the /sh/ sound, as in the word <u>ocean</u>.

지도: 단어 상자에 있는 대상 단어를 읽으십시오. 첫 번째 열에는 cell이라는 단어에서와 같이 /s/ 소리가 나는 문자"c"가 있는 단어를 씁니다. 두 번째 열에는 다음과 같은 문자"c"가 포함된 단어를 쓰십시오. /sh/ 소리, ocean이라는 단어에서처럼.

Target Word Box				
commercial	delicious	office	place	lacy
technician	gallinacean	spices	cement	artificial
circus	proficient	prince	race	decided
omniscient	twice	optician	conscious	socialize

Soft letter "c" has the /s/ sound as in the word <u>cell</u>

- lacy
- race
- place
- twice
- circus
- office
- spices
- prince
- cement
- decided

Soft letter "c" has the /sh/ sound as in the word <u>ocean</u>

- socialize
- optician
- artificial
- delicious
- conscious
- proficient
- omniscient
- gallinacean
- technician
- commercial

Unit C Lesson 3.6

Learn To Read English With Directions In Korean

 Name: _____ Date: ___/___/_____ Score: _____

Lesson 3.7

Reading Words with the "ch" Letter Combination

✓ Lesson Check Point

 Directions: Read each target word. Circle the word in the column that has the same "ch" sound as the target word.
지도: 각 대상 단어를 읽으십시오. 대상 단어와 같은 "ch" 소리가 나는 열의 단어에 동그라미를 치십시오.

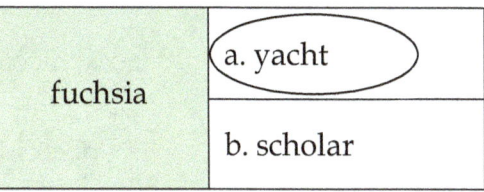

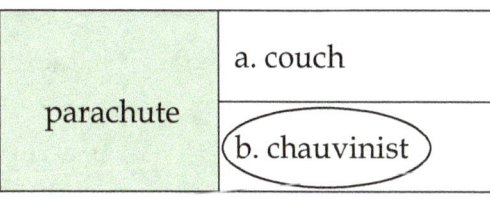

 Directions: Read each target word. Put a check (✓) under the correct column heading.
지도: 각 대상 단어를 읽으십시오. 올바른 열 제목 아래에 체크(✓)를 하십시오.

Target Words	"ch" has the /ch/ sound as in the word <u>chain</u>	"ch" has the /sh/ sound as in the word <u>chef</u>	"ch" has the /k/ sound as in the word <u>chaos</u>	"ch" is silent as in the word <u>yacht</u>
1. chicken	✓			
2. fuchsia				✓
3. anchor			✓	
4. parachute		✓		

Classwork

 Name: _____ Date: ___/___/_____ Score: _____

Lesson 3.8

Reading Words with the "cc" Letter Combination

✓ Lesson Check Point

 Directions: Read each target word. Circle the word in the column that has the same "cc" sound(s) as the target word.

지도: 각 대상 단어를 읽으십시오. 대상 단어와 동일한"cc" 소리가 나는 열의 단어에 동그라미를 치십시오.

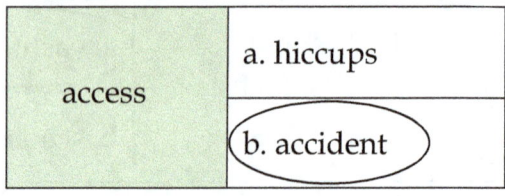

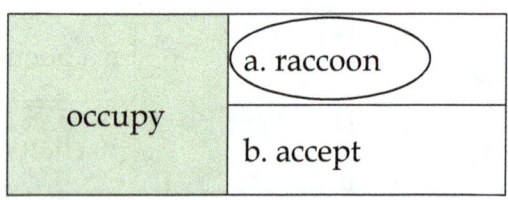 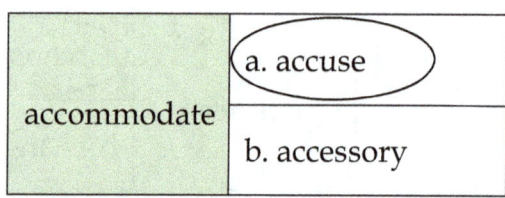

 Directions: Read each target word.   Put a check (✓) under the correct column heading.

지도: 각 대상 단어를 읽으십시오. 올바른 열 제목 아래에 체크(✓)를하십시오.

Target Words	"cc" has the /k/ sound as in the word <u>soccer</u>	"cc" has the /k/ + /s/ sounds as in the word <u>accept</u>
1. access		✓
2. succeed		✓
3. occupy	✓	
4. accommodate	✓	

Learn To Read English With Directions In Korean

Name: _____ Date: ___/___/_____ Score: _____

Lesson 3.9

Reading Words with a Silent Letter "c"

✓ **Lesson Check Point**

 Directions: Read the target words in the word box. Write the words that have a silent letter "c" in the first column. Write the words that do not have a silent letter "c" in the second column.

지도: 단어 상자에 있는 대상 단어를 읽으십시오. 첫 번째 열에 묵음 문자"c"가 있는 단어를 쓰십시오. 두 번째 열에 묵음 문자"c"가 없는 단어를 쓰십시오.

Target Word Box				
czar	scent	scalp	cake	acquit
occupy	corpuscle	muscle	excited	scissors
citizens	produce	congress	scenery	ascend
classic	yacht	increase	court	scale

Letter "c" is silent	Letter "c" has the /k/, /s/ or /sh/ sound
czar	cake
scent	court
yacht	scale
acquit	scalp
ascend	classic
occupy	citizens
scissors	excited
muscle	produce
scenery	increase
corpuscle	congress

Unit C Lesson 3.9

Classwork

Name: _____ Date: ___/___/_____ Score: _____

The Reading Challenge

Lesson 3.10

Reading Multisyllable Words

✓ **Lesson Check Point**

Directions: Read and divide each target word into syllables. Write each word and place a hyphen (-) between the syllables in the second column. Write the number of syllables in the third column. Use a dictionary or the Internet to check your answers.

지도: 각 대상 단어를 읽고 음절로 나눕니다. 각 단어를 쓰고 두 번째 열의 음절 사이에 하이픈(-)을 넣습니다. 세 번째 열에 음절 수를 쓰십시오. 사전이나 인터넷을 사용하여 답을 확인하십시오.

Target Words	Words Divided into Syllables	Number of Syllables
1. climber	climb-er	2
2. cleaner	clean-er	2
3. climbing	climb-ing	2
4. crayons	cray-ons	2
5. construction	con-struc-tion	3
6. cereal	ce-re-al	3
7. crocodile	croc-o-dile	3
8. creditors	cred-i-tors	3
9. crackers	crack-ers	2
10. camping	camp-ing	2

Name: _____ Date: ___/___/_____ Score: _____

The Reading Challenge

Lesson 3.10

Reading Multisyllable Words

✓ **Lesson Check Point**

Directions: Read each target word. Circle the word in the row that is divided correctly into syllables. Use a dictionary or the Internet to check your answers.

지도: 각 대상 단어를 읽으십시오. 음절로 올바르게 나누어진 행에 있는 단어에 동그라미를 치십시오. 사전이나 인터넷을 사용하여 답을 확인하십시오.

Model

| calculus | a. calcu-lus | (b. cal-cu-lus) | c. cal-culus |

| 1. chipmunk | (a. chip-munk) | b. chip-mu-nk | c. ch-ipmu-nk |

| 2. calendar | a. ca-lend-ar | (b. cal-en-dar) | c. ca-le-ndar |

| 3. circuit | a. cir-cu-it | b. circu-it | (c. cir-cuit) |

| 4. compound | (a. com-pound) | b. co-mpou-nd | c. com-po-und |

| 5. cereal | (a. ce-re-al) | b. cer-e-al | c. c-ere-al |

| 6. charisma | a. char-isma | b. cha-rism-a | (c. cha-ris-ma) |

| 7. cinema | (a. cin-e-ma) | b. cine-ma | c. ci-ne-ma |

| 8. cylinder | a. cy-lin-der | (b. cyl-in-der) | c. cylin-der |

Learn To Read English With Directions In Korean

Classwork

Name: _____ Date: ___/___/_____ Score: _____

Lesson 3.11

Reading and Writing

Proper and Common Nouns and Adjectives

✓ Lesson Check Point

Directions: Read the words in the word box. Put an (X) on the line next to each word that is written incorrectly. Remember that all proper nouns and proper adjectives are capitalized. Use a dictionary or the Internet to check your answers.

지도: 단어 상자에 있는 단어를 읽으십시오. 잘못 쓰여진 각 단어 옆의 줄에 (X)를 표시하십시오. 모든 고유 명사와 고유 형용사는 대문자임을 기억하십시오. 사전이나 인터넷을 사용하여 답을 확인하십시오.

Word Box					
__	China	X	cliniC	__	camp
X	cleveland	X	College	__	Colombia
__	cities	__	castle	X	charles
X	chicago	X	chinese	__	cherry

Directions: Read each unedited sentence and underline the word that is written incorrectly. Write each sentence correctly on the line.

지도: 편집되지 않은 각 문장을 읽고 잘못 쓰여진 단어에 밑줄을긋습 니다. 각 문장을 줄에 올바르게 쓰십시오.

Model
The <u>Camp</u> in Cleveland is closed.
<u>The camp in Cleveland is closed.</u>

1. The crickets chirp loudly on <u>clement</u> Cliff.
<u>The crickets chirp loudly on Clement Cliff.</u>

2. Do you like <u>cindy's</u> corn and chili?
<u>Do you like Cindy's corn and chili?</u>

3. The City of Chicago is cold and <u>Chilly</u>.
<u>The City of Chicago is cold and chilly.</u>

4. The <u>coyotes</u> is the name of our chess team.
<u>The Coyotes is the name of our chess team.</u>

Name: _____ Date: ___/___/_____ Score: _____

Lesson 4.1

Reading Words with the Letter D/d

✓ Lesson Check Point

Directions: Read each target word. Find the letter "d" and put a check (✓) in the column that identifies its position: beginning, within or end.
지도: 각 대상 단어를 읽으십시오. 문자"d"를 찾아 위치를 나타내는 열에 체크(✓)를 하십시오: 시작, 내부 또는 끝.

Target Words	Beginning (First Letter)	Within	End (Last Letter)
1. calendar		✓	
2. dusting	✓		
3. garden		✓	
4. hard			✓
5. dictionary	✓		

Directions: Read each sentence and underline the words that begin with the letter "d." Write all the underlined words in alphabetical order on the lines below.
지도: 각 문장을 읽고 문자"d"로 시작하는 단어에 밑줄을 긋습니다. 아래 줄에 밑줄 친 단어를 알파벳 순서로 모두 쓰십시오.

6. Brandon has a <u>dark</u> blue <u>drum</u>.

7. The barking <u>dogs</u> are on the <u>deck</u>.

8. The <u>driver</u> is <u>driving</u> a big blue bus.

9. My <u>daughter</u> ate the biggest <u>drumstick</u>.

10. Candice <u>designed</u> a beautiful black <u>dress</u>.

dark _____   daughter _____   deck _____
designed _____   dogs _____   dress _____
driver _____   driving _____   drum _____
                     drumstick _____

Learn To Read English With Directions In Korean   43

Classwork

Name: _____ Date: ___/___/_____ Score: _____

Lesson 4.2

Reading Letter "d" Words with the /d/ Sound & /j/ Sound

✓ **Lesson Check Point**

Directions: Read each target word. Circle the word in the column that has the same "d" sound as the target word.
지도: 각 대상 단어를 읽으십시오. 대상 단어와 "d" 소리가 같은 열의 단어에 동그라미를 치십시오.

London	a. handle (circled)
	b. nodule

golden	a. glandular
	b. field (circled)

education	a. explode
	b. schedule (circled)

modulate	a. soldier (circled)
	b. modify

Directions: Read each target word. Put a check (✓) under the correct column heading.
지도: 각 대상 단어를 읽으십시오. 올바른 열 제목 아래에 체크(✓)를 하십시오.

Target Words	"d" has the /d/ sound as in the word <u>doctor</u>	"d" has the /j/ sound as in the word <u>educate</u>
1. London	✓	
2. golden	✓	
3. education		✓
4. modulate		✓

Name: _____ Date:___/___/_____ Score:_____

Lesson 4.2

Reading Words with the "dr" Letter Combination

Dictionary Skills/ Vocabulary

✓ Lesson Check Point

Directions: Read each target word and its definition. Write the letter of the definition on the line of each target word. Use a dictionary or the Internet to check your answers.

지도: 각 대상 단어와 그 정의를 읽으십시오. 각 대상 단어의 행에 정의의 문자를 씁니다. 사전이나 인터넷을 사용하여 답을 확인하십시오.

Target Words	Definitions
1. _c_ dreams	a. to have fallen unintentionally
2. _d_ driveway	b. the cooked leg of a chicken, duck or turkey
3. _e_ driving	c. visualizing events that happen during sleep
4. _a_ dropped	d. a short path that leads to a house or garage
5. _b_ drumstick	e. the process of operating a vehicle

Directions: Read each sentence. Underline the word in the parentheses that correctly completes each sentence. Then, write the underlined word on the line.

지도: 각 문장을 읽으십시오. 각 문장을 올바르게 완성하는 괄호 안에 있는 단어에 밑줄을 긋습니다. 그런 다음 밑줄 친 단어를 줄에 쓰십시오.

6. I drove the blue car into the _____driveway_____. (dreams, <u>driveway</u>)

7. The boy _____dropped_____ his big chocolate donut. (<u>dropped</u>, driving)

8. At night, Dan _____dreams_____ about big animals. (<u>dreams</u>, driveway)

9. I am _____driving_____ my car to Denver, Colorado. (<u>driving</u>, drumstick)

10. At dinner, David ate a delicious _____drumstick_____. (dropped, <u>drumstick</u>)

Classwork

Name: _____ Date: ___/__/_____ Score: _____

Lesson 4.3

Reading Words with the "ed" Suffix/ Past Tense Verbs

✓ **Lesson Check Point**

Directions: Read each target word. Circle the word in the column that has the same "ed" sound(s) as the target word.

지도: 각 대상 단어를 읽으십시오. 대상 단어와 동일한"ed" 소리(들)가있는열의 단어에 동그라미를 치십시오.

| missed | a. ended |
| | (b. trapped) |

| burned | (a. grabbed) |
| | b. planted |

| named | a. snapped |
| | (b. pulled) |

| ended | a. signed |
| | (b. traded) |

Directions: Read each target word. Put a check (✓) under the correct column heading.

지도: 각 대상 단어를 읽으십시오. 올바른 열 제목 아래에 체크(✓)를하십시오.

Target Words	"ed" has the /i/ + /d/ sounds as in the word <u>rested</u>	"ed" has the /d/ sound as in the word <u>hugged</u>	"ed" has the /t/ sound as in the word <u>tipped</u>
1. missed			✓
2. burned		✓	
3. named		✓	
4. ended	✓		

 Name: _____ Date:___/___/_____ Score:_____

Lesson 4.4

Reading Words with a Silent Letter "d"

✓ **Lesson Check Point**

 Directions: Read the target words in the word box. Write the words that have a silent letter "d" in the first column. Write the words that do not have a silent letter "d" in the second column.

지도: 단어 상자에 있는 대상 단어를 읽으십시오. 첫 번째 열에 묵음문자 "d"가 있는 단어를 쓰십시오. 두 번째 열에 묵음 문자"d"가 없는 단어를 쓰십시오.

Target Word Box				
handicap	Cambridge	dock	Windsor	elder
does	conduct	handsome	adjourn	adjustment
judge	adjacent	director	handkerchief	discuss
padlock	doctor	footbridge	Wednesday	depend

Letter "d" is silent

judge
adjacent
adjourn
Windsor
footbridge
handsome
Wednesday
Cambridge
adjustment
handkerchief

Letter "d" has the /d/ sound

does
dock
doctor
elder
discuss
padlock
conduct
depend
director
handicap

Classwork

Name: _____   Date: ___/___/_____   Score: _____

The Reading Challenge

Lesson 4.5

Reading Multisyllable Words

 Lesson Check Point

Directions: Read and divide each target word into syllables. Write each word and place a hyphen (-) between the syllables in the second column. Write the number of syllables in the third column. Use a dictionary or the Internet to check your answers.

지도: 각 대상 단어를 읽고 음절로 나눕니다. 각 단어를 쓰고 두 번째 열의 음절 사이에 하이픈(-)을 넣습니다. 세 번째 열에 음절 수를 쓰십시오. 사전이나 인터넷을 사용하여 답을 확인하십시오.

Target Words	Words Divided into Syllables	Number of Syllables
1. demonstrate	dem-on-strate	3
2. duplicate	du-pli-cate	3
3. diagram	di-a-gram	3
4. decimal	dec-i-mal	3
5. descendent	de-scen-dent	3
6. digital	dig-i-tal	3
7. disengaged	dis-en-gaged	3
8. doormat	door-mat	2
9. discomfort	dis-com-fort	3
10. driver	driv-er	2

 Name: _____ Date:___/___/_____ Score: _____

The Reading Challenge

Lesson 4.5

Reading Multisyllable Words

✓ Lesson Check Point

 Directions: Read each target word. Circle the word in the row that is divided correctly into syllables. Use a dictionary or the Internet to check your answers.
지도: 각 대상 단어를 읽으십시오. 음절로 올바르게 나누어진 행에 있는 단어에 동그라미를 치십시오. 사전이나 인터넷을 사용하여 답을 확인하십시오.

Model

| dictionary | a. di-ction-ary | b. dic-tion-ar-y ⭕ | c. dic-tiona-ry |

1. disciple	a. di-sci-ple	b. dis-cip-le	c. dis-ci-ple ⭕
2. deceptive	a. de-cep-tive ⭕	b. dec-ep-tive	c. de-cept-ive
3. Dakota	a. Dako-ta	b. Da-kot-a	c. Da-ko-ta ⭕
4. disgruntle	a. dis-grun-tle ⭕	b. di-sgrun-tle	c. dis-grunt-le
5. dimension	a. dim-e-nsion	b. dim-en-sion	c. di-men-sion ⭕
6. domino	a. dom-i-no ⭕	b. do-min-o	c. dom-in-o
7. decelerate	a. decel-er-ate	b. dec-el-er-ate	c. de-cel-er-ate ⭕
8. distribute	a. dist-rib-ute	b. dis-tri-bute	c. dis-trib-ute ⭕

Classwork

Name: _____ Date:___/___/_____ Score:_____

Lesson 4.6

Reading and Writing

Proper and Common Nouns and Adjectives

✓ **Lesson Check Point**

Directions: Read the words in the word box. Put an (X) on the line next to each word that is written incorrectly. Remember that all proper nouns and proper adjectives are capitalized. Use a dictionary or the Internet to check your answers.

지도: 단어 상자에 있는 단어를 읽으십시오. 잘못 쓰여진 각 단어 옆의 줄에 (X)를 표시하십시오. 모든 고유 명사와 고유 형용사는 대문자임을 기억하십시오. 사전이나 인터넷을 사용하여 답을 확인하십시오.

Word Box					
X	Daughter	X	denmark	__	Dutch
__	Dana	X	detroit	__	director
__	Denver	__	diner	X	danish
X	dakota	__	door	X	Detective

Directions: Read each unedited sentence and underline the word that is written incorrectly. Write each sentence correctly on the line.

지도: 편집되지 않은 각 문장을 읽고 잘못 쓰여진 단어에 밑줄을긋습 니다. 각 문장을 줄에 올바르게 쓰십시오.

Model
Dan said, "My daughter's name is <u>donna</u>."
<u>Dan said, "My daughter's name is Donna."</u>

1. Drake's <u>Dictionary</u> is not on his desk.
   <u>Drake's dictionary is not on his desk.</u>

2. The dark blue <u>Doormat</u> has one big dot.
   <u>The dark blue doormat has one big dot.</u>

3. The diploma belongs to <u>doctor</u> Davis.
   <u>The diploma belongs to Doctor Davis.</u>

4. The <u>danish</u> pastries, pancakes, and donuts cost five dollars.
   <u>The Danish pastries, pancakes, and donuts cost five dollars.</u>

Name: _____ Date: ___/___/_____ Score: _____

Lesson 5.1

Reading Words with the Letter E/e

✓ **Lesson Check Point**

Directions: Read each target word. Find the letter "e" and put a check (✓) in the column that identifies its position: beginning, within or end.
지도: 각 대상 단어를 읽으십시오. 문자 "e"를 찾아 체크 표시(✓)위치를 식별하는 열에서 시작, 내부 또는 끝.

Target Words	Beginning (First Letter)	Within	End (Last Letter)
1. eating	✓		
2. belong		✓	
3. cake			✓
4. father		✓	
5. embark	✓		

Directions: Read each target word. Read the words in the row and circle the word that has a different vowel "e" sound.
지도: 각 대상 단어를 읽으십시오. 줄에 있는 단어를 읽고 모음 "e" 소리가 다른 단어에 동그라미를 치세요.

Target Words				
6. beds	leg	(she)	check	pet
7. men	(be)	ten	vet	hen
8. decks	yet	pen	(we)	set
9. stem	hem	(me)	net	fled
10. them	(he)	send	less	test

Classwork

 Name: _____ Date: ___/___/_____ Score: _____

Lesson 5.2

Reading Words with the Short Vowel "e" Sound

✓ Lesson Check Point

 Directions: Read the words in the four boxes. Circle two words with the short vowel /ĕ/ sound. The anchor word for the short vowel /ĕ/ sound is <u>egg</u>.

지도: 네 개의 상자에 있는 단어를 읽으십시오. 짧은 모음 /ĕ/ 소리로 두 단어에 동그라미를 치십시오. 단모음 /ĕ/ 소리의 앵커 워드는 egg입니다.

cake	(web)		bead	(speck)		ease	choose
(check)	theme		bee	(fed)		(dwelt)	(hem)

(Fred)	mean		(well)	(them)		(sped)	beat
eat	(hedge)		Pete	free		(yell)	mate

 Directions: Read the words in the four boxes. Circle two words that rhyme. Rhyming words have the same ending sound, such as <u>set</u> and <u>wet</u>.

지도: 네 개의 상자에 있는 단어를 읽으십시오. 운이 맞는 두 단어에 동그라미를 치십시오. 운율이 있는 단어는 set 및 wet와 같이 끝 소리가 같습니다.

bean	(neck)		gem	stem		(bell)	each
wise	(deck)		deal	pie		true	(spell)

shoe	meat		toe	(bed)		(edge)	zeal
(men)	(ten)		(red)	heal		(pledge)	they

Name: _____   Date: ___/___/_____   Score: _____

Lesson 5.2

Reading & Writing Words with the Short Vowel "e" Sound

✓ **Lesson Check Point**

Directions: Read each sentence and underline three words with the short vowel /ĕ/ sound. Then, write the underlined words on the lines below. The anchor word for the short vowel /ĕ/ sound is <u>egg</u>.

지도: 각 문장을 읽고 세 단어에 짧은 모음 /ĕ/ 소리에 밑줄을 긋습니다. 그런 다음 밑줄 친 단어를 아래 줄에 쓰십시오. 단모음 /ĕ/ 소리의 기준어는 egg입니다.

Model

She placed her <u>legs</u> on the <u>wet</u> <u>deck</u>.

legs _____   wet _____   deck _____

1. She will not <u>let</u> us <u>get</u> a <u>pet</u>.

    let _____   get _____   pet _____

2. We <u>smell</u> the three <u>wet</u> <u>hens</u>.

    smell _____   wet _____   hens _____

3. Andre <u>bent</u> his <u>leg</u> and <u>fell</u>.

    bent _____   leg _____   fell _____

4. Eve <u>went</u> to <u>Ed's</u> summer <u>wedding</u>.

    went _____   Ed's _____   wedding _____

5. We have to go to <u>bed</u> by <u>ten</u> o'clock for a <u>restful</u> night's sleep.

    bed _____   ten _____   restful _____

Unit E Lesson 5.2

Classwork

 Name: _____ Date: ___/___/_____ Score: _____

Lesson 5.3

Reading Words with the Long Vowel "e" Sound

✓ **Lesson Check Point**

 Directions: Read the words in the four boxes. Circle two words with the long vowel /ē/ sound. The anchor word for the long vowel /ē/ sound is <u>me</u>.

지도: 네 개의 상자에 있는 단어를 읽으십시오. 장모음 /ē/ 소리로두단어에 동그라미를 치십시오. 장모음 /ē/ 소리의 기준어는 me입니다.

break	(east)		cease	(scene)		chest	(these)
(pea)	spell		clever	here		cakes	(zebra)

(zero)	scent		(east)	next		(heal)	trend
(believe)	come		(eating)	beard		where	(react)

 Directions: Read the words in the four boxes. Circle two words that rhyme. Rhyming words have the same ending sound, such as <u>beep</u> and <u>reap</u>.

지도: 네 개의 상자에 있는 단어를 읽으십시오. 운이 맞는 두 단어에동그라미를 치십시오. 운율이 있는 단어는 beep 및 reap과 같이 끝 소리가같습니다.

(speed)	(read)		lead	(eat)		(see)	were
bread	felt		when	(heat)		held	(tea)

(tease)	fence		head	(theme)		realm	temp
(lease)	there		(scheme)	deck		(leave)	(weave)

Name: _____ Date: ___/___/_____ Score: _____

Lesson 5.3

Reading & Writing Words with the Long Vowel "e" Sound

✓ **Lesson Check Point**

Directions: Read each sentence and underline three words with the long vowel /ē/ sound. Then, write the underlined words on the lines below. The anchor word for the long vowel /ē/ sound is <u>me</u>.

지도: 각 문장을 읽고 장모음 /ē/ 소리로 세 단어에 밑줄을 긋습니다. 그런 다음 밑줄 친 단어를 아래 줄에 쓰십시오. 장모음 /ē/ 소리의 기준어는 <u>me</u> 입니다.

Model

<u>We</u> are <u>reading</u> an article entitled, "<u>Eagles</u> Bird of Prey."

　　We　　　　　　reading　　　　　　Eagles
　　‾‾‾‾‾　　　　　‾‾‾‾‾‾‾　　　　　‾‾‾‾‾‾

1. <u>Irene</u> and <u>Lee</u> are relaxing under the <u>tree</u> with their pets.

　　Irene　　　　　　Lee　　　　　　tree
　　‾‾‾‾‾　　　　　‾‾‾‾‾　　　　　‾‾‾‾‾

2. The ten <u>Guyanese</u> <u>teams</u> are <u>extremely</u> talented.

　　Guyanese　　　　teams　　　　　extremely
　　‾‾‾‾‾‾‾‾　　　　‾‾‾‾‾　　　　　‾‾‾‾‾‾‾‾‾

3. This <u>evening</u>, Esther <u>received</u> a <u>speeding</u> ticket.

　　evening　　　　　received　　　　speeding
　　‾‾‾‾‾‾‾　　　　　‾‾‾‾‾‾‾‾　　　　‾‾‾‾‾‾‾‾

4. The <u>speaker</u> said, "<u>Lean</u> <u>meats</u> have relatively low-fat content."

　　speaker　　　　　Lean　　　　　meats
　　‾‾‾‾‾‾‾　　　　　‾‾‾‾　　　　　‾‾‾‾‾

5. The students will <u>speak</u> to the <u>dean</u> about the new <u>teachers</u>.

　　speak　　　　　　dean　　　　　teachers
　　‾‾‾‾‾　　　　　‾‾‾‾　　　　　‾‾‾‾‾‾‾‾

Learn To Read English With Directions In Korean

Classwork

Name: _____   Date: ___/___/_____   Score: _____

Review Lessons 5.2 & 5.3

Reading Short Vowel and Long Vowel Words

Directions: Read the target words in the word box. In the first column, write the words that have the short vowel /ĕ/ sound, as in the word <u>egg</u>. In the second column, write the words that have the long vowel /ē/ sound, as in the word <u>me</u>.

지도: 단어 상자에 있는 대상 단어를 읽으십시오. 첫 번째 칸에는 egg라는 단어처럼 단모음 /ĕ/ 소리가 나는 단어를 씁니다. 두 번째 칸에는 me라는 단어처럼 장모음 /ē/ 소리가 나는 단어를 쓰세요.

Target Word Box				
fled	theme	left	temp	went
these	step	scene	seeing	speed
held	athlete	complete	then	increase
extreme	self	west	free	test

Letter "e" has the /ĕ/ sound as in the word <u>egg</u>

- fled
- left
- test
- step
- held
- then
- self
- west
- went
- temp

Letter "e" has the /ē/ sound as in the word <u>me</u>

- free
- these
- theme
- scene
- seeing
- speed
- athlete
- complete
- increase
- extreme

 Name: _____ Date: ___/___/_____ Score: _____

Lesson 5.4

Reading Words with Letter "e" Vowel Pairs

 Lesson Check Point

Directions: Read each target word. Circle the word in the column that has the same vowel "ea," "ee," "ei," "eo" or "eu" sound as the target word.
지도: 각 대상 단어를 읽으십시오. 같은 모음 "ea," "ee," "ei," "eo" 또는 "eu"가 대상 단어와 동일한 열의 단어에 동그라미를 치십시오.

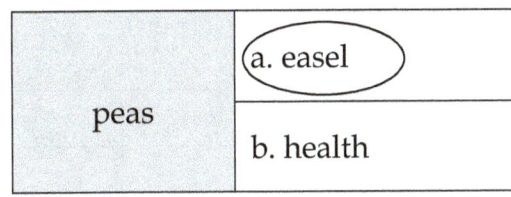
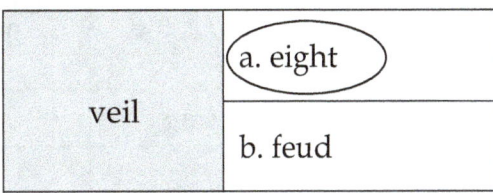
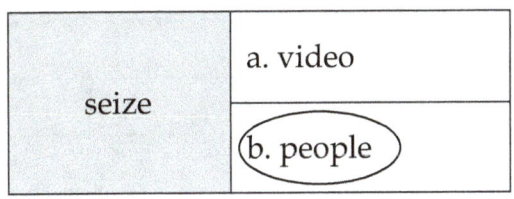
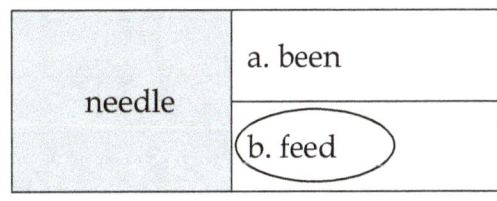

 Directions: Read each target word. Put a check (✓) under the correct column heading.
지도: 각 대상 단어를 읽으십시오. 올바른 열 제목 아래에 체크(✓)를 하십시오.

Target Words	Words have the long "e" sound as in the word <u>tea</u>	Words do not have the long "e" sound
1. peas	✓	
2. veil		✓
3. seize	✓	
4. needle	✓	

Classwork

 Name: _____ Date: ___/___/_____ Score: _____

Lesson 5.5

Reading Words with the Final Letter "e"

✓ **Lesson Check Point**

 Directions: Read each target word. Find the letter "e" and put a check (✓) in the column that identifies its position within the syllable.
지도: 각 대상 단어를 읽으십시오. 문자"e"를 찾아 체크 표시(✓)음 절 내에서 위치를 식별하는 열에서.

Target Words	"e" is at the end of a one syllable word	"e" is at the end of the first syllable	"e" is at the end of a multi-syllable word
1. becoming		✓	
2. he	✓		
3. recording		✓	
4. multiple			✓
5. we	✓		

 Directions: Read each target word. Put a check (✓) under the correct column heading.
지도: 각 대상 단어를 읽으십시오. 올바른 열 제목 아래에 체크(✓)를하십시오.

Target Words	"e" has the /ĕ/ sound as in the word egg	"e" has the /ē/ sound as in the word me	"e" has the /ə/ sound as in the word item	"e" is silent as in the word great
6. prefix		✓		
7. made				✓
8. marvel			✓	
9. season		✓		
10. travel			✓	

Name: _____ Date: __/__/_____ Score: _____

Lesson 5.6

Reading Letter "e" Words with the Schwa Vowel Sound

✓ Lesson Check Point

Directions: Read each target word. Circle the word in the column that has the same "e" sound as the target word.

지도: 각 대상 단어를 읽으십시오. 목표 단어와 같은 "e" 소리가 나는 열의 단어에 동그라미를 치십시오.

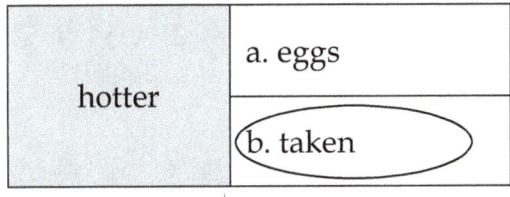
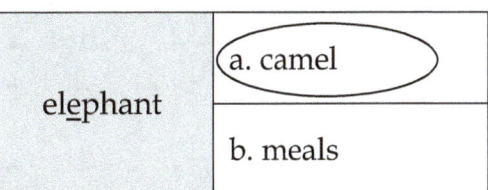
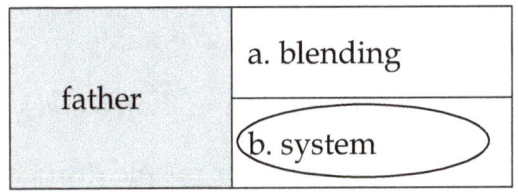
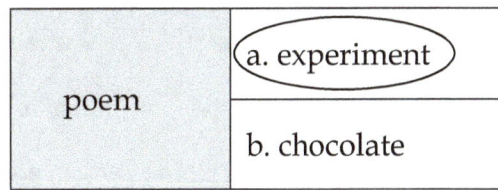

 Directions: Read each sentence and underline the letter "e" word that has the schwa vowel /ə/ sound. The anchor word for the letter "e" schwa vowel sound is item.

지도: 각 문장을 읽고 슈와 모음 /ə/ 소리가 있는 문자 "e" 단어에 밑줄을 긋습니다. "e" 슈와 모음 소리의 앵커 단어는 item입니다.

1. At <u>dinner</u>, I ate a slice of roast beef.

2. Five <u>movers</u> organized my bedroom set.

3. Every year, we <u>celebrated</u> Andrew's birthday.

4. Three large <u>barrels</u> are located next to cabinets.

5. Our <u>fishermen</u> sailed their ships twenty miles from shore.

6. Large animal populations are <u>scattered</u> throughout Africa.

Classwork

Name: _____ Date: ___/___/_____ Score: _____

Lesson 5.7

Reading Words with the "er" Letter Combination

Dictionary Skills/ Vocabulary

✓ Lesson Check Point

Directions: Read each target word and its definition. Write the letter of the definition on the line of each target word. Use a dictionary or the Internet to check your answers.

지도: 각 대상 단어와 그 정의를 읽으십시오. 각 대상 단어의 행에 정의의 문자를 씁니다. 사전이나 인터넷을 사용하여 답을 확인하십시오.

Target Words	Definitions
1. _b_ river	a. something very bad or unacceptable
2. _e_ sister	b. a body of water that is larger than a creek
3. _a_ terrible	c. a small fruit that has red or purple drupelets
4. _c_ raspberry	d. a verbal or written response to a question
5. _d_ answer	e. a female who has the same parent(s) as another

Directions: Read each sentence and write the target word that correctly completes the sentence.

지도: 각 문장을 읽고 문장을 올바르게 완성하는 목표 단어를 쓰십시오.

6. My younger _____sister_____ eats berries and cherries.

7. Jerry did not _____answer_____ Sherry's difficult questions.

8. Have you ever eaten a sweet, juicy _____raspberry_____?

9. Sherry's baked herring tasted _____terrible_____.

10. We are going to take a ferry ride along the _____river_____.

 Name: _____ Date:___/___/_____ Score:_____

Lesson 5.8

Reading Words with the "eu" and "ew" Letter Combinations

✓ **Lesson Check Point**

 Directions: Read each sentence and underline the word that has a silent letter "e."
지도: 각 문장을 읽고 묵음 문자"e"가 있는 단어에 밑줄을 긋습니다.

Model
My father said, "The apricot streusel is very tasty."

1. In Germany, I bought many elegant gifts with euros.

2. Jennifer and Cathy painted the ceiling a neutral color.

3. The European bound flight will depart at eleven o'clock.

4. The bridal party was euphoric during the wonderful wedding.

 Directions: Read each sentence and underline the word with an "eu" or "ew" letter combination that has the long vowel /yo͞o/ or /o͞o/ sound, as in the words feud and flew.
지도: 각 문장을 읽고 단어 feud 그리고 flew에서와 같이 장모음 /yo͞o/ 또는 /o͞o/ 소리가 있는 "eu" 또는 "ew" 문자 조합으로 단어에 밑줄을 긋습니다.

5. Mom's apple streusel is delicious.

6. Lieutenant Edwards is a strong leader.

7. The engineering students ate grapes and cashews.

8. Eddie learned a lot of interesting information about Zeus.

9. The Elton family is feuding over Grandmother's possessions.

10. The shower was extremely clean after Jane used mildew remover.

Classwork

 Name: _____ Date: ___/ ___/ _____ Score: _____

Lesson 5.9

Reading Words with the "ey" Letter Combination

✓ Lesson Check Point

 Directions: Read each target word. Put a check (✓) under the correct column heading.

지도: 각 대상 단어를 읽으십시오. 올바른 열 제목 아래에 체크(✓)를 하십시오.

Target Words	"ey" has the long /ē/ sound as in the word honey	"ey" has the long /ā/ sound as in the word hey
1. monkey	✓	
2. survey		✓
3. convey		✓
4. kidney	✓	

 Directions: Read each sentence and underline the word with the "ey" letter combination. Put a check (✓) under the correct column heading.

지도: 각 문장을 읽고 "ey" 문자 조합으로 단어에 밑줄을 긋습니다. 올바른 열 제목 아래에 체크(✓)를 하십시오.

	"ey" has the long /ē/ sound as in the word honey	"ey" has the long /ā/ sound as in the word hey
5. The survey has ten questions.		✓
6. Lee received a new team jersey.	✓	
7. Today, they will have a yard sale.		✓
8. I did not obey my teachers' rules.		✓
9. Ethan enjoys playing volleyball.	✓	
10. The jockey's horse is on the track.	✓	

Name: _____ Date: ___/___/_____ Score: _____

Lesson 5.10

Reading Words with a Silent Letter "e"

✓ **Lesson Check Point**

 Directions: Read the target words in the word box. Write the words that have a silent letter "e" in the first column. Write the words that do not have a silent letter "e" in the second column.

지도: 단어 상자에 있는 대상 단어를 읽으십시오. 첫 번째 열에 묵음 문자"e"가 있는 단어를 쓰십시오. 두 번째 열에 묵음 문자"e"가 없는 단어를 쓰십시오.

Target Word Box				
eating	cells	friends	game	vote
seat	base	depend	effect	fresh
tone	size	tube	beds	came
face	zebras	clue	drive	meal

Letter "e" is silent

- clue
- vote
- base
- tone
- size
- tube
- came
- face
- drive
- game

Letter "e" has a letter "e" sound

- beds
- cells
- seat
- meal
- effect
- fresh
- eating
- zebras
- friends
- depend

Classwork

Name: _____ Date: ___/___/_____ Score: _____

Unit Review – E/e

Reading Words with Vowel "e" Sounds: /ĕ/, /ē/, /ə/ & Silent

✓ **Lesson Check Point**

Directions: Read each target word. Circle the word in the column that has the same "e" sound as the target word.
지도: 각 대상 단어를 읽으십시오. 목표 단어와 같은 "e" 소리가 나는 열의 단어에 동그라미를 치십시오.

| eating | (a. coffee) |
| | b. bake |

| barrel | (a. oxygen) |
| | b. these |

| pollen | a. beat |
| | (b. benefit) |

| check | a. rakes |
| | (b. cells) |

Directions: Read each target word. Put a check (✓) under the correct column heading.
지도: 각 대상 단어를 읽으십시오. 올바른 열 제목 아래에 체크(✓)를 하십시오.

Target Words	"e" has the /ĕ/ sound as in the word <u>egg</u>	"e" has the /ē/ sound as in the word <u>me</u>	"e" has the /ə/ sound as in the word <u>item</u>	"e" is silent as in the word <u>great</u>
1. eating		✓		
2. barrel			✓	
3. pollen			✓	
4. check	✓			

Learn To Read English With Directions In Korean

Name: _____ Date:___/___/_____ Score:_____

The Reading Challenge

Lesson 5.11

Reading Multisyllable Words

✓ Lesson Check Point

 Directions: Read and divide each target word into syllables. Write each word and place a hyphen (-) between the syllables in the second column. Write the number of syllables in the third column. Use a dictionary or the Internet to check your answers.

지도: 각 대상 단어를 읽고 음절로 나눕니다. 각 단어를 쓰고 두 번째 열의 음절 사이에 하이픈(-)을 넣습니다. 세 번째 열에 음절 수를 쓰십시오. 사전이나 인터넷을 사용하여 답을 확인하십시오.

Target Words	Words Divided into Syllables	Number of Syllables
1. decreasing	de-creas-ing	3
2. between	be-tween	2
3. peanut	pea-nut	2
4. shipwreck	ship-wreck	2
5. nutmeg	nut-meg	2
6. leghorn	leg-horn	2
7. farewell	fare-well	2
8. anthem	an-them	2
9. modem	mo-dem	2
10. itemize	i-tem-ize	3

Unit E
Lesson 5.11

Classwork

 Name: _____ Date:___/___/_____ Score:_____

The Reading Challenge

Lesson 5.11

Reading Multisyllable Words

✓ **Lesson Check Point**

Directions: Read each target word. Circle the word in the row that is divided correctly into syllables. Use a dictionary or the Internet to check your answers.

지도: 각 대상 단어를 읽으십시오. 음절로 올바르게 나누어진 행에 있는 단어에 동그라미를 치십시오. 사전이나 인터넷을 사용하여 답을 확인하십시오.

Model

| megabyte | a. me-ga-byte | (b. meg-a-byte) | c. me-gaby-te |

| 1. awaken | a. aw-a-ken | (b. a-wak-en) | c. a-wa-ken |

| 2. legacy | a. le-ga-cy | (b. leg-a-cy) | c. leg-ac-y |

| 3. forgiven | (a. for-giv-en) | b. for-gi-ven | c. fo-rgi-ven |

| 4. acknowledge | a. ack-now-ledge | b. ac-know-ledge | (c. ac-knowl-edge) |

| 5. turtleneck | (a. tur-tle-neck) | b. turt-len-eck | c. turt-le-neck |

| 6. celebrate | a. cel-eb-rate | (b. cel-e-brate) | c. ce-le-brate |

| 7. federal | a. fe-de-ral | b. fed-e-ral | (c. fed-er-al) |

| 8. ascending | (a. as-cend-ing) | b. asc-end-ing | c. as-cen-ding |

Unit E
Lesson 5.11

Name: _____ Date: ___/___/_____ Score: _____

Lesson 5.12

Reading and Writing

Proper and Common Nouns and Adjectives

✓ Lesson Check Point

Directions: Read the words in the word box. Put an (X) on the line next to each word that is written incorrectly. Remember that all proper nouns and proper adjectives are capitalized. Use a dictionary or the Internet to check your answers.

지도:
단어 상자에 있는 단어를 읽으십시오. 잘못 쓰여진 각 단어 옆의 줄에 (X)를 표시하십시오. 모든 고유 명사와 고유 형용사는 대문자임을 기억하십시오. 사전이나 인터넷을 사용하여 답을 확인하십시오.

Word Box					
X	eiffel Tower	X	Educator	X	east Asia
__	England	X	egyptian	X	el Dorado
__	egocentric	__	Estonia	__	editor
X	Envelope	__	European	__	environment

Directions: Read each unedited sentence and underline the word that is written incorrectly. Write each sentence correctly on the line.

路线：读每个未经编辑的句子，并给书写错误的词加下划线。在线 上写上正确的句子。

Model
All my friends are <u>Excited</u> about the class trip to Europe.
All my friends are excited about the class trip to Europe.

1. I will meet my friend, <u>eileen</u>, at five o'clock EST.
I will meet my friend, Eileen, at five o'clock EST.

2. <u>evan</u> said, "Many of the citizens of Ethiopia speak English."
Evan said, "Many of the citizens of Ethiopia speak English."

3. The address on the envelope indicates that the letter is from <u>egypt</u>.
The address on the envelope indicates that the letter is from Egypt.

4. On Earth Day, Mr. <u>eglon's</u> class will discuss environmental issues.
On Earth Day, Mr. Eglon's class will discuss environmental issues.

Classwork

Name: _____ Date: ___/___/_____ Score: _____

Lesson 6.1

Reading Words with the Letter F/f

✓ **Lesson Check Point**

Directions: Read each target word. Find the letter "f" and put a check (✓) in the column that identifies its position: beginning, within or end.
지도: 각 대상 단어를 읽으십시오. 문자 "f"를 찾아 체크 표시(✓)위치를 식별하는 열에서 시작, 내부 또는 끝.

Target Words	Beginning (First Letter)	Within	End (Last Letter)
1. flip	✓		
2. fresh	✓		
3. leaf			✓
4. defrost		✓	
5. comfort		✓	

Directions: Read each sentence and underline the words that begin with the letter "f." Write all the underlined words in alphabetical order on the lines below.
지도: 각 문장을 읽고 "f"로 시작하는 단어에 밑줄을 긋습니다. 밑줄친모든 단어를 아래 줄에 알파벳 순서로 쓰십시오.

6. Ashley and <u>Fred</u> are citizens of <u>France</u>.

7. Brad and Alex are <u>fabulous</u> <u>flute</u> players.

8. The <u>fence</u> in <u>front</u> of the house is dark blue.

9. The <u>flowers</u> in the <u>field</u> are extremely beautiful.

10. The <u>flag</u> of Belgium is <u>flying</u> high over the building.

fabulous   fence   field
flag   flowers   flute
flying   France   Fred
                  front

Unit F Lesson 6.1

Learn To Read English With Directions In Korean   Copyrighted Material

 Name: _____ Date: ___/___/_____ Score: _____

Lesson 6.2

Reading Words with the "fr" Letter Combination

Dictionary Skills/ Vocabulary

✓ **Lesson Check Point**

 Directions: Read each target word and its definition. Write the letter of the definition on the line of each target word. Use a dictionary or the Internet to check your answers.
지도: 각 대상 단어와 그 정의를 읽으십시오. 각 대상 단어의 행에 정의의 문자를 씁니다. 사전이나 인터넷을 사용하여 답을 확인하십시오.

Target Words	Definitions
1. _d_ frog	a. to have broken or cracked something
2. _e_ framed	b. a branch of a business chain
3. _b_ franchise	c. to be ahead of someone or something
4. _a_ fractured	d. a small, smooth, tailless and wet-skinned animal
5. _c_ front	e. evidence or testimony presented to falsely incriminate

 Directions: Read each sentence. Underline the word in the parentheses that correctly completes each sentence. Then, write the underlined word on the line.
지도: 각 문장을 읽으십시오. 각 문장을 올바르게 완성하는 괄호 안에 있는 단어에 밑줄을 긋습니다. 그런 다음 밑줄 친 단어를 줄에 쓰십시오.

6. The ____frog____ is croaking by the water. (<u>frog</u>, framed)

7. On the bus, Freda sat in ____front____ of Frankie. (<u>front</u>, franchise)

8. At the game, Flo fell and ____fractured____ her ankle. (frog, <u>fractured</u>)

9. Frank was ____framed____ for a crime he didn't commit. (front, <u>framed</u>)

10. Flossy purchased a fast food ____franchise____. (<u>franchise</u>, framed)

Classwork

Name: _____ Date: ___/___/_____ Score: _____

Lesson 6.3

Reading Words with the "fl" Letter Combination

Dictionary Skills/ Vocabulary

✓ **Lesson Check Point**

Directions: Read each target word and its definition. Write the target word on the line in front of its meaning. Use a dictionary or the Internet to check your answers.

지도: 각 대상 단어와 그 정의를 읽으십시오. 의미 앞 줄에 대상단어 를 쓰십시오. 사전이나 인터넷을 사용하여 답을 확인하십시오.

Target Word Box				
fleet	flash	flower	fluently	fly

1. __fly_____   to travel through the air with wings
2. __flower_____   the colorful part of a plant that contains seeds
3. __fleet_____   a number of vehicles owned as a unit
4. __flash_____   a device that provides light to brighten a picture
5. __fluently___   the ability to speak a language correctly

Directions: Read each sentence. Underline the word in the parentheses that correctly completes each sentence. Then, write the underlined word on the line.

지도: 각 문장을 읽으십시오. 각 문장을 올바르게 완성하는 괄호 안에 있는 단어에 밑줄을 긋습니다. 그런 다음 밑줄 친 단어를 줄에 쓰십시오.

6. Fred's camera has a built-in ____flash_____. (<u>flash</u>, flower)

7. Flamingos can ___fly____ up to 40 mph in the air. (flash, <u>fly</u>)

8. My friend speaks French and Finnish ___fluently____. (<u>fluently</u>, flash)

9. The florist made a beautiful __flower__ arrangement. (fluently, <u>flower</u>)

10. After the funeral, a __fleet__ of cars drove down the avenue. (fly, <u>fleet</u>)

Name: _____ Date: ___/___/_____ Score: _____

Lesson 6.3

Reading Words with the "fle" Letter Combination

✓ Lesson Check Point

 Directions: Read each target word. Find the "fle" letter combination and put a check (✓) in the column that identifies its position: beginning, within or end.

지도: 각 대상 단어를 읽으십시오. "fle" 문자 조합을 찾아해당 위치를식 별하는열에 체크(✓)를 하십시오: 시작, 내부 또는 끝.

Target Words	Beginning (First 3 Letters)	Within	End (Last 3 Letters)
1. waffle			✓
2. flesh	✓		
3. fleet	✓		
4. reflect		✓	
5. duffle			✓

 Directions: Read each target word. Put a check (✓) in the "yes" column if the "fle" letter combination has the /f/ + /ə/ + /l/ sounds. Put a check (✓) in the "no" column if the "fle" letter combination does not have the /f/ + /ə/ + /l/ sounds.

지도: 각 대상 단어를 읽으십시오. "fle" 문자 조합에/f/ + /ə/ + /l/ 소리가있으면 "yes" 열에 체크(✓)를 하십시오. "fle" 문자 조합에/f/ + /ə/ + /l/ 소리가"no" 아 니오" 열에 체크(✓)를 하십시오.

Target Words	Yes	No
6. waffle	✓	
7. flesh		✓
8. fleet		✓
9. reflect		✓
10. duffle	✓	

Classwork

 Name: _____ Date:___/___/_____ Score:_____

Lesson 6.4

Reading Words with the "ft," "lf" and "ff" Letter Combinations

Dictionary Skills/ Vocabulary

✓ Lesson Check Point

 Directions: Read each target word and its definition. Write the letter of the definition on the line of each target word. Use a dictionary or the Internet to check your answers.
지도: 각 대상 단어와 그 정의를 읽으십시오. 각 대상 단어의 행에 정의의 문자를 씁니다. 사전이나 인터넷을 사용하여 답을 확인하십시오.

Target Words	Definitions
1. _d_ giraffe	a. a piece of writing that is not finalized
2. _e_ Gulf	b. to move along by wind or water
3. _a_ draft	c. a vehicle that can fly in the air
4. _c_ aircraft	d. the tallest land animal with dark spots
5. _b_ drift	e. a large body of water partially enclosed by land

 Directions: Read each sentence and write the target word that correctly completes the sentence.
지도: 각 문장을 읽고 문장을 올바르게 완성하는 목표 단어를 쓰십시오.

6. I will write the first _____draft_____ of the report in class.

7. The _____aircraft_____ flew from New York City to Atlantic City.

8. At sunset, the boats and rafts will _____drift_____ along the lake.

9. The hurricane damaged the houses along the _____Gulf_____ Coast.

10. The guide said, "The _____giraffe_____ is the tallest African animal."

Name: _____ Date: ___/___/_____ Score: _____

Lesson 6.5

Reading Words with a Silent Letter "f"

✓ **Lesson Check Point**

 Directions: Read the target words in the word box. Write the words that have a silent letter "f" in the first column. Write the words that do not have a silent letter "f" in the second column.

지도: 단어 상자에 있는 대상 단어를 읽으십시오. 첫 번째 열에 묵음문자 "f"가 있는 단어를 쓰십시오. 두 번째 열에 묵음 문자"f"가 없는 단어를 쓰십시오.

Target Word Box				
muffin	buffalo	infancy	faces	suffocate
wife	after	afresh	afford	flying
defect	effect	cliff	caffeine	officially
fitness	coffee	bullfrog	fast	taffy

Letter "f" is silent

- cliff
- taffy
- effect
- afford
- muffin
- coffee
- caffeine
- buffalo
- suffocate
- officially

Letter "f" has the /f/ sound

- wife
- fast
- defect
- after
- afresh
- faces
- flying
- fitness
- infancy
- bullfrog

Classwork

 Name: _____ Date: ___/___/_____ Score: _____

Lesson 6.6

Reading Singular and Plural forms of Words Ending in "-f" & "-fe"

✓ **Lesson Check Point**

 Directions: Read each target word. Put a check (✓) in the second column if the plural form of the target word ends with "-ves." Put a check (✓) in the third column if the plural form of the target word ends with "-s" or "-es."

지도: 각 대상 단어를 읽으십시오. 대상 단어의 복수형이 "-ves"로 끝나는 경우 두 번째 열에 체크(✓)를 하십시오. 대상 단어의 복수형이 "-s" 또는 "-es."로 끝나는 경우 세 번째 열에 체크(✓)를 하십시오.

Target Words	The plural form of the target word ends with "-ves"	The plural form of the target word ends with "-s" or "-es"
1. roof		✓
2. half	✓	
3. life	✓	
4. thief	✓	
5. chef		✓

 **Directions:** Read each sentence. Complete each sentence by writing the plural form of the word on the line.

지도: 각 문장을 읽으십시오. 단어의 복수형을 줄에 써서 각 문장을 완성하세요.

6. Doctors save _____lives_____ every day. (life)

7. The men gave flowers to their _____wives_____. (wife)

8. Frank built five _____shelves_____ by himself. (shelf)

9. The girls filmed the events by _____themselves_____. (herself)

10. Many _____wolves_____ attacked the farmer's chicken. (wolf)

Name: _____ Date:___/___/_____ Score:_____

The Reading Challenge

Lesson 6.7

Reading Multisyllable Words

✓ **Lesson Check Point**

 Directions: Read and divide each target word into syllables. Write each word and place a hyphen (-) between the syllables in the second column. Write the number of syllables in the third column. Use a dictionary or the Internet to check your answers.

지도: 각 대상 단어를 읽고 음절로 나눕니다. 각 단어를 쓰고 두 번째 열의 음절 사이에 하이픈(-)을 넣습니다. 세 번째 열에 음절 수를 쓰십시오. 사전이나 인터넷을 사용하여 답을 확인하십시오.

Target Words	Words Divided into Syllables	Number of Syllables
1. fencing	fenc-ing	2
2. fabulous	fab-u-lous	3
3. friendship	friend-ship	2
4. facial	fa-cial	2
5. flawless	flaw-less	2
6. franchising	fran-chis-ing	3
7. falcon	fal-con	2
8. finalist	fi-nal-ist	3
9. florist	flo-rist	2
10. football	foot-ball	2

Classwork

 Name: _____ Date: ___/___/_____ Score: _____

The Reading Challenge

Lesson 6.7

Reading Multisyllable Words

✓ **Lesson Check Point**

 Directions: Read each target word. Circle the word in the row that is divided correctly into syllables. Use a dictionary or the Internet to check your answers.

지도: 각 대상 단어를 읽으십시오. 음절로 올바르게 나누어진 행에 있는 단어에 동그라미를 치십시오. 사전이나 인터넷을 사용하여 답을 확인하십시오.

Model

| factory | a. fac-tor-y | (b. fac-to-ry) | c. fa-cto-ry |

1. flexible	b. fle-x-ible	b. fle-xi-ble	(c. flex-i-ble)
2. festival	a. fest-i-val	b. fe-stiv-al	(c. fes-ti-val)
3. fabricate	(a. fab-ri-cate)	b. fa-bri-cate	c. fabr-ic-ate
4. finale	a. fin-al-e	(b. fi-nal-e)	c. fina-le
5. forensic	a. for-e-nsic	b. for-en-sic	(c. fo-ren-sic)
6. fortify	a. fort-i-fy	(b. for-ti-fy)	c. for-tif-y
7. familiar	(a. fa-mil-iar)	b. fam-i-liar	c. fam-il-iar
8. flavoring	(a. fla-vor-ing)	b. flav-or-ing	c. flav-o-ring

Name: _____ Date: ___/___/_____ Score: _____

Lesson 6.8

Reading and Writing

Proper and Common Nouns and Adjectives

✓ Lesson Check Point

Directions: Read the words in the word box. Put an (X) on the line next to each word that is written incorrectly. Remember that all proper nouns and proper adjectives are capitalized. Use a dictionary or the Internet to check your answers.

지도: 단어 상자에 있는 단어를 읽으십시오. 잘못 쓰여진 각 단어 옆의 줄에 (X)를 표시하십시오. 모든 고유 명사와 고유 형용사는 대문자임을 기억하십시오. 사전이나 인터넷을 사용하여 답을 확인하십시오.

Word Box					
__	flower	__	Florida	X	far East
X	franklin	__	flock	X	france
X	french	X	Finalist	__	fashion
__	flamingo	X	frankfort	__	florist

Directions: Read each unedited sentence and underline the word that is written incorrectly. Write each sentence correctly on the line.

지도: 편집되지 않은 각 문장을 읽고 잘못 쓰여진 단어에 밑줄을긋습 니다. 각 문장을 줄에 올바르게 쓰십시오.

Model
Fiji is my <u>Florist's</u> favorite holiday destination.
<u>Fiji is my florist's favorite holiday destination.</u>

1. Flossy and Frank were born in <u>france</u>.
<u>Flossy and Frank were born in France.</u>

2. <u>francis</u> speaks English and French fluently.
<u>Francis speaks English and French fluently.</u>

3. Freda works by <u>fort</u> Hamilton Parkway.
<u>Freda works by Fort Hamilton Parkway.</u>

4. Fred's baseball game is at <u>frankfurt</u> Field.
<u>Fred's baseball game is at Frankfurt Field.</u>

Classwork

 Name: _____ Date: ___/___/_____ Score: _____

Lesson 7.1

Reading Words with the Letter G/g

✓ **Lesson Check Point**

 Directions: Read each target word. Find the letter "g" and put a check (✓) in the column that identifies its position: beginning, within or end.
지도: 각 대상 단어를 읽으십시오. 문자"g"를 찾아 체크 표시(✓)위치를 식별하는 열에서 시작, 내부 또는 끝.

Target Words	Beginning (First Letter)	Within	End (Last Letter)
1. glossary	✓		
2. hexagon		✓	
3. landing			✓
4. oblong			✓
5. government	✓		

 Directions: Read each sentence and underline the words that begin with the letter "g." Write all the underlined words in alphabetical order on the lines below.
지도: 각 문장을 읽고 문자"g"로 시작하는 단어에 밑줄을 긋습니다. 밑줄 친 모든 단어를 아래 줄에 알파벳 순서로 쓰십시오.

6. Billy and Fran ate <u>green</u> <u>grapes</u>.

7. All the boys earned <u>good</u> <u>grades</u>.

8. My <u>guests</u> are <u>going</u> to the airport.

9. The <u>girls</u> forgot to put <u>gas</u> in the car.

10. The <u>golfers</u> play a challenging <u>game</u>.

game_____   gas_____   girls_____
going_____ golfers_____ good_____
grades_____ grapes_____ green_____
                 guests_____

Name: _____ Date: ___/___/_____ Score: _____

Lesson 7.1

Reading Words with the Hard Letter "g"

✓ Lesson Check Point

Directions: Read each target word. Put a check (✓) under the correct column heading.

지도: 각 대상 단어를 읽으십시오. 올바른 열 제목 아래에 체크(✓)를하십시오.

Target Words	Hard "g" has the /g/ sound as in the word <u>gum</u>	Soft "g" has the /j/ sound as in the word <u>gem</u>
1. gills	✓	
2. golden	✓	
3. gentle		✓
4. geese	✓	
5. gallops	✓	

Directions: Read each sentence and underline the words that have the hard "g" sound. The anchor word for the hard "g" sound is <u>gum</u>. Write all the underlined words in alphabetical order on the lines below.

지도: 각 문장을 읽고 단단한"g" 소리가 나는 단어에 밑줄을 긋습니다. 단단한"g" 소리의 기준어는 gum입니다. 밑줄 친 모든 단어를 아래 줄에알파벳 순서로 쓰십시오.

6. <u>Gloria</u> and Gina have beautiful blue <u>glasses</u>.

7. Today, Georgette saw a cow, a <u>goat</u> and a <u>gazelle</u>.

8. Jennifer is <u>growing</u> geraniums in her <u>greenhouse</u>.

9. The children in Ms. George's class have <u>good</u> <u>grades</u>.

10. My <u>grandfather</u> has ginger chicken and corn on the <u>grill</u>.

gazelle _____   glasses _____   Gloria _____
goat _____   good _____   grades _____
grandfather _____ greenhouse _____ grill _____
                        growing _____

Classwork

Name: _____ Date: ___/___/_____ Score: _____

Lesson 7.2

Reading Words with the Soft Letter "g"

✓ Lesson Check Point

Directions: Read each target word. Put a check (✓) under the correct column heading.

지도: 각 대상 단어를 읽으십시오. 올바른 열 제목 아래에 체크(✓)를하십시오.

Target Words	Soft "g" has the /j/ or /zh/ sound as in the words gem & massage	Hard "g" has the /g/ sound as in the word gum	Both soft "g" and hard "g" sounds as in the word gauge
1. garage			✓
2. gear		✓	
3. intelligent	✓		
4. progress		✓	
5. grammar		✓	

Directions: Read each sentence and underline the words that have the soft "g" sound. The anchor word for the soft "g" sound is gem. Write all the underlined words in alphabetical order on the lines below.

지도: 각 문장을 읽고 부드러운"g" 소리가 나는 단어에 밑줄을 긋습니다. 부드러운"g" "g" 소리의 기준어는 gem입니다. 밑줄 친 모든 단어를 아래 줄에 알파벳 순서로 쓰십시오.

6. Gloria's giant gem glistens in the sun.

7. Gianna is chewing gum in the gymnasium.

8. Ginny got a great grade in her biology class.

9. For graduation, I received a gigantic package.

10. The teenagers felt guilty because they did not go to the gym.

biology _____   gem _____   Gianna _____
giant _____   gigantic _____   Ginny _____
gym _____   gymnasium _____   package _____
                   teenagers _____

Name: _____ Date: ___/___/_____ Score: _____

Review Lessons 7.1 & 7.2

Reading Hard Letter "g" and Soft Letter "g" Words

Directions: Read each target word. Put a check (✓) under the correct column heading.

지도: 각 대상 단어를 읽으십시오. 올바른 열 제목 아래에 체크(✓)를 하십시오.

Target Words	Soft "g" has the /j/ or /zh/ sound as in the words gem & massage	Hard "g" has the /g/ sound as in the word gum	Both soft "g" and hard "g" sounds as in the word gauge
1. get		✓	
2. biology	✓		
3. ground		✓	
4. ingested	✓		
5. fragrant		✓	

Directions: Read each sentence and underline the words that have the hard "g" sound. The anchor word for the hard "g" sound is gum. Write all the underlined words in alphabetical order on the lines below.

지도: 각 문장을 읽고 단단한 "g" 소리가 나는 단어에 밑줄을 긋습니다. 단단한 "g" 소리의 기준어는 gum입니다. 밑줄 친 모든 단어를 아래 줄에 알파벳 순서로 쓰십시오.

6. Georgette has <u>good</u> <u>grades</u>.

7. <u>Greg</u> enjoys <u>going</u> to the gym.

8. Gina's <u>eyeglasses</u> are <u>glamorous</u>.

9. Ben <u>gave</u> me a bronze chain as a <u>gift</u>.

10. My friend, Gio, <u>graduated</u> and traveled to <u>Guyana</u>.

eyeglasses   gave   gift
glamorous   going   good
grades   graduated   Greg
                      Guyana

Classwork

Name: _____   Date: ___/___/_____   Score: _____

Review Lessons 7.1 & 7.2

Reading Hard Letter "g" and Soft Letter "g" Words

 Directions: Read the target words in the word box. In the first column, write the words with the letter "g" that have the /g/ sound, as in the word gum. In the second column, write the words with the letter "g" that have the /j/ sound, as in the word gem.

지도: 단어 상자에 있는 대상 단어를 읽으십시오. 첫 번째 열에는 단어 gum 에서와 같이 /g/ 소리가 나는 문자 "g"가 있는 단어를 씁니다. 두 번째 열에 "g"가 포함된 단어를 쓰십시오. /j/ 소리, gem이라는 단어에서와 같이.

Target Word Box				
digital	green	geese	ginger	page
germs	greet	gems	organ	gulf
grandson	glasses	large	sugar	engine
gate	gifts	gym	stage	orange

Hard letter "g" has the /g/ sound as in the word gum

- gifts
- gate
- green
- greet
- sugar
- gulf
- geese
- organ
- glasses
- grandson

Soft letter "g" has the /j/ sound as in the word gem

- gym
- page
- gems
- stage
- large
- germs
- orange
- digital
- engine
- ginger

Name: _____ Date: ___/___/_____ Score: _____

Lesson 7.3

Reading Words with the "gr" Letter Combination

Dictionary Skills/ Vocabulary

✓ **Lesson Check Point**

Directions: Read each target word and its definition. Write the letter of the definition on the line of each target word. Use a dictionary or the Internet to check your answers.

지도: 각 대상 단어와 그 정의를 읽으십시오. 각 대상 단어의 행에 정의의 문자를 씁니다. 사전이나 인터넷을 사용하여 답을 확인하십시오.。

Target Words	Definitions
1. _b_ grabs	a. to make a big, positive impression
2. _a_ grand	b. to take something quickly with one's hand(s)
3. _e_ gravel	c. something that contains or is covered with oil
4. _c_ greasy	d. to hold something firmly with one's hand(s)
5. _d_ grip	e. a mixture of very small rocks and pebbles

Directions: Read each sentence. Underline the word in the parentheses that correctly completes each sentence. Then, write the underlined word on the line.

지도: 각 문장을 읽으십시오. 각 문장을 올바르게 완성하는 괄호 안에 있는 단어에 밑줄을 긋습니다. 그런 다음 밑줄 친 단어를 줄에 쓰십시오.

6. Grandpa's driveway is made of _____gravel_____. (greasy, <u>gravel</u>)

7. I can't eat the burger because it is too _____greasy_____. (grabs, <u>greasy</u>)

8. The gloves give me a better _____grip_____ on the bars. (<u>grip</u>, grabbed)

9. Greg _____grabs_____ the books with both hands. (<u>grabs</u>, gravel)

10. At the dance, the girls made a _____grand_____ entrance. (<u>grand</u>, greasy)

Classwork

Name: _____ Date:___/___/_____ Score:_____

Lesson 7.4

Reading Words with the "gl" Letter Combination

Dictionary Skills/ Vocabulary

✓ **Lesson Check Point**

Directions: Read each target word and its definition. Write the target word on the line in front of its meaning. Use a dictionary or the Internet to check your answers.

지도: 각 대상 단어와 그 정의를 읽으십시오. 의미 앞 줄에 대상 단어를 쓰십시오. 사전이나 인터넷을 사용하여 답을 확인하십시오.

Target Word Box				
glaze	globe	gloom	glossary	glowing

1. __glowing__ to shine brightly like a light or the sun
2. __gloom__   a state of sadness, hopelessness and/or depression
3. __glaze__   to spread a thin layer of something on a surface
4. __globe__   a three-dimensional, sphere shaped model of the earth
5. __glossary__ an alphabetical list of text-related words with definitions

Directions: Read each sentence. Underline the word in the parentheses that correctly completes each sentence. Then, write the underlined word on the line.

지도: 각 문장을 읽으십시오. 각 문장을 올바르게 완성하는 괄호 안에 있는 단어에 밑줄을 긋습니다. 그런 다음 밑줄 친 단어를 줄에 쓰십시오.

6. The beautiful, blushing bride is __glowing__. (gloom, <u>glowing</u>)

7. Gerald plans to travel around the __globe__. (<u>globe</u>, glowing)

8. Gloria __glazed__ the chicken with barbecue sauce. (<u>glazed</u>, globe)

9. The bad report brought deep __gloom__ to the family. (glossary, <u>gloom</u>)

10. The book's __glossary__ helps me define difficult words. (<u>glossary</u>, glowing)

 Name: _____ Date: ___/___/_____ Score: _____

Lesson 7.4

Reading Words with the "gle" Letter Combination

✓ **Lesson Check Point**

 Directions: Read each target word. Find the "gle" letter combination and put a check (✓) in the column that identifies its position: beginning, within or end.
지도: 각 대상 단어를 읽으십시오. "gle" 문자 조합을 찾아 위치를 식별하는 열에 체크(✓)를 하십시오: 시작, 내부 또는 끝.

Target Words	Beginning (First 3 Letters)	Within	End (Last 3 Letters)
1. glee	✓		
2. angle			✓
3. mangled		✓	
4. gleaming	✓		
5. triangle			✓

 Directions: Read each target word. Put a check (✓) in the "yes" column if the "gle" letter combination has the /g/ + /ə/ + /l/ sounds. Put a check (✓) in the "no" column if the "gle" letter combination does not have the /g/ + /ə/ + /l/ sounds.
지도: 각 대상 단어를 읽으십시오. "gle" 문자 조합에 /g/ + /ə/ + /l/ 소리가 있으면 "yes" 열에 체크(✓)를 하십시오. "gle" 문자 조합에 /g/ + /ə/ + /l/ 소리가 없으면 "no" 열에 체크(✓)를 하십시오.

Target Words	Yes	No
6. glee		✓
7. angle	✓	
8. mangled	✓	
9. gleaming		✓
10. triangle	✓	

Classwork

 Name: _____ Date: ___/___/_____ Score: _____

Lesson 7.5

Reading Words with the "gh" Letter Combination

✓ Lesson Check Point

 Directions: Read each target word. Circle the word in the column that has the same "gh" sound as the target word.
지도: 각 대상 단어를 읽으십시오. 대상 단어와 같은 "gh" 소리가 나는 열의 단어에 동그라미를 치십시오.

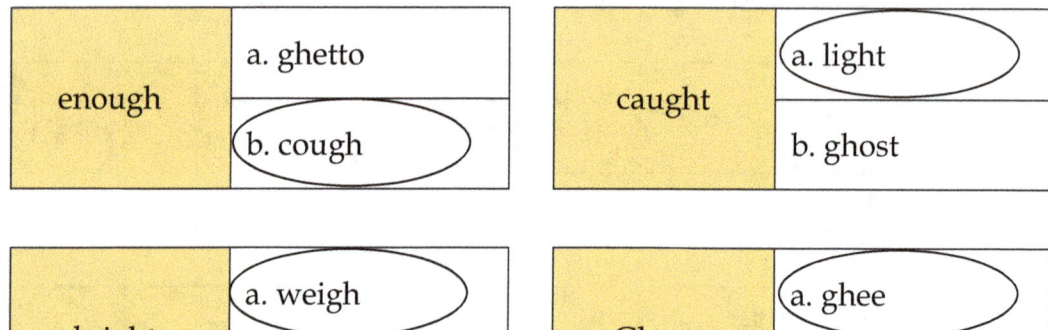

 Directions: Read each target word. Put a check (✓) under the correct column heading.
지도: 각 대상 단어를 읽으십시오. 올바른 열 제목 아래에 체크(✓)를 하십시오.

Target Words	"gh" has the /g/ sound as in the word ghetto	"gh" has the /f/ sound as in the word laugh	"gh" is silent as in the word light
1. enough		✓	
2. caught			✓
3. bright			✓
4. Ghana	✓		

 Name: _____ Date:___/___/_____ Score:_____

Lesson 7.6

Reading Words with the "gn" Letter Combination

✓ Lesson Check Point

 Directions: Read each target word. Circle the word in the column that has the same "gn" sound(s) as the target word.
지도: 각 대상 단어를 읽으십시오. 대상 단어와 같은 "gn" 소리가 나는 열의 단어에 동그라미를 치십시오.

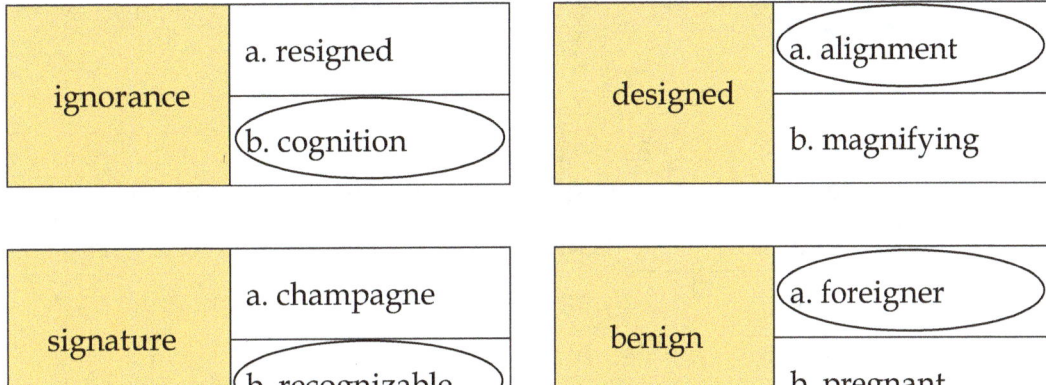

 Directions: Read each target word. Put a check (✓) under the correct column heading.
지도: 각 대상 단어를 읽으십시오. 올바른 열 제목 아래에 체크(✓)를 하십시오.

Target Words	"gn" has the /g/ + /n/ sounds as in the word <u>ignite</u>	"gn" has the silent "g" + /n/ sound as in the word <u>sign</u>
1. ignorance	✓	
2. designed		✓
3. signature	✓	
4. benign		✓

Classwork

 Name: _____ Date: ___/___/_____ Score: _____

Lesson 7.7

Reading Words with a Silent Letter "g"

✓ **Lesson Check Point**

 Directions: Read the target words in the word box. Write the words that have a silent letter "g" in the first column. Write the words that do not have a silent letter "g" in the second column.

지도: 단어 상자에 있는 대상 단어를 읽으십시오. 첫 번째 열에 묵음문자 "g"가 있는 단어를 쓰십시오. 두 번째 열에 묵음 문자"g"가 없는 단어를 쓰십시오.

Target Word Box				
daughter	sleigh	image	hunger	signal
glance	fight	thought	campaign	dough
frog	dignify	sign	magnify	regent
elegant	neighbor	assign	grand	weigh

Letter "g" is silent	Letter "g" has the /g/ or /j/ sound
sign	frog
fight	image
dough	glance
assign	dignify
weigh	grand
sleigh	elegant
thought	signal
neighbor	regent
daughter	hunger
campaign	magnify

Learn To Read English With Directions In Korean

Name: _____ Date: ___/___/_____ Score: _____

The Reading Challenge

Lesson 7.8

Reading Multisyllable Words

✓ **Lesson Check Point**

 Directions: Read and divide each target word into syllables. Write each word and place a hyphen (-) between the syllables in the second column. Write the number of syllables in the third column. Use a dictionary or the Internet to check your answers.

지도: 각 대상 단어를 읽고 음절로 나눕니다. 각 단어를 쓰고 두 번째 열의 음절 사이에 하이픈(-)을 넣습니다. 세 번째 열에 음절 수를 쓰십시오. 사전이나 인터넷을 사용하여 답을 확인하십시오.

Target Words	Words Divided into Syllables	Number of Syllables
1. grocery	gro-cer-y	3
2. Guyana	Guy-a-na	3
3. gardening	gar-den-ing	3
4. general	gen-er-al	3
5. glamorize	glam-or-ize	3
6. grandfather	grand-fa-ther	3
7. girlfriend	girl-friend	2
8. generous	gen-er-ous	3
9. guardian	guard-i-an	3
10. genetic	ge-net-ic	3

Unit G Lesson 7.8

Classwork

Name: _____ Date: ___/___/_____ Score: _____

The Reading Challenge

Lesson 7.8

Reading Multisyllable Words

✓ **Lesson Check Point**

Directions: Read each target word. Circle the word in the row that is divided correctly into syllables. Use a dictionary or the Internet to check your answers.

지도: 각 대상 단어를 읽으십시오. 음절로 올바르게 나누어진 행에 있는 단어에 동그라미를 치십시오. 사전이나 인터넷을 사용하여 답을 확인하십시오.

Model

| galaxy | a. ga-lax-y | b. (gal-ax-y) | c. gal-a-xy |

1. glycerol	a. (glyc-er-ol)	b. gly-cer-ol	c. glyc-e-rol
2. governess	a. go-ver-ness	b. gov-ern-ess	c. (gov-er-ness)
3. general	a. (gen-er-al)	b. ge-ner-al	c. gene-r-al
4. graduate	a. gra-du-ate	b. (grad-u-ate)	c. grad-uat-e
5. granola	a. gra-nol-a	b. (gra-no-la)	c. gran-ol-a
6. gestation	a. gest-a-tion	b. ge-sta-tion	c. (ges-ta-tion)
7. germinate	a. (ger-mi-nate)	b. germ-i-nate	c. ge-rmi-nate
8. gratify	a. (grat-i-fy)	b. gra-tif-y	c. gr-ati-fy

Name: _____ Date: ___/___/_____ Score: _____

Lesson 7.9

Reading and Writing

Proper and Common Nouns and Adjectives

Directions: Read the words in the word box. Put an (X) on the line next to each word that is written incorrectly. Remember that all proper nouns and proper adjectives are capitalized. Use a dictionary or the Internet to check your answers.

지도: 단어 상자에 있는 단어를 읽으십시오. 잘못 쓰여진 각 단어 옆의 줄에 (X)를 표시하십시오. 모든 고유 명사와 고유 형용사는 대문자임을 기억하십시오. 사전이나 인터넷을 사용하여 답을 확인하십시오.

Word Box					
X	Geology	X	gandhi	__	groom
X	Gym	X	Group	__	grammar
__	Greece	__	globe	X	georgetown
__	Guyana	X	germany	__	Ghana

Directions: Read each unedited sentence and underline the word that is written incorrectly. Write each sentence correctly on the line.

지도: 편집되지 않은 각 문장을 읽고 잘못 쓰여진 단어에 밑줄을긋습 니다. 각 문장을 줄에 올바르게 쓰십시오.

Model
Ginger and <u>gene</u> are going to Georgetown, Guyana.
Ginger and Gene are going to Georgetown, Guyana.

1. The Gambia and <u>ghana</u> are amazing African countries.
The Gambia and Ghana are amazing African countries.

2. The bride and the <u>Groom</u> are getting married in Grenada.
The bride and the groom are getting married in Grenada.

3. Everyone says that Mr. Grant will be Georgia's <u>Governor</u>.
Everyone says that Mr. Grant will be Georgia's governor.

4. George and <u>gem</u> said, "Grandma has beautiful new glasses."
George and Gem said, "Grandma has beautiful new glasses."

Classwork

Name: _____ Date: ___/___/_____ Score: _____

Lesson 8.1

Reading Words with the Letter H/h

✓ **Lesson Check Point**

Directions: Read each target word. Find the letter "h" and put a check (✓) in the column that identifies its position: beginning, within or end.
지도: 각 대상 단어를 읽으십시오. 문자"h"를 찾아 체크 표시(✓)위치를 식별하는 열에서 시작, 내부 또는 끝.

Target Words	Beginning (First Letter)	Within	End (Last Letter)
1. inch			✓
2. cheeta_h_			✓
3. hallway	✓		
4. Fahrenheit		✓	
5. Savannah			✓

Directions: Read each sentence and underline the words that begin with the letter "h." Write all the underlined words in alphabetical order on the lines below.
지도: 각 문장을 읽고"h"로 시작하는 단어에 밑줄을 긋습니다. 밑줄 친 모든 단어를 아래 줄에 알파벳 순서로 쓰십시오.

6. Barry's <u>home</u> is on top of the <u>hill</u>.

7. <u>Henry</u> lives in the center of <u>Houston</u>.

8. The <u>hummingbirds'</u> eggs are <u>hatching</u>.

9. The cats and <u>hamsters</u> are very <u>hungry</u>.

10. <u>Heather</u> Carrington is an <u>honest</u> person.

hamster _____   hatching _____   Heather _____
Henry _____   hill _____   home _____
honest _____   Houston _____   hummingbirds' _____
                 hungry _____

Name: _____ Date: ___/___/_____ Score: _____

Lesson 8.2

Reading Words with the Letter "h" Combinations:
"sh," "wh," "ch," "th," "rh," "ph" and "gh"

✓ Lesson Check Point

Directions: Read the target words in the word box. Identify the words with the following letter combinations: "sh," "wh," "ch," "th," "rh," "ph" and "gh." Write the word on the line that shows the position of the letter combination: beginning, within or end.

지도: 단어 상자에 있는 대상 단어를 읽으십시오. "sh," "wh," "ch," "th," "rh," "ph" 및 "gh" 문자 조합으로 단어를 식별합니다. 문자 조합의 위치를 나타내는 줄에 단어를 쓰십시오: 시작, 내부 또는 끝.

Target Word Box				
wheel	thanks	rhino	kitchen	sheep
dishes	paragraph	anywhere	phone	laugh
overheard	ghost	myrrh	nephew	brother
chocolate	south	goldfish	reach	caught

	Beginning	Within	End
sh	1. sheep	2. dishes	3. goldfish
wh	4. wheel	5. anywhere	
ch	6. chocolate	7. kitchen	8. reach
th	9. thanks	10. brother	11. south
rh	12. rhino	13. overheard	14. myrrh
ph	15. phone	16. nephew	17. paragraph
gh	18. ghost	19. caught	20. laugh

Learn To Read English With Directions In Korean

Classwork

Name: _____ Date: ___/___/_____ Score: _____

Lesson 8.2

Reading Words with the Letter "h" Combinations:
"sh," "wh," "ch," "th," "rh," "ph," "gh" and "sch"

✓ **Lesson Check Point**

Directions: Read the target words in the word box. Identify the words with the following letter combinations: "sh," "wh," "ch," "th," "rh," "ph," "gh" and "sch." Write the target word that correctly completes each sentence on the line.

지도: 단어 상자에 있는 대상 단어를 읽습니다: "sh," "wh," "ch," "th," "rh," "ph," "gh" 및 "sch"의 문자 조합으로 단어를 식별합니다. 각 문장을 올바르게 완성하는 대상 단어를 줄에 쓰십시오.

Target Word Box		
shower	Ghana	Children
Whales	theater	through
phones		Chemicals
school		rhombus

1. I am learning to read and write in _____school_____.

2. We are not allowed to have cellular ___phones___ in school.

3. The sun was shining brightly ____through____ the window.

4. Yesterday, Trevor used liquid soap during his ___shower___.

5. Brenda used her ruler to draw the shape of a ___rhombus___.

6. __Children__ should obey their parents and teachers.

7. __Whales__ are the largest mammals that live in the ocean.

8. The people from ____Ghana____ speak many languages.

9. Thelma is hosting her birthday party at the movie __theater__.

10. __Chemicals__ found in processed foods may harm your health.

Unit H Lesson 8.2

Name: _____ Date: ___/___/_____ Score: _____

Lesson 8.3

Reading Words with a Silent Letter "h"

✓ **Lesson Check Point**

 Directions: Read the target words in the word box. Write the words that have a silent letter "h" in the first column. Write the words that do not have a silent letter "h" in the second column.

지도: 단어 상자에 있는 대상 단어를 읽습니다. 첫 번째 열에 묵음문자 "h"가 있는 단어를 쓰십시오. 두 번째 열에 묵음 문자"h"가 없는 단어를 쓰십시오.

Target Word Box				
inherent	beehive	unhappy	myrrh	dehydrate
exhibit	white	fright	hundred	holding
silhouette	behind	exhaust	honor	Fahrenheit
heirloom	house	comprehend	perhaps	whales

Letter "h" is silent

- fright
- white
- exhaust
- whales
- myrrh
- exhibit
- honor
- heirloom
- silhouette
- Fahrenheit

Letter "h" has the /h/ sound

- house
- behind
- holding
- hundred
- beehive
- inherent
- unhappy
- perhaps
- dehydrate
- comprehend

Classwork

 Name: _____ Date: ___/___/_____ Score: _____

The Reading Challenge

Lesson 8.4

Reading Multisyllable Words

✓ Lesson Check Point

 Directions: Read and divide each target word into syllables. Write each word and place a hyphen (-) between the syllables in the second column. Write the number of syllables in the third column. Use a dictionary or the Internet to check your answers.

지도: 각 대상 단어를 읽고 음절로 나눕니다. 각 단어를 쓰고 두 번째 열의 음절 사이에 하이픈(-)을 넣습니다. 세 번째 열에 음절 수를 쓰십시오. 사전이나 인터넷을 사용하여 답을 확인하십시오.

Target Words	Words Divided into Syllables	Number of Syllables
1. hallway	hall-way	2
2. heartache	heart-ache	2
3. honeycomb	hon-ey-comb	3
4. hyperlink	hy-per-link	3
5. headlights	head-lights	2
6. harmonize	har-mo-nize	3
7. homonym	hom-o-nym	3
8. hardware	hard-ware	2
9. hesitant	hes-i-tant	3
10. hazelnut	ha-zel-nut	3

Name: _____ Date: ___/___/_____ Score: _____

The Reading Challenge

Lesson 8.4

Reading Multisyllable Words

✓ **Lesson Check Point**

 Directions: Read each target word. Circle the word in the row that is divided correctly into syllables. Use a dictionary or the Internet to check your answers.

지도: 각 대상 단어를 읽으십시오. 음절로 올바르게 나누어진 행에 있는 단어에 동그라미를 치십시오. 사전이나 인터넷을 사용하여 답을 확인하십시오.

Model

heroic	a. he-roi-c	b. her-o-ic	c. he-ro-ic ⭕
1. hatchet	a. hatch-et ⭕	b. ha-tch-et	c. hatc-het
2. hazelnut	a. haz-e-lnut	b. haz-el-nut	c. ha-zel-nut ⭕
3. hexagon	a. he-xa-gon	b. hex-a-gon ⭕	c. hex-ag-on
4. historic	a. hi-stor-ic	b. his-tor-ic ⭕	c. hist-or-ic
5. halogen	a. hal-og-en	b. hal-o-gen ⭕	c. ha-lo-gen
6. hairdresser	a. hair-dress-er ⭕	b. ha-ir-dresser	c. hair-dresse-r
7. harvesting	a. harv-est-ing	b. har-ves-ting	c. har-vest-ing ⭕
8. handicap	a. hand-i-cap ⭕	b. han-dic-ap	c. hand-ic-ap

Classwork

Name: _____ Date: ___/___/_____ Score: _____

Lesson 8.5

Reading and Writing

Proper and Common Nouns and Adjectives

✓ **Lesson Check Point**

Directions: Read the words in the word box. Put an (X) on the line next to each word that is written incorrectly. Remember that all proper nouns and proper adjectives are capitalized. Use a dictionary or the Internet to check your answers.

지도: 단어 상자에 있는 단어를 읽으십시오. 잘못 쓰여진 각 단어 옆의 줄에 (X)를 표시하십시오. 모든 고유 명사와 고유 형용사는 대문자임을 기억하십시오. 사전이나 인터넷을 사용하여 답을 확인하십시오.

	Word Box				
__	Haiti	X	House	X	halifax
X	hebrew	X	Hexagon	__	Hawaii
__	horses	X	Haiku	__	hiccup
__	home	__	Hindu	X	hispanic

Directions: Read each unedited sentence and underline the word that is written incorrectly. Write each sentence correctly on the line.

路线: 读每个未经编辑的句子，并给书写错误的词加下划线。在线 上写上正确的句子。

Model
Mr. Hitt has a big house on <u>hope</u> Avenue.
<u>Mr. Hitt has a big house on Hope Avenue.</u>

1. Henry is studying <u>haitian</u> history at Hunter College.
<u>Henry is studying Haitian history at Hunter College.</u>

2. The local historian lives in <u>hartford's</u> Historic District.
<u>The local historian lives in Hartford's Historic District.</u>

3. The thoroughbred <u>Horses</u> are galloping along Houston Harbor.
<u>The thoroughbred horses are galloping along Houston Harbor.</u>

4. <u>heather</u> is a hard working housekeeper at the Hilton Garden Hotel.
<u>Heather is a hard working housekeeper at the Hilton Garden Hotel.</u>

Name: _____ Date: ___/___/_____ Score: _____

Lesson 9.1

Reading Words with the Letter I/i

✓ Lesson Check Point

 Directions: Read each target word. Find the letter "i" and put a check (✓) in the column that identifies its position: beginning, within or end.
지도: 각 대상 단어를 읽으십시오. 문자"i"를 찾아 체크 표시(✓)위치 를 식별하는 열에서 시작, 내부 또는 끝.

Target Words	Beginning (First Letter)	Within	End (Last Letter)
1. incapable	✓		
2. Fuji			✓
3. alive		✓	
4. broccoli			✓
5. Ireland	✓		

 Directions: Read each target word. Read the words in the row and circle the word that has a different vowel "i" sound.
지도: 각 대상 단어를 읽으십시오. 행에 있는 단어를 읽고 모음"i" 소리가 다른 단어에 동그라미를 치십시오.

Target Words				
6. blimp	(child)	this	grim	lid
7. spin	fix	pin	dip	(bike)
8. trip	hip	(nine)	fin	pit
9. crib	big	dim	(mild)	six
10. king	hill	(kite)	grin	ship

Classwork

 Name: _____ Date:___/___/_____ Score:_____

Lesson 9.2

Reading Words with the Short Vowel "i" Sound

✓ **Lesson Check Point**

 Directions: Read the words in the four boxes. Circle two words with the short vowel /ĭ/ sound. The anchor word for the short vowel /ĭ/ sound is <u>insect</u>.

지도: 네 개의 상자에 있는 단어를 읽으십시오. 짧은 모음/ĭ/ 소리로 두 단어에 동그라미를 치십시오. 단모음/ĭ/ 소리의 기준어는 insect입니다.

(bin)	(sip)	bike	(big)	(dig)	(slim)
child	mile	(hid)	fine	bite	pike

line	kite	(tint)	(will)	(twin)	pint
(crib)	(blip)	like	nine	taxi	(list)

 Directions: Read the words in the four boxes. Circle two words that rhyme. Rhyming words have the same ending sound, such as <u>hip</u> and <u>dip</u>.

지도: 네 개의 상자에 있는 단어를 읽으십시오. 운이 맞는 두 단어에동그라미를 치십시오. 운율이 있는 단어는 hip와dip과 같이 끝 소리가같습니다.

pine	(bib)	(clip)	wife	(fit)	(sit)
hike	(rib)	rice	(slip)	life	nice

mile	lime	hide	(him)	(win)	pipe
(six)	(mix)	(dim)	mice	(tin)	side

Learn To Read English With Directions In Korean

Name: _____ Date: ___/___/_____ Score: _____

Lesson 9.2

Reading & Writing Words with the Short Vowel "i" Sound

✓ **Lesson Check Point**

Directions: Read each sentence and underline three words with the short vowel /ĭ/ sound. Then, write the underlined words on the lines below. The anchor word for the short vowel /ĭ/ sound is <u>insect</u>.

지도: 각 문장을 읽고 세 단어에 짧은 모음/ĭ/ 소리에 밑줄을 긋습니다. 그런 다음 밑줄 친 단어를 아래 줄에 쓰십시오. 단모음/ĭ/ 소리의 기준 어는 insect입니다.

Model

<u>Jim</u> placed a <u>big</u> cup of ice on the <u>windowsill</u>.

Jim   big   windowsill

1. Irene gave <u>Jill</u> a <u>big</u> <u>wig</u>.

   Jill   big   wig

2. The <u>kids</u> <u>did</u> not <u>kick</u> the ball on the field.

   kids   did   kick

3. <u>Billy</u> said, "<u>Tim</u> <u>licked</u> the ice pop."

   Billy   Tim   licked

4. <u>Milly</u> <u>sipped</u> the medium-sized <u>drink</u>.

   Milly   sipped   drink

5. The <u>big</u> <u>dishes</u> used to serve the pizza are by the <u>sink</u>.

   big   dishes   sink

Classwork

 Name: _____ Date: ___/___/_____ Score: _____

Lesson 9.3

Reading Words with the Long Vowel "i" Sound

✓ **Lesson Check Point**

 Directions: Read the words in the four boxes. Circle two words with the long vowel /ī/ sound. The anchor word for the long vowel /ī/ sound is <u>ice</u>.

지도: 네 개의 상자에 있는 단어를 읽으십시오. 장모음/ī/ 소리로 두 단어에 동그라미를 치십시오. 장모음/ī/ 소리의 기준어는 ice입니다.

brain	(wild)	bill	(bike)	(hike)	taxi
kick	(fine)	(lime)	mini	sick	(dice)

(mine)	pink	chili	sing	pain	(vile)
train	(tile)	(mime)	(tide)	miss	(side)

 Directions: Read the words in the four boxes. Circle two words that rhyme. Rhyming words have the same ending sound, such as <u>rice</u> and <u>nice</u>.

지도: 네 개의 상자에 있는 단어를 읽으십시오. 운이 맞는 두 단어에 동그라미를 치십시오. 운율이 있는 단어는 rice와 nice와 같은 끝 소리가 같습니다.

lift	(dime)	(nine)	link	(bite)	fill
pick	(time)	kids	(pine)	(kite)	crib

(line)	skill	(like)	(pike)	(life)	rib
(vine)	Mali	drill	dim	lick	(wife)

Name: _____ Date: ___/___/_____ Score: _____

Lesson 9.3

Reading & Writing Words with the Long Vowel "i" Sound

✓ **Lesson Check Point**

Directions: Read each sentence and underline three words with the long vowel /ī/ sound. Then, write the underlined words on the lines below. The anchor word for the long vowel /ī/ sound is <u>ice</u>.

지도: 각 문장을 읽고 장모음/ī/ 소리로 세 단어에 밑줄을 긋습니다. 그런 다음 밑줄 친 단어를 아래 줄에 쓰십시오. 장모음/ī/ 소리의 기준어는 ice 입니다.

Model

David and <u>I</u> flew our big, <u>white</u> <u>kite</u> along the riverbank.

    I   white   kite

1. <u>Brian</u> has to fix his mountain <u>bike's</u> <u>tire</u>.

   Brian   bike's   tire

2. <u>Mike</u> went <u>outside</u> to <u>climb</u> the steep hill.

   Mike   outside   climb

3. Jill said, "The <u>bride</u> has a <u>nice</u>, <u>white</u> dress."

   bride   nice   white

4. <u>Irene's</u> husband <u>retired</u> from working as a <u>firefighter</u>.

   Irene's   retired   firefighter

5. The principal <u>invited</u> the <u>entire</u> class to his <u>tiny</u> office.

   invited   entire   tiny

Classwork

Name: _____ Date: ___/___/_____ Score: _____

Review Lessons 9.2 & 9.3

Reading Short Vowel and Long Vowel Words

✓ **Lesson Check Point**

Directions: Read the target words in the word box. In the first column, write the words that have the short vowel /ĭ/ sound, as in the word <u>insect</u>. In the second column, write the words that have the long vowel /ī/ sound, as in the word <u>ice</u>.

지도: 단어 상자에 있는 대상 단어를 읽습니다. 첫 번째 열에는 insect라는 단어와 같이 단모음 /ĭ/ 소리가 나는 단어를 씁니다. 두 번째 열에는 ice 라는 단어에서처럼 장모음 /ī/ 소리가 나는 단어를 씁니다.

Target Word Box				
child	dinner	trip	bill	gift
tie	hint	I	pink	diner
hi	bike	diet	skim	client
inward	pie	lint	ripe	disk

Letter "i" has the /ĭ/ sound as in the word <u>insect</u>

- lint
- trip
- bill
- gift
- disk
- hint
- pink
- skim
- inward
- dinner

Letter "i" has the /ī/ sound as in the word <u>ice</u>

- I
- hi
- pie
- tie
- bike
- diet
- ripe
- child
- client
- diner

 Name: _____ Date: ___/___/_____ Score: _____

Lesson 9.4

Reading Words with Letter "i" Vowel Pairs

✓ **Lesson Check Point**

 Directions: Read each target word. Circle the word in the column that has the same vowel "ia," "ie," "io" or "iu" sound(s) as the target word.
지도: 각 대상 단어를 읽으십시오. 대상 단어와 같은 모음"ia," "ie," "io" 또는"iu" 소리가 있는 열의 단어에 동그라미를 치십시오.

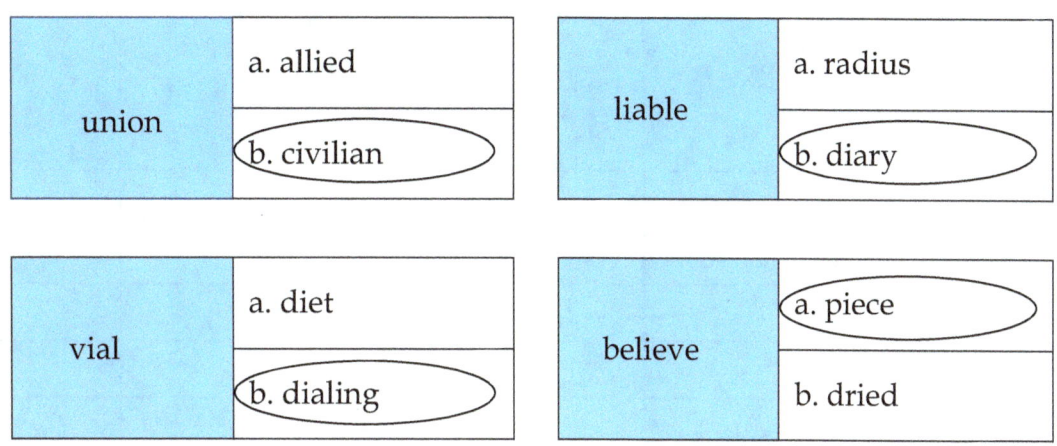

 Directions: Read each target word. Put a check (✓) under the correct column heading.
지도: 각 대상 단어를 읽으십시오. 올바른 열 제목 아래에 체크(✓)를하십시오.

Target Words	Words have the long "i" sound as in the word <u>dial</u>	Words do not have the long "i" sound
1. union		✓
2. liable	✓	
3. vial	✓	
4. believe		✓

Classwork

 Name: _____ Date: ___/___/_____ Score: _____

Lesson 9.5

Reading Words with the Final Letter "i"

✓ Lesson Check Point

 Directions: Read each target word. Find the letter "i" and put a check (✓) in the column that identifies its position within the syllable.
지도: 각 대상 단어를 읽으십시오. 문자"i"를 찾아 체크 표시(✓)음절내에서 위치를 식별하는 열에서.

Target Words	"i" is at the end of a one syllable word	"i" is at the end of the first syllable	"i" is at the end of a multi-syllable word
1. hi	✓		
2. final		✓	
3. alibi			✓
4. iron		✓	
5. dinosaur		✓	

 Directions: Read each target word. Put a check (✓) under the correct column heading.
지도: 각 대상 단어를 읽으십시오. 올바른 열 제목 아래에 체크(✓)를 하십시오.

Target Words	"i" has the /ĭ/ sound as in the word insect	"i" has the /ī/ sound as in the word bike	"i" has the /ə/ sound as in the word pencil	"i" is silent as in the word maid
6. kite		✓		
7. pilgrim			✓	
8. himself	✓			
9. business				✓
10. utensil			✓	

 Name: _____ Date: ___/___/_____ Score: _____

Lesson 9.6

Reading Letter "i" Words with the Schwa Vowel Sound

✓ Lesson Check Point

 Directions: Read each target word. Circle the word in the column that has the same "i" sound as the target word.
지도: 각 대상 단어를 읽으십시오. 목표 단어와 동일한"i" 소리가 나는 열의 단어에 동그라미를 치십시오.

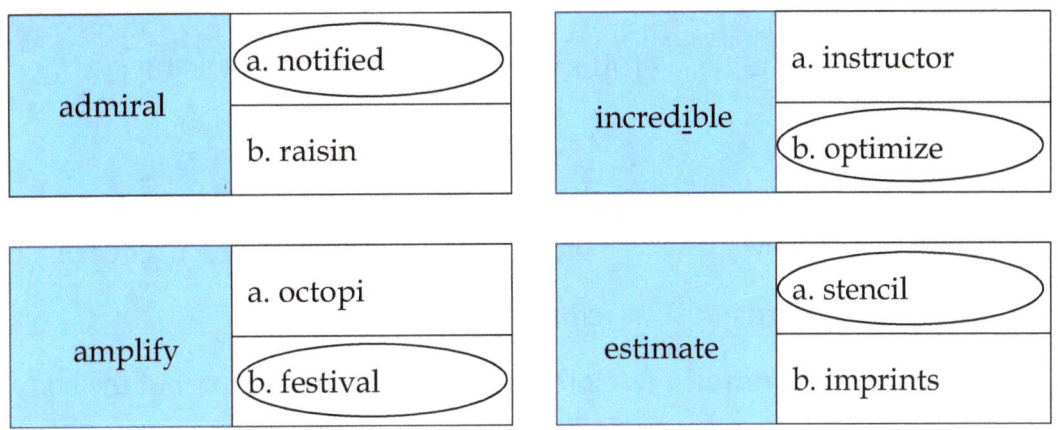

 Directions: Read each sentence and underline the letter "i" word that has the schwa vowel /ə/ sound. The anchor word for the letter "i" schwa vowel sound is <u>pencil</u>.
지도: 각 문장을 읽고 슈와 모음 /ə/ 소리가 있는 문자"i" 단어에 밑줄을 긋습니다. 문자"i" 슈와 모음 소리의 앵커 단어는 pencil입니다.

1. I will <u>notify</u> the girls about the field trip.

2. The child is experiencing pain in his <u>nostrils</u>.

3. Trinidad's <u>carnival</u> is a major cultural event.

4. The <u>binoculars</u> are inside my white briefcase.

5. I bought vanilla ice cream at the <u>convenience</u> store.

6. The president encouraged every <u>individual</u> to vote.

Classwork

 Name: _____ Date: ___/___/_____ Score: _____

Lesson 9.7

Reading Words with the "ir" Letter Combination

Dictionary Skills/ Vocabulary

✓ Lesson Check Point

 Directions: Read each target word and its definition. Write the letter of the definition on the line of each target word. Use a dictionary or the Internet to check your answers.

지도: 각 대상 단어와 그 정의를 읽으십시오. 각 대상 단어의 행에 정의의 문자를 씁니다. 사전이나 인터넷을 사용하여 답을 확인하십시오.

Target Words	Definitions
1. _c_ shirt	a. a bushy-tailed rodent that lives in a tree or a burrow
2. _e_ birds	b. females
3. _a_ squirrel	c. clothing worn on the upper part of the body
4. _d_ twirl	d. to spin or turn something around with one's fingers
5. _b_ girls	e. egg-laying animals that have wings

 Directions: Read each sentence and write the target word that completes the sentence.

지도: 각 문장을 읽고 문장을 완성하는 목표어를 쓰세요.

6. My white ____shirt____ has a clean collar.

7. The cheerleaders ____twirl____ their batons.

8. The ____girls____ like to eat ice cream cones.

9. Millions of ____birds____ migrate along the flyway.

10. The ____squirrel____ climbed up the tree quickly.

 Name: _____ Date: ___/___/_____ Score: _____

Lesson 9.8

Reading Letter "i" Words with the Long Vowel "e" Sound

✓ **Lesson Check Point**

 Directions: Read each target word. Circle the word in the column that has the same "i" sound as the target word.
지도: 각 대상 단어를 읽으십시오. 목표 단어와 동일한"i" 소리가 나는 열의 단어에 동그라미를 치십시오.

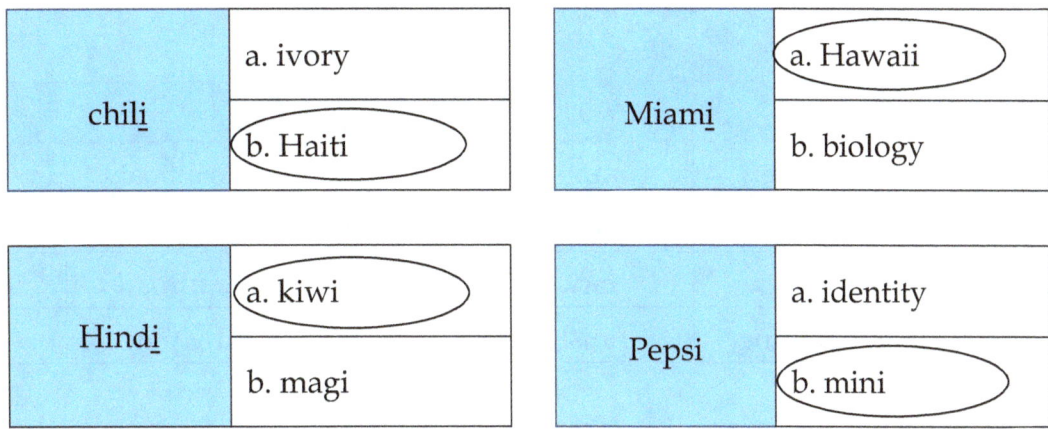

 Directions: Read each sentence and underline the letter "i" word that has the long vowel /ē/ sound. Then, write the word on the line. The anchor word, taxi has a letter "i" that represents the long vowel /ē/ sound.
지도: 각 문장을 읽고 장모음 /ē/ 소리가 나는"i" 단어에 밑줄을 긋습니다. 그런 다음 줄에 단어를 쓰십시오. 앵커 단어인 taxi에는 장모음 /ē/ 소리를 나타내는 문자"i"가 있습니다.

1. It is not wise to go <u>skiing</u> at night.   _skiing_

2. Jim and Mike enjoy eating <u>pita</u> bread.   _pita_

3. The children admire the <u>police</u> officers.   _police_

4. My family likes to eat dinner on the <u>patio</u>.   _patio_

5. I will use the sewing <u>machine</u> to sew a pillow.   _machine_

6. Baked <u>ziti</u> is a classic Italian-American dish.   _ziti_

Classwork

Name: _____ Date: ___/___/_____ Score: _____

Lesson 9.9

Reading Words with a Silent Letter "i"

✓ **Lesson Check Point**

Directions: Read the target words in the word box. Write the words that have a silent letter "i" in the first column. Write the words that do not have a silent letter "i" in the second column.

지도: 단어 상자에 있는 대상 단어를 읽습니다. 첫 번째 열에 묵음문자 "i"가 있는 단어를 쓰십시오. 두 번째 열에 묵음 문자"i"가 없는 단어를 쓰십시오.

Target Word Box				
aside	camping	Jamaica	sailboat	stained
waist	afraid	giggles	bail	fifteen
bigger	city	hiking	railroad	distinct
attaining	finish	suit	helping	again

Letter "i" is silent

- suit
- bail
- again
- waist
- afraid
- stained
- railroad
- Jamaica
- sailboat
- attaining

Letter "i" has a letter "i" sound

- city
- aside
- finish
- hiking
- bigger
- giggles
- helping
- distinct
- fifteen
- camping

 Name: _____   Date: ___/___/_____   Score: _____

Unit Review - I/i

Reading Words with Vowel "i" Sounds: /ĭ/, /ī/, /ə/ & Silent

✓ Lesson Check Point

 Directions: Read each target word. Circle the word in the column that has the same "i" sound as the target word.

지도: 각 대상 단어를 읽으십시오. 목표 단어와 동일한 "i" 소리가 나는 열의 단어에 동그라미를 치십시오.

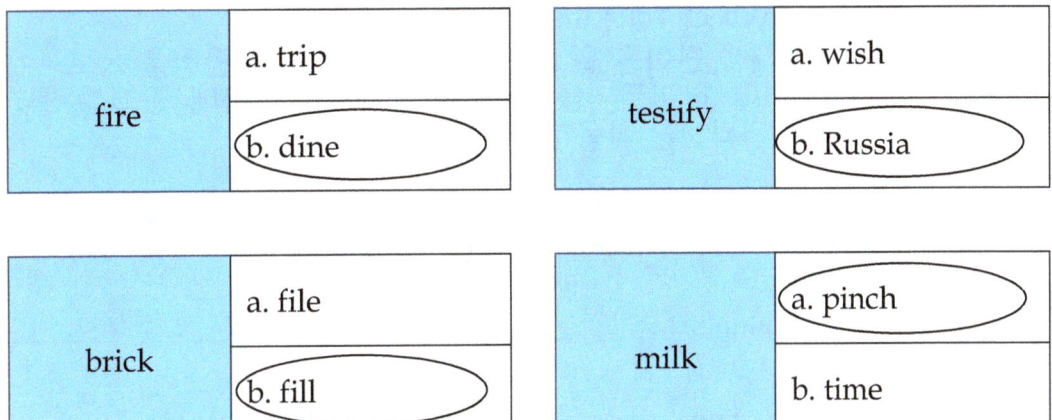

 Directions: Read each target word. Put a check (✓) under the correct column heading.

지도: 각 대상 단어를 읽으십시오. 올바른 열 제목 아래에 체크(✓)를 하십시오.

Target Words	"i" has the /ĭ/ sound as in the word <u>insect</u>	"i" has the /ī/ sound as in the word <u>bike</u>	"i" has the /ə/ sound as in the word <u>pencil</u>	"i" is silent as in the word <u>maid</u>
1. fire		✓		
2. testify			✓	
3. brick	✓			
4. milk	✓			

Classwork

 Name: _____ Date: ___/___/_____ Score: _____

The Reading Challenge

Lesson 9.10

Reading Multisyllable Words

✓ **Lesson Check Point**

 Directions: Read and divide each target word into syllables. Write each word and place a hyphen (-) between the syllables in the second column. Write the number of syllables in the third column. Use a dictionary or the Internet to check your answers.

지도: 각 대상 단어를 읽고 음절로 나눕니다. 각 단어를 쓰고 두 번째 열의 음절 사이에 하이픈(-)을 넣습니다. 세 번째 열에 음절 수를 쓰십시오. 사전이나 인터넷을 사용하여 답을 확인하십시오.

Target Words	Words Divided into Syllables	Number of Syllables
1. drinking	drink-ing	2
2. mentoring	men-tor-ing	3
3. spider	spi-der	2
4. Haiti	Hai-ti	2
5. kiwi	ki-wi	2
6. providing	pro-vid-ing	3
7. diner	din-er	2
8. beside	be-side	2
9. mineral	min-er-al	3
10. fictional	fic-tion-al	3

Unit I Lesson 9.10

Name: _____ Date: ___/___/_____ Score: _____

The Reading Challenge

Lesson 9.10

Reading Multisyllable Words

✓ Lesson Check Point

Directions: Read each target word. Circle the word in the row that is divided correctly into syllables. Use a dictionary or the Internet to check your answers.

지도: 각 대상 단어를 읽으십시오. 음절로 올바르게 나누어진 행에 있는 단어에 동그라미를 치십시오. 사전이나 인터넷을 사용하여 답을 확인하십시오.

Model

| interesting | (a. in-ter-est-ing) | b. int-er-est-ing | c. inte-rest-ing |

1. bifocal	a. bif-o-cal	(b. bi-fo-cal)	c. bi-foc-al
2. hibernate	(a. hi-ber-nate)	b. hib-er-nate	c. hi-bern-ate
3. Malawi	(a. Ma-la-wi)	b. Ma-law-i	c. Mal-a-wi
4. tribunal	a. trib-un-al	b. trib-u-nal	(c. tri-bu-nal)
5. safari	(a. sa-fa-ri)	b. saf-a-ri	c. sa-far-i
6. unicorn	(a. u-ni-corn)	b. un-i-corn	c. u-nic-orn
7. imagine	a. im-a-gine	b. i-ma-gine	(c. i-mag-ine)
8. dialect	a. di-ale-ct	(b. di-a-lect)	c. dial-e-ct

Classwork

Name: _____ Date: ___/___/_____ Score: _____

Lesson 9.11

Reading and Writing

Proper and Common Nouns and Adjectives

✓ Lesson Check Point

Directions: Read the words in the word box. Put an (X) on the line next to each word that is written incorrectly. Remember that all proper nouns and proper adjectives are capitalized. Use a dictionary or the Internet to check your answers.

지도: 단어 상자에 있는 단어를 읽으십시오. 잘못 쓰여진 각 단어 옆의 줄에 (X)를 표시하십시오. 모든 고유 명사와 고유 형용사는 대문자임을 기억하십시오. 사전이나 인터넷을 사용하여 답을 확인하십시오.

Word Box					
__	identify	X	illinois	X	Invincible
__	Iroquois	X	Insanity	__	illusion
__	Indo-European	__	itching	__	Ivory Coast
X	italy	X	irish	X	ida Mount

Directions: Read each unedited sentence and underline the word that is written incorrectly. Write each sentence correctly on the line.

지도: 편집되지 않은 각 문장을 읽고 잘못 쓰여진 단어에 밑줄을 긋습 니다. 각 문장을 줄에 올바르게 쓰십시오.

Model
New Delhi and Indore are beautiful cities in <u>india</u>.
New Delhi and Indore are beautiful cities in India.

1. My teacher said, "The <u>incas</u> inhabited the Americas."
My teacher said, "The Incas inhabited the Americas."

2. In April, Isabella will attend <u>iowa</u> Community College.
In April, Isabella will attend Iowa Community College.

3. Ida looked up information about <u>indonesia</u> on the Internet.
Ida looked up information about Indonesia on the Internet.

4. On <u>independence</u> Day, Ian ignited a massive display of fireworks.
On Independence Day, Ian ignited a massive display of fireworks.

Name: _____ Date: ___/___/_____ Score: _____

Lesson 10.1

Reading Words with the Letter J/j

✓ Lesson Check Point

 Directions: Read each target word. Find the letter "j" and put a check (✓) in the column that identifies its position: beginning, within or end.
지도: 각 대상 단어를 읽으십시오. 문자"j"를 찾아 체크 표시(✓)위치를 식별하는 열에서 시작, 내부 또는 끝.

Target Words	Beginning (First Letter)	Within	End (Last Letter)
1. conjunct		✓	
2. jacket	✓		
3. jersey	✓		
4. reject		✓	
5. jumbo	✓		

 Directions: Read each sentence and underline the words that begin with the letter "j." Write all the underlined words in alphabetical order on the lines below.
지도: 각 문장을 읽고"j"로 시작하는 단어에 밑줄을 긋습니다. 밑줄 친 모든 단어를 아래 줄에 알파벳 순서로 쓰십시오.

6. Henry has a <u>jug</u> of apple <u>juice</u>.

7. The <u>jockey's</u> horse is named <u>Jupiter</u>.

8. We flew in a <u>jet</u> from New York to <u>Japan</u>.

9. Hadia took a long <u>journey</u> through the <u>jungle</u>.

10. In <u>January</u>, Mrs. Adams is going to <u>Jacksonville</u>, Florida.

Jacksonville   January   Japan
jet   jockey's   journey
juice   jug   jungle
           Jupiter

Classwork

 Name: _____ Date:___/___/_____ Score:_____

The Reading Challenge

Lesson 10.2

Reading Multisyllable Words

✓ **Lesson Check Point**

 Directions: Read and divide each target word into syllables. Write each word and place a hyphen (-) between the syllables in the second column. Write the number of syllables in the third column. Use a dictionary or the Internet to check your answers.

지도: 각 대상 단어를 읽고 음절로 나눕니다. 각 단어를 쓰고 두 번째 열의 음절 사이에 하이픈(-)을 넣습니다. 세 번째 열에 음절 수를 쓰십시오. 사전이나 인터넷을 사용하여 답을 확인하십시오.

Target Words	Words Divided into Syllables	Number of Syllables
1. jackpot	jack-pot	2
2. joey	jo-ey	2
3. jealous	jeal-ous	2
4. judgmental	judg-men-tal	3
5. journal	jour-nal	2
6. judo	ju-do	2
7. Japanese	Jap-a-nese	3
8. joyously	joy-ous-ly	3
9. justify	jus-ti-fy	3
10. juicy	juic-y	2

Name: _____ Date: ___/___/_____ Score: _____

The Reading Challenge

Lesson 10.2

Reading Multisyllable Words

✓ **Lesson Check Point**

 Directions: Read each target word. Circle the word in the row that is divided correctly into syllables. Use a dictionary or the Internet to check your answers.

지도: 각 대상 단어를 읽으십시오. 음절로 올바르게 나누어진 행에 있는 단어에 동그라미를 치십시오. 사전이나 인터넷을 사용하여 답을 확인하십시오.

Model

| janitor | a. ja-ni-tor | b. jan-it-or | c. jan-i-tor ⭕ |

1. January	a. Jan-u-ar-y ⭕	b. Jan-u-ary	c. Jan-uar-y
2. jeopardize	a. jeop-ard-ize ⭕	b. jeop-ar-dize	c. jeo-pard-ize
3. jubilant	a. ju-bila-nt	b. ju-bi-lant ⭕	c. ju-bil-ant
4. javelin	a. javel-in	b. jave-lin ⭕	c. ja-vel-in
5. judgmental	a. judg-men-tal ⭕	b. jud-gmen-tal	c. judg-ment-al
6. jubilance	a. ju-bi-lance ⭕	b. ju-bil-ance	c. jub-i-lance
7. justify	a. ju-sti-fy	b. jus-tif-y	c. jus-ti-fy ⭕
8. jalopy	a. jal-o-py	b. ja-lop-y ⭕	c. jal-op-y

Classwork

Name: _____ Date: ___/___/_____ Score: _____

Lesson 10.3

Reading and Writing

Proper and Common Nouns and Adjectives

Directions: Read the words in the word box. Put an (X) on the line next to each word that is written incorrectly. Remember that all proper nouns and proper adjectives are capitalized. Use a dictionary or the Internet to check your answers.
지도: 단어 상자에 있는 단어를 읽으십시오. 잘못 쓰여진 각 단어 옆의 줄에 (X)를 표시하십시오. 모든 고유 명사와 고유 형용사는 대문자임을 기억하십시오. 사전이나 인터넷을 사용하여 답을 확인하십시오.

Word Box					
__	Jasmine	X	jupiter	__	jigsaw
X	june	__	jelly	X	january
__	jersey	__	jockey	X	Juice
X	japan	X	Jewelry	__	Jackson

Directions: Read each unedited sentence and underline the word that is written incorrectly. Write each sentence correctly on the line.
지도: 편집되지 않은 각 문장을 읽고 잘못 쓰여진 단어에 밑줄을긋습 니다. 각 문장을 줄에 올바르게 쓰십시오.

Model
Joey and his family live in New jersey.
Joey and his family live in New Jersey.

1. In january, Jack will wear a warm jacket.
   In January, Jack will wear a warm jacket.

2. In june, Jordan had five jars of jalapenos.
   In June, Jordan had five jars of jalapenos.

3. The kids are playing with a Jigsaw puzzle and a jet.
   The kids are playing with a jigsaw puzzle and a jet.

4. jillian has a new job at Johnson and Johnson Incorporated.
   Jillian has a new job at Johnson and Johnson Incorporated.

Name: _____ Date: ___/___/_____ Score: _____

Lesson 11.1

Reading Words with the Letter K/k

✓ Lesson Check Point

 Directions: Read each target word. Find the letter "k" and put a check (✓) in the column that identifies its position: beginning, within or end.
지도: 각 대상 단어를 읽으십시오. 문자"k"를 찾아 체크 표시(✓)위치를 식별하는 열에서 시작, 내부 또는 끝.

Target Words	Beginning (First Letter)	Within	End (Last Letter)
1. shock			✓
2. king	✓		
3. choke		✓	
4. homework			✓
5. keycard	✓		

 Directions: Read each sentence and underline the words that begin with the letter "k." Write all the underlined words in alphabetical order on the lines below.
지도: 각 문장을 읽고 문자"k"로 시작하는 단어에 밑줄을 긋습니다. 밑줄 친 모든 단어를 아래 줄에 알파벳 순서로 쓰십시오.

6. Kangaroos and koalas live in Australia.

7. Alex is learning to kick in his karate class.

8. King George III had a very powerful kingdom.

9. My friend, Karen, was born in Kingston, Jamaica.

10. Some keys on the computer keyboard are not working.

Kangaroos   karate   Karen
keyboard   keys   kick
King   kingdom   Kingston
                 koalas

Classwork

Name: _____ Date: ___/___/_____ Score: _____

Lesson 11.2

Reading Words with the Letter "k" and "ck" Letter Combination

✓ **Lesson Check Point**

Directions: Read each target word. Put a check (✓) in the second column if the target word has one vowel. Put a check (✓) in the third column if the target word has two vowels.

지도: 각 대상 단어를 읽으십시오. 대상 단어에 모음이 하나 있는 경우 두 번째 열에 체크(✓)를 합니다. 대상 단어에 두 개의 모음이 있는경우제삼 열에 체크(✓)를 합니다.

Target Words	Words with 1 Vowel	Words with 2 Vowels
1. pike		✓
2. smack	✓	
3. sneak		✓
4. lock	✓	
5. broke		✓

Directions: Read each target word in the first column and write the number of vowels within the word in the second column. Read each target word in the third column and write the number of vowels within the word in the fourth column.

지도: 첫 번째 열의 각 대상 단어를 읽고 두 번째 열의 단어 내 모음 수를 쓰십시오. 세 번째 열의 각 대상 단어를 읽고 네 번째 열의 단어에 포함된 모음의 수를 쓰십시오.

Target Words	Number of Vowels	Target Words	Number of Vowels
6. stoke	2	stock	1
7. smock	1	smoke	2
8. Blake	2	black	1
9. tack	1	take	2
10. pick	1	pike	2

Unit K Lesson 11.2

Learn To Read English With Directions In Korean

 Name: _____ Date: ___/___/_____ Score: _____

Lesson 11.3

Reading Words with the "kle" Letter Combination

✓ **Lesson Check Point**

 Directions: Read each target word. Find the "kle" letter combination and put a check (✓) in the column that identifies its position: beginning, within or end.
지도: 각 대상 단어를 읽으십시오. "kle" 문자 조합을 찾아 해당 위치를 식별하는 열에 체크(✓)를 하십시오: 시작, 내부 또는 끝.

Target Words	Beginning (First 3 Letters)	Within	End (Last 3 Letters)
1. knuckle			✓
2. Kleenex	✓		
3. anklets		✓	
4. sparkles		✓	
5. wrinkle			✓

 Directions: Read each target word. Put a check (✓) in the "yes" column if the "kle" letter combination has the /k/ + /ə/ + /l/ sounds. Put a check (✓) in the "no" column if the "kle" letter combination does not have the /k/ + /ə/ + /l/ sounds.
지도: 각 대상 단어를 읽으십시오. "kle" 문자 조합에 /k/ + /ə/ + /l/ 소리가있으 면 "yes" 열에 체크(✓)를 하십시오. "kle" 문자 조합에 /k/ + /ə/ + /l/ 소리가없으 면 "no" 열에 체크(✓)를 하십시오.

Target Words	Yes	No
6. knuckle	✓	
7. Kleenex		✓
8. anklets		✓
9. sparkles	✓	
10. wrinkle	✓	

Classwork

 Name: _____ Date: ___/___/_____ Score: _____

Lesson 11.4

Reading Words with a Silent Letter "k"

✓ **Lesson Check Point**

 **Directions:** Read the target words in the word box. Write the words that have a silent letter "k" in the first column. Write the words that do not have a silent letter "k" in the second column.

지도: 단어 상자에 있는 대상 단어를 읽으십시오. 첫 번째 열에 묵음문자 "k"가 있는 단어를 쓰십시오. 두 번째 열에 묵음 문자"k"가 없는 단어를 쓰십시오.

Target Word Box				
knee	known	doorknob	seeking	knead
shaking	parking	knocking	keyboard	knew
keeping	karate	kennel	knap	sharks
knish	knives	knuckle	milky	kneed

Letter "k" is silent	Letter "k" has the /k/ sound
knee	milky
knew	knish
knap	sharks
knead	karate
kneed	kennel
known	parking
knives	seeking
knuckle	shaking
doorknob	keeping
knocking	keyboard

Learn To Read English With Directions In Korean

Name: _____ Date:___/___/_____ Score:_____

The Reading Challenge

Lesson 11.5

Reading Multisyllable Words

✓ **Lesson Check Point**

 Directions: Read and divide each target word into syllables. Write each word and place a hyphen (-) between the syllables in the second column. Write the number of syllables in the third column. Use a dictionary or the Internet to check your answers.

지도: 각 대상 단어를 읽고 음절로 나눕니다. 각 단어를 쓰고 두 번째 열의 음절 사이에 하이픈(-)을 넣습니다. 세 번째 열에 음절 수를 쓰십시오. 사전이나 인터넷을 사용하여 답을 확인하십시오.

Target Words	Words Divided into Syllables	Number of Syllables
1. kayak	kay-ak	2
2. Kenya	Ken-ya	2
3. Korean	Ko-re-an	3
4. kindly	kind-ly	2
5. ketchup	ketch-up	2
6. keyboard	key-board	2
7. Kuwaiti	Ku-wait-i	3
8. kidnap	kid-nap	2
9. knowledge	knowl-edge	2
10. kudos	ku-dos	2

Learn To Read English With Directions In Korean

Classwork

Name: _____ Date: ___/___/_____ Score: _____

The Reading Challenge

Lesson 11.5

Reading Multisyllable Words

✓ **Lesson Check Point**

Directions: Read each target word. Circle the word in the row that is divided correctly into syllables. Use a dictionary or the Internet to check your answers.

지도: 각 대상 단어를 읽으십시오. 음절로 올바르게 나누어진 행에 있는 단어에 동그라미를 치십시오. 사전이나 인터넷을 사용하여 답을 확인하십시오.

Model

kangaroo	a. kang-a-roo	(b. kan-ga-roo)	c. kan-gar-oo
1. karate	(a. ka-ra-te)	b. ka-rate	c. kar-ate
2. kilobyte	a. ki-lo-byte	(b. kil-o-byte)	c. kil-ob-yte
3. Kentucky	a. Ken-tuc-ky	b. Kent-uck-y	(c. Ken-tuck-y)
4. kilowatt	a. ki-lo-watt	(b. kil-o-watt)	c. ki-low-att
5. keratin	a. ke-ra-tin	b. ker-at-in	(c. ker-a-tin)
6. Korea	a. Ko-r-ea	(b. Ko-re-a)	c. Kor-e-a
7. koala	(a. ko-a-la)	b. koa-la	c. ko-ala
8. kilogram	a. ki-log-ram	b. ki-lo-gram	(c. kil-o-gram)

Name: _____ Date: ___/___/_____ Score: _____

Lesson 11.6

Reading and Writing

Proper and Common Nouns and Adjectives

 Lesson Check Point

Directions: Read the words in the word box. Put an (X) on the line next to each word that is written incorrectly. Remember that all proper nouns and proper adjectives are capitalized. Use a dictionary or the Internet to check your answers.

지도: 단어 상자에 있는 단어를 읽으십시오. 잘못 쓰여진 각 단어 옆의 줄에 (X)를 표시하십시오. 모든 고유 명사와 고유 형용사는 대문자임을 기억하십시오. 사전이나 인터넷을 사용하여 답을 확인하십시오.

Word Box		
__ Kenya	X key Largo	__ Korea
X Kept	__ Kensington	X Know
X Kid	__ knock	__ knight
X kansas	X kentucky	__ kind

Directions: Read each unedited sentence and underline the word that is written incorrectly. Write each sentence correctly on the line.

지도: 편집되지 않은 각 문장을 읽고 잘못 쓰여진 단어에 밑줄을긋습 니다. 각 문장을 줄에 올바르게 쓰십시오.

Model
Helen <u>keller</u> was a kind person.
<u>Helen Keller was a kind person.</u>

1. <u>karen</u> and Kim speak Korean fluently.
<u>Karen and Kim speak Korean fluently.</u>

2. Kimberly is going to <u>kingston</u>, Jamaica.
<u>Kimberly is going to Kingston, Jamaica.</u>

3. My best friend, Kara, is from <u>kuwait</u>.
<u>My best friend, Kara, is from Kuwait.</u>

4. Kennedy and I are reading about <u>king</u> George III.
<u>Kennedy and I are reading about King George III.</u>

Classwork

L Name: _____ Date: ___/___/_____ Score: _____

Lesson 12.1

Reading Words with the Letter L/l

✓ **Lesson Check Point**

Directions: Read each target word. Find the letter "l" and put a check (✓) in the column that identifies its position: beginning, within or end.
지도: 각 대상 단어를 읽으십시오. 문자"l"을 찾아 체크 표시(✓)위치를 식별하는 열에서 시작, 내부 또는 끝.

Target Words	Beginning (First Letter)	Within	End (Last Letter)
1. kneel			✓
2. imply		✓	
3. leave	✓		
4. juvenile		✓	
5. lasting	✓		

Directions: Read each sentence and underline the words that begin with the letter "l." Write all the underlined words in alphabetical order on the lines below.
지도: 각 문장을 읽고 문자"l"로 시작하는 단어에 밑줄을 긋습니다. 밑줄 친 모든 단어를 아래 줄에 알파벳 순서로 쓰십시오.

6. The <u>little</u> <u>light</u> bulb is very bright.

7. We are <u>learning</u> about <u>Lewis</u> and Clark.

8. Abraham <u>Lincoln</u> was a brilliant <u>lawyer</u>.

9. My friend, Tim, enjoys <u>licking</u> cherry <u>lollipops</u>.

10. Everyone in my <u>Latin</u> class speaks another <u>language</u>.

language	Latin	lawyer
learning	Lewis	licking
light	Lincoln	little
	lollipops	

Name: _____ Date: ___/___/_____ Score: _____

Lesson 12.2

Reading Words with the Letter "l" Combinations:
"cl," "fl," "pl" & "sl"

Dictionary Skills/ Vocabulary

✓ **Lesson Check Point**

Directions: Read each target word and its definition. Write the target word on the line in front of its meaning. Use a dictionary or the Internet to check your answers.
지도: 각 대상 단어와 그 정의를 읽으십시오. 의미 앞 줄에 대상 단어 를 쓰십시오. 사전이나 인터넷을 사용하여 답을 확인하십시오.

Target Word Box				
class	flowers	placed	play	sleet

1. __play__   the act of doing something fun
2. __sleet__   small icy pieces that fall from the sky
3. __flowers__   the colorful part of a plant that contains seeds
4. __placed__   to put something in a particular position or location
5. __class__   group of students who is taught by the same teacher

Directions: Read each sentence. Underline the word in the parentheses that correctly completes each sentence. Then, write the underlined word on the line.
지도: 각 문장을 읽으십시오. 각 문장을 올바르게 완성하는 괄호 안에 있는 단어에 밑줄을 긋습니다. 그런 다음 밑줄 친 단어를 줄에 쓰십시오.

6. I _____placed_____ two plants in large pots. (class, <u>placed</u>)

7. The kids like to _____play_____ at the playground. (placed, <u>play</u>)

8. The _____sleet_____ caused the skiers to stop skiing. (<u>sleet</u>, flowers)

9. The garden in your backyard has beautiful __flowers__ . (<u>flowers</u>, play)

10. Ms. Brown's _____class_____ is going on an exciting trip. (<u>class</u>, sleet)

Classwork

 Name: _____ Date:___/___/_____ Score: _____

Lesson 12.3

Reading Words with a Silent Letter "l"

✓ Lesson Check Point

 Directions: Read the target words in the word box. Write the words that have a silent letter "l" in the first column. Write the words that do not have a silent letter "l" in the second column.

지도: 단어 상자에 있는 대상 단어를 읽으십시오. 첫 번째 열에 묵음문자 "l"이 있는 단어를 쓰십시오. 두 번째 열에 묵음 문자"l"이 없는 단어를 쓰십 시오.

Target Word Box				
could	build	soul	cool	likes
yolk	halves	salmon	slam	behalf
calf	loves	talking	helpful	pencil
leaf	slime	chalk	should	almond

Letter "l" is silent	Letter "l" has the /l/ sound
calf	leaf
yolk	likes
chalk	slam
behalf	loves
could	soul
halves	cool
almond	build
should	slime
talking	pencil
salmon	helpful

Learn To Read English With Directions In Korean

Name: _____ Date: ___/___/_____ Score: _____

The Reading Challenge

Lesson 12.4

Reading Multisyllable Words

✓ **Lesson Check Point**

 Directions: Read and divide each target word into syllables. Write each word and place a hyphen (-) between the syllables in the second column. Write the number of syllables in the third column. Use a dictionary or the Internet to check your answers.

지도: 각 대상 단어를 읽고 음절로 나눕니다. 각 단어를 쓰고 두 번째 열의 음절 사이에 하이픈(-)을 넣습니다. 세 번째 열에 음절 수를 쓰십시오. 사전이나 인터넷을 사용하여 답을 확인하십시오.

Target Words	Words Divided into Syllables	Number of Syllables
1. limber	lim-ber	2
2. lumber	lum-ber	2
3. leveling	lev-el-ing	3
4. licensing	li-cens-ing	3
5. liberty	lib-er-ty	3
6. loyalty	loy-al-ty	3
7. landlord	land-lord	2
8. liable	li-a-ble	3
9. lioness	li-on-ess	3
10. leotard	le-o-tard	3

Classwork

 Name: _____ Date: ___/___/_____ Score: _____

The Reading Challenge

Lesson 12.4

Reading Multisyllable Words

✓ **Lesson Check Point**

 Directions: Read each target word. Circle the word in the row that is divided correctly into syllables. Use a dictionary or the Internet to check your answers.

지도: 각 대상 단어를 읽으십시오. 음절로 올바르게 나누어진 행에 있는 단어에 동그라미를 치십시오. 사전이나 인터넷을 사용하여 답을 확인하십시오.

Model

| liberty | a. li-ber-ty | b. lib-er-ty ⭕ | c. lib-ert-y |

1. luxury	a. lux-u-ry ⭕	b. lu-xu-ry	c. lux-ur-y
2. lasagna	a. las-a-gna	b. la-sa-gna ⭕	c. la-sag-na
3. lemonade	a. lem-o-nade	b. lem-on-ade ⭕	c. le-mo-nade
4. limited	a. lim-it-ed ⭕	b. li-mit-ed	c. lim-i-ted
5. levitate	a. le-vi-tate	b. lev-i-tate ⭕	c. lev-it-ate
6. lavender	a. lav-en-der ⭕	b. lave-n-der	c. la-ven-der
7. legislate	a. leg-i-slate	b. le-gis-late	c. leg-is-late ⭕
8. levity	a. le-vit-y	b. le-vi-ty	c. lev-i-ty ⭕

Name: _____ Date:___/___/_____ Score: _____

Lesson 12.5

Reading and Writing

Proper and Common Nouns and Adjectives

✓ Lesson Check Point

 Directions: Read the words in the word box. Put an (X) on the line next to each word that is written incorrectly. Remember that all proper nouns and proper adjectives are capitalized. Use a dictionary or the Internet to check your answers.

지도: 단어 상자에 있는 단어를 읽으십시오. 잘못 쓰여진 각 단어 옆의 줄에 (X)를 표시하십시오. 모든 고유 명사와 고유 형용사는 대문자임을 기억하십시오. 사전이나 인터넷을 사용하여 답을 확인하십시오.

Word Box					
__	ladder	__	leopard	X	Ladybug
X	lincoln	X	lebanon	__	language
__	Laos	X	Lobster	__	London
X	latin	__	Labrador	X	Lawyer

 Directions: Read each unedited sentence and underline the word that is written incorrectly. Write each sentence correctly on the line.

지도: 편집되지 않은 각 문장을 읽고 잘못 쓰여진 단어에 밑줄을긋습 니다. 각 문장을 줄에 올바르게 쓰십시오.

Model
I am studying <u>latin</u> at Lutheran Life Academy.
<u>I am studying Latin at Lutheran Life Academy.</u>

1. My family and I had a <u>Lovely</u> time in Liberia.
<u>My family and I had a lovely time in Liberia.</u>

2. Abraham <u>lincoln</u> was a loyal American president.
<u>Abraham Lincoln was a loyal American president.</u>

3. Lucy said, "The <u>labrador</u> Current is a cold ocean current."
<u>Lucy said, "The Labrador Current is a cold ocean current."</u>

4. Larry learned that the capital of Arkansas is <u>little</u> Rock.
<u>Larry learned that the capital of Arkansas is Little Rock.</u>

Classwork

Name: _____ Date:___/___/_____ Score:_____

Lesson 13.1

Reading Words with the Letter M/m

✓ **Lesson Check Point**

Directions: Read each target word. Find the letter "m" and put a check (✓) in the column that identifies its position: beginning, within or end.
지도: 각 대상 단어를 읽으십시오. 문자"m"을 찾아 체크 표시(✓)위치 를 식별하는 열에서 시작, 내부 또는 끝.

Target Words	Beginning (First Letter)	Within	End (Last Letter)
1. money	✓		
2. common		✓	
3. multiple	✓		
4. eardrum			✓
5. dilemma		✓	

Directions: Read each sentence and underline the words that begin with the letter "m." Write all the underlined words in alphabetical order on the lines below.
지도: 각 문장을 읽고 문자"m"으로 시작하는 단어에 밑줄을 긋습니다. 밑줄 친 모든 단어를 아래 줄에 알파벳 순서로 쓰십시오.

6. Danny has <u>more</u> <u>mittens</u> than gloves.

7. Our aunt, <u>Mary</u>, is baking <u>macaroons</u>.

8. Dan and <u>Madison</u> are from <u>Morocco</u>.

9. Did <u>Miller</u> eat the <u>mozzarella</u> cheese?

10. His <u>mom</u> baked <u>mini</u> pies for our snack.

<u>macaroons</u>　　　　<u>Madison</u>　　　　<u>Mary</u>
<u>Miller</u>　　　　　　<u>mini</u>　　　　　　<u>mittens</u>
<u>mom</u>　　　　　　<u>more</u>　　　　　<u>Morocco</u>
　　　　　　　　　　<u>mozzarella</u>

Unit M
Lesson 13.1

 Name: _____ Date: ___/___/_____ Score: _____

Lesson 13.2

Reading Words with a Silent Letter "m"

✓ Lesson Check Point

 Directions: Read each target word. Find the letter "m" and put a check (✓) in the column that identifies its position: beginning, within or end.
지도: 각 대상 단어를 읽으십시오. 문자"m"을 찾아 체크 표시(✓)위치 를 식별하는 열에서 시작, 내부 또는 끝.

Target Words	Beginning (First Letter)	Within	End (Last Letter)
1. program			✓
2. immediate		✓	
3. basement		✓	
4. submarine		✓	
5. moving	✓		

 Directions: Read each target word. Put a check (✓) in the "yes" column if the target word has a silent letter "m." Put a check (✓) in the "no" column if the target word does not have a silent letter "m."
지도: 각 대상 단어를 읽으십시오. 대상 단어에 묵음"m"이 있는 경우"yes" 열에 체크(✓) 표시 대상 단어에 묵음"m"이 없는 경우"no" 열에체크 (✓) 표시.

Target Words	Yes	No
6. mnemonic	✓	
7. immense	✓	
8. commit	✓	
9. compromise		✓
10. momentum		✓

Classwork

 Name: _____ Date: ___/___/_____ Score: _____

The Reading Challenge

Lesson 13.3

Reading Multisyllable Words

✓ **Lesson Check Point**

 Directions: Read and divide each target word into syllables. Write each word and place a hyphen (-) between the syllables in the second column. Write the number of syllables in the third column. Use a dictionary or the Internet to check your answers.

지도: 각 대상 단어를 읽고 음절로 나눕니다. 각 단어를 쓰고 두 번째 열의 음절 사이에 하이픈(-)을 넣습니다. 세 번째 열에 음절 수를 쓰십시오. 사전이나 인터넷을 사용하여 답을 확인하십시오.

Target Words	Words Divided into Syllables	Number of Syllables
1. menu	men-u	2
2. minuteman	min-ute-man	3
3. monsoon	mon-soon	2
4. meaningful	mean-ing-ful	3
5. migrant	mi-grant	2
6. monkey	mon-key	2
7. macaroni	mac-a-ro-ni	4
8. meadow	mead-ow	2
9. morsel	mor-sel	2
10. Mexico	Mex-i-co	3

Name: _____ Date: ___/___/_____ Score: _____

The Reading Challenge

Lesson 13.3

Reading Multisyllable Words

✓ **Lesson Check Point**

Directions: Read each target word. Circle the word in the row that is divided correctly into syllables. Use a dictionary or the Internet to check your answers.

지도: 각 대상 단어를 읽으십시오. 음절로 올바르게 나누어진 행에 있는 단어에 동그라미를 치십시오. 사전이나 인터넷을 사용하여 답을확인하십시오.

Model

magazine	a. mag-a-zine ✓	b. ma-ga-zine	c. mag-az-ine
1. mineral	a. mi-ner-al	b. min-er-al ✓	c. min-e-ral
2. magnify	a. mag-ni-fy ✓	b. mag-nif-y	c. ma-gni-fy
3. malpractice	a. mal-prac-tice ✓	b. mal-pract-ice	c. ma-lprac-tice
4. mechanics	a. mech-an-ics	b. me-cha-nics	c. me-chan-ics ✓
5. monopoly	a. mon-op-o-ly	b. mo-no-po-ly	c. mo-nop-o-ly ✓
6. metaphor	a. me-ta-phor	b. met-aph-or	c. met-a-phor ✓
7. monument	a. mon-um-ent	b. mon-u-ment ✓	c. mo-nu-ment
8. memorize	a. mem-o-rize ✓	b. mem-or-ize	c. me-mor-ize

Classwork

Lesson 13.4

Reading and Writing

Proper and Common Nouns and Adjectives

Directions: Read the words in the word box. Put an (X) on the line next to each word that is written incorrectly. Remember that all proper nouns and proper adjectives are capitalized. Use a dictionary or the Internet to check your answers.

지도: 단어 상자에 있는 단어를 읽으십시오. 잘못 쓰여진 각 단어 옆의 줄에 (X)를 표시하십시오. 모든 고유 명사와 고유 형용사는 대문자임을 기억하십시오. 사전이나 인터넷을 사용하여 답을 확인하십시오.

Word Box					
X	Manager	X	Monkey	__	menu
__	Manchester	__	market	__	mentor
X	manhattan	__	Margaret	X	Mailbox
X	malawi	X	malta	__	Mother

Directions: Read each unedited sentence and underline the word that is written incorrectly. Write each sentence correctly on the line.

지도: 편집되지 않은 각 문장을 읽고 잘못 쓰여진 단어에 밑줄을 긋습 니다. 각 문장을 줄에 올바르게 쓰십시오.

Model
My son, Mark, is going to attend MIT in <u>massachusetts</u>.
<u>My son, Mark, is going to attend MIT in Massachusetts.</u>

1. My <u>Mom</u> is cooking macaroni and cheese for dinner.
<u>My mom is cooking macaroni and cheese for dinner.</u>

2. Mary and <u>max</u> read a book about the planet Mars.
<u>Mary and Max read a book about the planet Mars.</u>

3. Beth and Mom will meet in Midtown <u>manhattan</u>.
<u>Beth and Mom will meet in Midtown Manhattan.</u>

4. I received my master's degree from <u>mombasa</u> College.
<u>I received my master's degree from Mombasa College.</u>

 Name: _____ Date: ___/___/_____ Score: _____

Lesson 14.1

Reading Words with the Letter N/n

✓ Lesson Check Point

 Directions: Read each target word. Find the letter "n" and put a check (✓) in the column that identifies its position: beginning, within or end.
지도: 각 대상 단어를 읽으십시오. 문자"n"을 찾아 체크 표시(✓)위치를 식별하는 열에서 시작, 내부 또는 끝.

Target Words	Beginning (First Letter)	Within	End (Last Letter)
1. university		✓	
2. glutton			✓
3. twin			✓
4. nurse	✓		
5. newspaper	✓		

 Directions: Read each sentence and underline the words that begin with the letter "n." Write all the underlined words in alphabetical order on the lines below.
지도: 각 문장을 읽고"n"으로 시작하는 단어에 밑줄을 긋습니다. 밑줄 친 모든 단어를 아래 줄에 알파벳 순서로 쓰십시오.

6. Mommy <u>never</u> tasted chicken <u>noodle</u> soup.

7. <u>Napoleon</u> read ten books about the <u>Nile</u> River.

8. My <u>neighbors</u> enjoy celebrating <u>New</u> Year's Eve.

9. <u>Nick</u> wants to move from Kansas to <u>North</u> Dakota.

10. Everyone knows that many <u>nice</u> people live in <u>Norway</u>.

Napoleon _____	neighbors _____	never _____
New _____	nice _____	Nick _____
Nile _____	noodle _____	North _____
	Norway _____	

Classwork

 Name: _____ Date:___/___/_____ Score:_____

Lesson 14.2

Reading Words with the "ng" Letter Combination

✓ Lesson Check Point

 Directions: Read each target word. Circle the word in the column that has the same "ng" sound(s) as the target word.
지도: 각 대상 단어를 읽으십시오. 대상 단어와 같은 "ng" 소리가 나는 열의 단어에 동그라미를 치십시오.

anger	a. exchange		congratulate	a. congruence (circled)	
	b. language (circled)			b. engineer	
congeniality	a. jingle		singer	a. boxing (circled)	
	b. danger (circled)			b. triangle	

 Directions: Read each target word. Put a check (✓) under the correct column heading.
지도: 각 대상 단어를 읽으십시오. 올바른 열 제목 아래에 체크(✓)를 하십시오.

Target Words	"ng" has the /n/ + /g/ sounds as in the word ingrain	"ng" has the /n/ + /j/ sounds as in the word ginger	"ng" has the /ng/ sound as in the word bang	"ng" has the /ng/ + /g/ sounds as in the word congress
1. anger				✓
2. congratulate	✓			
3. congeniality		✓		
4. singer			✓	

 Name: _____ Date: ___/___/_____ Score: _____

Lesson 14.3

Reading Words with a Silent Letter "n"

✓ **Lesson Check Point**

 Directions: Read the target words in the word box. Write the words that have a silent letter "n" in the first column. Write the words that do not have a silent letter "n" in the second column.

지도: 단어 상자에 있는 대상 단어를 읽으십시오. 첫 번째 열에 묵음문자 "n"이 있는 단어를 쓰십시오. 두 번째 열에 묵음 문자"n"이 없는 단어를 쓰십시오.

Target Word Box				
animals	hymn	encounter	botanical	annex
comments	behind	hunter	nouns	penny
autumn	annual	cinnamon	monsieur	condemn
chimneys	tennis	handy	nominate	columns

Letter "n" is silent

hymn
annex
tennis
penny
annual
autumn
monsieur
condemn
columns
cinnamon

Letter "n" has the /n/ sound

handy
nouns
hunter
animals
behind
botanical
comments
encounter
chimneys
nominate

Classwork

Name: _____ Date:___/___/_____ Score:_____

The Reading Challenge

Lesson 14.4

Reading Multisyllable Words

✓ Lesson Check Point

Directions: Read and divide each target word into syllables. Write each word and place a hyphen (-) between the syllables in the second column. Write the number of syllables in the third column. Use a dictionary or the Internet to check your answers.

지도: 각 대상 단어를 읽고 음절로 나눕니다. 각 단어를 쓰고 두 번째 열의 음절 사이에 하이픈(-)을 넣습니다. 세 번째 열에 음절 수를 쓰십시오. 사전이나 인터넷을 사용하여 답을 확인하십시오.

Target Words	Words Divided into Syllables	Number of Syllables
1. nighttime	night-time	2
2. nationwide	na-tion-wide	3
3. nuance	nu-ance	2
4. needlessly	need-less-ly	3
5. normalize	nor-mal-ize	3
6. ninety	nine-ty	2
7. nimbleness	nim-ble-ness	3
8. noble	no-ble	2
9. nectarine	nec-tar-ine	3
10. notion	no-tion	2

Name: _____ Date: ___/___/_____ Score: _____

The Reading Challenge

Lesson 14.4

Reading Multisyllable Words

✓ **Lesson Check Point**

 Directions: Read each target word. Circle the word in the row that is divided correctly into syllables. Use a dictionary or the Internet to check your answers.

지도: 각 대상 단어를 읽으십시오. 음절로 올바르게 나누어진 행에 있는 단어에 동그라미를 치십시오. 사전이나 인터넷을 사용하여 답을 확인하십시오.

Model

| napkin | a. na-pkin | b. napk-in | **c. nap-kin** |

1. neighbor	a. neighb-or	**b. neigh-bor**	c. nei-gh-bor
2. notify	**a. no-ti-fy**	b. no-tif-y	c. not-i-fy
3. natural	**a. nat-u-ral**	b. na-tu-ral	c. na-tur-al
4. nevermore	a. ne-ver-more	b. nev-erm-ore	**c. nev-er-more**
5. nobody	**a. no-bod-y**	b. no-body	c. no-bo-dy
6. newcomer	a. ne-wcom-er	b. new-co-mer	**c. new-com-er**
7. nutrition	**a. nu-tri-tion**	b. nut-ri-tion	c. nu-trit-ion
8. nausea	a. na-us-ea	b. n-au-sea	**c. nau-se-a**

Classwork

Name: _____ Date: ___/___/_____ Score: _____

Lesson 14.5

Reading and Writing

Proper and Common Nouns and Adjectives

Directions: Read the words in the word box. Put an (X) on the line next to each word that is written incorrectly. Remember that all proper nouns and proper adjectives are capitalized. Use a dictionary or the Internet to check your answers.

지도: 단어 상자에 있는 단어를 읽으십시오. 잘못 쓰여진 각 단어 옆의 줄에 (X)를 표시하십시오. 모든 고유 명사와 고유 형용사는 대문자임을 기억하십시오. 사전이나 인터넷을 사용하여 답을 확인하십시오.

Word Box					
X	Nugget	X	north Africa	X	nigeria
__	Nepal	X	nile	__	napkin
__	Napoleon	__	news	X	Noodle
__	New Delhi	X	Number	__	Nicaragua

Directions: Read each unedited sentence and underline the word that is written incorrectly. Write each sentence correctly on the line.

지도: 편집되지 않은 각 문장을 읽고 잘못 쓰여진 단어에 밑줄을굿습 니다. 각 문장을 줄에 올바르게 쓰십시오.

Model
Nick and Nancy live in the <u>netherlands</u>.
<u>Nick and Nancy live in the Netherlands.</u>

1. I received a <u>Needle</u> from Nurse Nutley.
<u>I received a needle from Nurse Nutley.</u>

2. The <u>Newscasters</u> collaborate about national news stories.
<u>The newscasters collaborate about national news stories.</u>

3. Mrs. Newton taught a lesson about the <u>Nervous</u> system.
<u>Mrs. Newton taught a lesson about the nervous system.</u>

4. The <u>nile</u> River derives its name from the Greek word, Nelios.
<u>The Nile River derives its name from the Greek word, Nelios.</u>

Name: _____ Date: ___/___/_____ Score: _____

Lesson 15.1

Reading Words with the Letter O/o

✓ **Lesson Check Point**

 Directions: Read each target word. Find the letter "o" and put a check (✓) in the column that identifies its position: beginning, within or end.
지도: 각 대상 단어를 읽으십시오. 문자"o"를 찾아 체크 표시(✓)위치 를 식별하는 열에서 시작, 내부 또는 끝.

Target Words	Beginning (First Letter)	Within	End (Last Letter)
1. combine		✓	
2. older	✓		
3. outreach	✓		
4. cargo			✓
5. embargo			✓

 Directions: Read each target word. Read the words in the row and circle the word that has a different vowel "o" sound.
지도: 각 대상 단어를 읽으십시오. 행에 있는 단어를 읽고 모음"o" 소리가 다른 단어에 동그라미를 치십시오.

Target Words					
6. almost	go	code	(song)	dole	
7. drop	(host)	prom	stop	clog	
8. solo	(lock)	joke	tone	coat	
9. gold	soap	(toss)	aloe	so	
10. shopping	rock	clock	frost	(poll)	

Classwork

 Name: _____ Date: ___/___/_____ Score: _____

Lesson 15.2

Reading Words with the Short Vowel "o" Sound

✓ **Lesson Check Point**

 Directions: Read the words in the four boxes. Circle two words with the short vowel /ŏ/ or /ô/ sound. The anchor word for the short vowel /ŏ/ and /ô/ sounds is <u>frog</u>.

지도: 네 개의 상자에 있는 단어를 읽으십시오. 짧은 모음/ŏ/ 또는 /ô/ 소리로 두 단어에 동그라미를 치십시오. 단모음/ŏ/ 및 /ô/ 소리의 앵커 단어는 frog입니다.

(stop)	poll	colt	(flog)	post	both
old	(plot)	host	(drop)	(slot)	(chop)

(fond)	(prom)	(blot)	mole	(rock)	(clop)
told	go	(knot)	don't	hold	roll

 Directions: Read the words in the four boxes. Circle two words that rhyme. Rhyming words have the same ending sound, such as <u>hot</u> and <u>not</u>.

지도: 네 개의 상자에 있는 단어를 읽으십시오. 운이 맞는 두 단어에 동그라미를 치십시오. 운율이 있는 단어는 hot 및 not과 같이 끝 소리가 같습니다.

(shot)	(spot)	(shop)	roll	hydro	phone
no	chosen	solo	(crop)	(bond)	(pond)

ago	(lock)	(boss)	(toss)	(long)	joke
gold	(dock)	ocean	hotel	(song)	sold

Learn To Read English With Directions In Korean

Name: _____ Date: ___/___/_____ Score: _____

Lesson 15.2

Reading & Writing Words with the Short Vowel "o" Sound

✓ **Lesson Check Point**

Directions: Read each sentence and underline three words with the short vowel /ŏ/ or /ô/ sound. Then, write the underlined words on the lines below. The anchor word for the short vowel /ŏ/ and /ô/ sounds is <u>frog</u>.

지도: 각 문장을 읽고 짧은 모음/ŏ/ 또는 /ô/ 소리로 세 단어에 밑줄을 긋습니다. 그런 다음 밑줄 친 단어를 아래 줄에 쓰십시오. 단모음/ŏ/ 및 /ô/ 소리의 앵커 단어는 frog입니다.

Model
Everyone saw the <u>frog</u> <u>hop</u> close to the <u>rock</u>.

    frog   hop   rock

1. The ropes <u>on</u> the <u>mop</u> are very <u>soft</u>.

    on   mop   soft

2. The policeman <u>stopped</u> the <u>robber</u> in the <u>office</u>.

    stopped   robber   office

3. <u>Tom</u> walked around the <u>block</u> in his <u>socks</u>.

    Tom   block   socks

4. Joan's <u>job</u> assignment is to <u>mop</u> the <u>spotty</u> tiles.

    job   mop   spotty

5. <u>Moss</u> develops <u>from</u> spores and grows in damp <u>logs</u>.

    Moss   from   logs

Classwork

 Name: _____   Date: ___/___/_____   Score: _____

Lesson 15.3

Reading Words with the Long Vowel "o" Sound

✓ **Lesson Check Point**

 Directions: Read the words in the four boxes. Circle two words with the long vowel /ō/ sound. The anchor word for the long vowel /ō/ sound is <u>open</u>.

지도: 네 개의 상자에 있는 단어를 읽으십시오. 장모음 /ō/ 소리로 두 단어에 동그라미를 치십시오. 장모음 /ō/ 소리의 기준어는 open입니다.

cross	(yo-yo)	boss	(joke)	rock	took
(roll)	lock	lost	(so)	(pony)	(sold)

(both)	pond	drop	shop	prompt	(soap)
(boat)	sock	(poke)	(toad)	floss	(poll)

 Directions: Read the words in the four boxes. Circle two words that rhyme. Rhyming words have the same ending sound, such as <u>hope</u> and <u>soap</u>.

지도: 네 개의 상자에 있는 단어를 읽으십시오. 운이 맞는 두 단어에 동그라미를 치십시오. 운율이 있는 단어는 hope 및 soap과 같이 끝 소리가 같습니다.

go	(folk)	(boat)	(coat)	toss	home
(yolk)	clock	rose	song	(post)	(most)

frost	(pole)	so	(cold)	poet	(roast)
told	(role)	strong	(sold)	(toast)	spot

Name: _____   Date: ___/___/_____   Score: _____

Lesson 15.3

Reading & Writing Words with the Long Vowel "o" Sound

✓ **Lesson Check Point**

Directions: Read each sentence and underline three words with the long vowel /ō/ sound. Then, write the underlined words on the lines below. The anchor word for the long vowel /ō/ sound is open.

지도: 각 문장을 읽고 장모음 /ō/소리로 세 단어에 밑줄을 긋습니다. 그런 다음 밑줄 친 단어를 아래 줄에 쓰십시오. 장모음 /ō/ 소리의 앵커 단어는 open입니다.

Model

We will go to the rodeo and limbo competitions for fun.

    go   rodeo   limbo

1. Owen said hello to the ponies in the zoo.

    Owen   hello   ponies

2. The hotel's frozen donuts do not taste good.

    hotel's   frozen   donuts

3. The coeducational golf team is going to enroll in the competition.

    coeducational   going   enroll

4. Tom, the yodeler, will change his tempo in a moment.

    yodeler   tempo   moment

5. My son said, "Both hippos and dodo birds are interesting animals."

    Both   hippos   dodo

Classwork

Name: _____ Date: ___/___/_____ Score: _____

Review Lessons 15.2 & 15.3

Reading Short Vowel and Long Vowel Words

Directions: Read the target words in the word box. In the first column, write the words that have the short vowel /ŏ/ or /ô/ sound, as in the word <u>frog</u>. In the second column, write the words that have the long vowel /ō/ sound, as in the word <u>open</u>.

지도: 단어 상자에 있는 대상 단어를 읽으십시오. 첫 번째 열에는 frog라는 단어에서와 같이 단모음/ŏ/또는 /ô/소리가 나는 단어를 씁니다. 두번째 열에는 open이라는 단어에서와 같이 장모음 /ō/ 소리가 나는 단어를 씁니다.

Target Word Box				
scaffold	cross	billfold	prompt	shopping
disposal	postal	bonding	going	rocking
stock	revolt	lost	enroll	grocery
plot	clock	mostly	strong	hippos

Letter "o" has the /ŏ/ or /ô/ sound as in the word <u>frog</u>

- plot
- lost
- clock
- cross
- stock
- strong
- prompt
- rocking
- bonding
- shopping

Letter "o" has the /ō/ sound as in the word <u>open</u>

- enroll
- revolt
- grocery
- mostly
- postal
- hippos
- going
- billfold
- scaffold
- disposal

 Name: _____   Date:___/___/_____   Score:_____

Lesson 15.4

Reading Words with Letter "o" Vowel Pairs

✓ **Lesson Check Point**

 Directions: Read each target word. Circle the word in the column that has the same vowel "oa," "oe," "oo" or "ou" sound(s) as the target word.
지도: 각 대상 단어를 읽으십시오. 대상 단어와 동일한 모음 "oa," "oe," "oo" 또는 "ou" 소리가 있는 열의 단어에 동그라미를 치십시오.

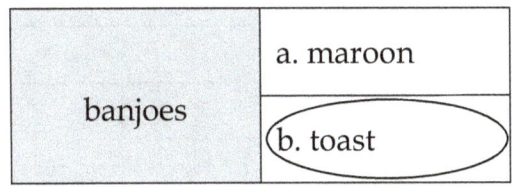

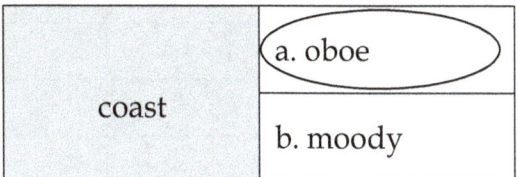

 Directions: Read each target word. Put a check (✓) under the correct column heading.
지도: 각 대상 단어를 읽으십시오. 올바른 열 제목 아래에 체크(✓)를 하십시오.

Target Words	Words have the long "o" sound as in the word <u>coat</u>	Words do not have the long "o" sound
1. carousel		✓
2. gloat	✓	
3. banjoes	✓	
4. coast	✓	

Classwork

 Name: _____ Date: ___/___/_____ Score: _____

Lesson 15.5

Reading Words with the Final Letter "o"

✓ Lesson Check Point

 Directions: Read each target word. Find the letter "o" and put a check (✓) in the column that identifies its position within the syllable.
지도: 각 대상 단어를 읽으십시오. 문자"o"를 찾아 체크 표시(✓)음절 내에서 위치를 식별하는 열에서.

Target Words	"o" is at the end of a one syllable word	"o" is at the end of the first syllable	"o" is at the end of a multi-syllable word
1. m<u>o</u>tor		✓	
2. piano			✓
3. chosen		✓	
4. go	✓		
5. ago			✓

 Directions: Read each target word. Put a check (✓) under the correct column heading.
지도: 각 대상 단어를 읽으십시오. 올바른 열 제목 아래에 체크(✓)를 하십시오.

Target Words	"o" has the /ŏ/ sound as in the word <u>frog</u>	"o" has the /ō/ sound as in the word <u>go</u>	"o" has the /ə/ sound as in the word <u>carrot</u>	"o" is silent as in the word <u>people</u>
6. roaches		✓		
7. turbo		✓		
8. contain			✓	
9. mopping	✓			
10. vaporize			✓	

Learn To Read English With Directions In Korean

Name: _____   Date:___/___/_____   Score:_____

Lesson 15.6

Reading Letter "o" Words with the Schwa Vowel Sound

✓ Lesson Check Point

 Directions: Read each target word. Circle the word in the column that has the same "o" sound as the target word.

지도: 각 대상 단어를 읽으십시오. 대상 단어와 동일한 "o" 소리가 나는 열의 단어에 동그라미를 치십시오.

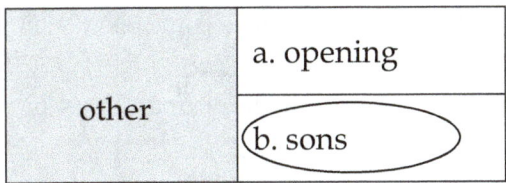
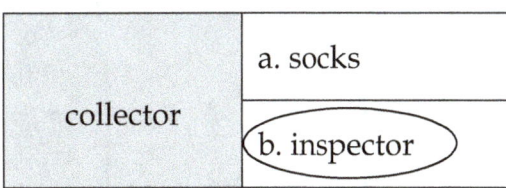
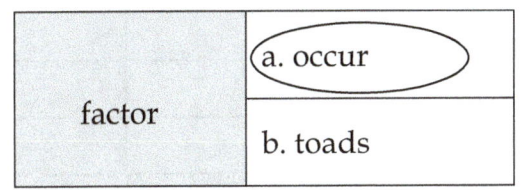
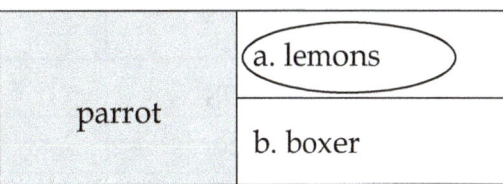

 Directions: Read each sentence and underline the letter "o" word that has the schwa vowel /ə/ sound or short vowel /ŭ/ sound. The anchor word for the letter "o" schwa vowel /ə/ sound is <u>carrot</u> and the letter "o" short vowel /ŭ/ sound is <u>dove</u>.

지도: 각 문장을 읽고 슈와 모음/ə/ 소리 또는 단모음/ŭ/ 소리가 있는 문자 "o" 단어에 밑줄을 긋습니다. 문자 "o" 슈와 모음/ə/ 소리의 앵커 단어는 carrot이고 문자 "o" 단모음/ŭ/ 소리는 dove입니다.

1. The orange <u>sponge</u> is in the old pot.

2. The boys <u>won</u> the bowling tournament.

3. Mommy enjoys eating <u>onion</u> noodle soup.

4. This year, our school will start at eight <u>o'clock</u>.

5. On <u>Monday</u>, I closed the window before the storm.

6. In October, my <u>doctor</u> gave me an intensive examination.

Classwork

 Name: _____ Date:___/___/_____ Score:_____

Lesson 15.7

Reading Words with Vowel "o" Sounds: /ŏ/, /ō/ & /o͞o/

✓ Lesson Check Point

 Directions: Read each target word. Put a check (✓) under the correct column heading.
지도: 각 대상 단어를 읽으십시오. 올바른 열 제목 아래에 체크(✓)를 하십시오.

Target Words	"o" has the /ŏ/ sound as in the word frog	"o" has the /ō/ sound as in the word go	"o" has the /o͞o/ sound as in the word to
1. mopping	✓		
2. who			✓
3. moving			✓
4. October	✓		
5. soul		✓	

 Directions: Read each sentence and underline the word that has a letter "o" that has the vowel /o͞o/ sound, as in the word two.
지도: 각 문장을 읽고 two라는 단어에서처럼 모음/o͞o/소리가 있는 문자 "o"가 있는 단어에 밑줄을 긋습니다.

6. <u>Do</u> we have a box of colorful rocks?

7. On Monday, Ron and Tom will <u>move</u> out.

8. We may <u>lose</u> our money in the stock market.

9. <u>Who</u> read the book about the fox in the woods?

10. The outspoken lawyer <u>proved</u> that his client is not guilty.

Name: _____   Date: ___/___/_____   Score: _____

Lesson 15.8

Reading Words with the "or" Letter Combination

✓ **Lesson Check Point**

Directions: Read each target word. Circle the word in the column that has the same "o" + "r" sounds as the target word.

지도: 각 대상 단어를 읽으십시오. 가 있는 열에 있는 단어에 동그라미를 치십시오. 동일한 "o" + "r"이 대상 단어로 들립니다.

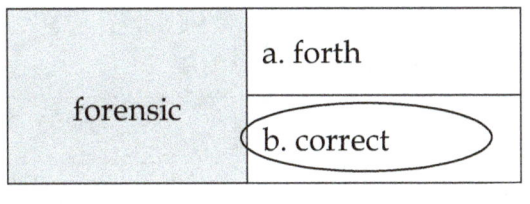

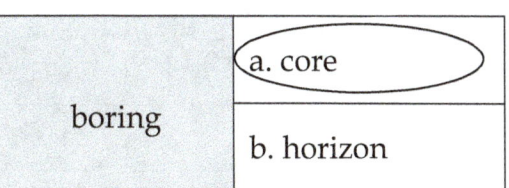

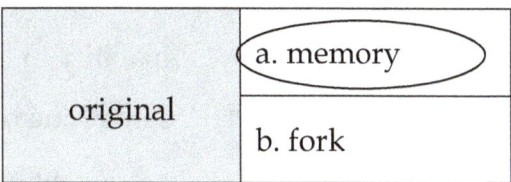

Directions: Read each target word. Put a check (✓) under the correct column heading.

지도: 각 대상 단어를 읽으십시오. 올바른 열 제목 아래에 체크(✓)를 하십시오.

Target Words	"or" has the /ô/ + /r/ sounds as in the word <u>door</u>	"or" has the /ə/ + /r/ sounds as in the word <u>doctor</u>
1. forensic		✓
2. boring	✓	
3. portion	✓	
4. original		✓

Classwork

Name: _____ Date:___/___/_____ Score:_____

Lesson 15.8

Reading Words with the "or" Letter Combination

Dictionary Skills/ Vocabulary

✓ **Lesson Check Point**

Directions: Read each target word and its definition. Write the target word on the line in front of its meaning. Use a dictionary or the Internet to check your answers.

지도: 각 대상 단어와 그 정의를 읽으십시오. 의미 앞 줄에 대상 단어 를 쓰십시오. 사전이나 인터넷을 사용하여 답을 확인하십시오.

Target Word Box				
worn	orbits	important	story	forgot

1. __forgot__   inability to remember
2. __important__   something or someone of great value
3. __worn__   fabric that has become thinner or damaged
4. __orbits__   the act of moving around another object
5. __story__   a spoken or written description of characters and events

Directions: Read each sentence and write the target word that correctly completes the sentence.

지도: 각 문장을읽고 다음과 같은 목표 단어를 쓰십시오. 장을올바르게 완성합니다.

6. My old blue jeans are ____worn____ out.

7. The science teacher said, "The Earth __orbits__ the Sun."

8. It is ____important____ to attend school every day.

9. Molly told the teacher she ____forgot____ to do her homework.

10. The ____story____ "The Fox and the Wise Owl" has a great plot.

Name: _____ Date: ___/___/_____ Score: _____

Lesson 15.9

Reading Words with a Silent Letter "o"

✓ **Lesson Check Point**

 Directions: Read the target words in the word box. Write the words that have a silent letter "o" in the first column. Write the words that do not have a silent letter "o" in the second column.

지도: 단어 상자에 있는 대상 단어를 읽으십시오. 첫 번째 열에 묵음 문자"o"가 있는 단어를 쓰십시오. 두 번째 열에 묵음 문자"o"가 없는 단어를 쓰십시오.

Target Word Box				
combat	leopards	horse	Phoenician	subpoena
body	jeopardy	subpoenas	know	hold
Leonard	assort	open	leopard	collect
expose	phoenix	people	octopus	jeopardize

Letter "o" is silent	Letter "o" has a letter "o" sound
leopards	open
jeopardy	horse
leopard	know
people	body
phoenix	hold
subpoena	assort
subpoenas	combat
Leonard	collect
jeopardize	expose
Phoenician	octopus

Classwork

 Name: _____ Date:___/___/_____ Score:_____

Unit Review - O/o

Reading Words with Vowel "o" Sounds: /ŏ/, /ō/, /ə/ & Silent

✓ **Lesson Check Point**

 Directions: Read each target word. Circle the word in the column that has the same "o" sound as the target word.
지도: 각 대상 단어를 읽으십시오. 대상 단어와 동일한 "o" 소리가 나는 열의 단어에 동그라미를 치십시오.

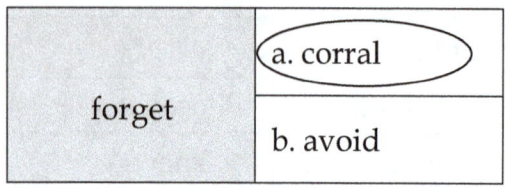

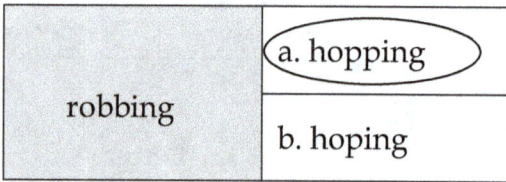

 Directions: Read each target word. Put a check (✓) under the correct column heading.
지도: 각 대상 단어를 읽으십시오. 올바른 열 제목 아래에 체크(✓)를 하십시오.

Target Words	"o" has the /ŏ/ sound as in the word <u>frog</u>	"o" has the /ō/ sound as in the word <u>go</u>	"o" has the /ə/ sound as in the word <u>carrot</u>	"o" is silent as in the word <u>people</u>
1. forget			✓	
2. toaster		✓		
3. jeopardy				✓
4. robbing	✓			

Name: _____ Date: ___/___/_____ Score: _____

The Reading Challenge

Lesson 15.10

Reading Multisyllable Words

✓ **Lesson Check Point**

Directions: Read and divide each target word into syllables. Write each word and place a hyphen (-) between the syllables in the second column. Write the number of syllables in the third column. Use a dictionary or the Internet to check your answers.

지도: 각 대상 단어를 읽고 음절로 나눕니다. 각 단어를 쓰고 두 번째 열의 음절 사이에 하이픈(-)을 넣습니다. 세 번째 열에 음절 수를 쓰십시오. 사전이나 인터넷을 사용하여 답을 확인하십시오.

Target Words	Words Divided into Syllables	Number of Syllables
1. solar	so-lar	2
2. motel	mo-tel	2
3. token	to-ken	2
4. composer	com-pos-er	3
5. Romania	Ro-ma-ni-a	4
6. lotion	lo-tion	2
7. orderly	or-der-ly	3
8. rodent	ro-dent	2
9. provoking	pro-vok-ing	3
10. Bohemian	Bo-he-mi-an	4

Classwork

 Name: _____ Date: ___/___/_____ Score: _____

The Reading Challenge

Lesson 15.10

Reading Multisyllable Words

✓ **Lesson Check Point**

 Directions: Read each target word. Circle the word in the row that is divided correctly into syllables. Use a dictionary or the Internet to check your answers.

지도: 각 대상 단어를 읽으십시오. 음절로 올바르게 나누어진 행에 있는 단어에 동그라미를 치십시오. 사전이나 인터넷을 사용하여 답을 확인하십시오.

Model

| proposal | a. prop-o-sal | b. pro-po-sal | c. (pro-pos-al) |

1. portable	a. por-table	b. (por-ta-ble)	c. port-a-ble
2. asteroid	a. as-te-roid	b. ast-e-roid	c. (as-ter-oid)
3. corporate	a. (cor-po-rate)	b. corpo-ra-te	c. corp-o-rate
4. potato	a. pot-at-o	b. (po-ta-to)	c. pot-a-to
5. repertoire	a. (rep-er-toire)	b. re-pert-oire	c. re-per-toire
6. investor	a. (in-ves-tor)	b. in-vest-or	c. i-nvest-or
7. cockatoo	a. cock-at-oo	b. co-cka-too	c. (cock-a-too)
8. October	a. Oct-o-ber	b. (Oc-to-ber)	c. Oct-ob-er

Learn To Read English With Directions In Korean

Name: _____ Date: ___/___/_____ Score: _____

Lesson 15.11

Reading and Writing

Proper and Common Nouns and Adjectives

Directions: Read the words in the word box. Put an (X) on the line next to each word that is written incorrectly. Remember that all proper nouns and proper adjectives are capitalized. Use a dictionary or the Internet to check your answers.

지도: 단어 상자에 있는 단어를 읽으십시오. 잘못 쓰여진 각 단어 옆의 줄에 (X)를 표시하십시오. 모든 고유 명사와 고유 형용사는 대문자임을 기억하십시오. 사전이나 인터넷을 사용하여 답을 확인하십시오.

Word Box		
__ Oxbridge	__ octopus	X orlando
X ontario	__ Onega Bay	__ organizer
__ Old English	X october	X Atlantic ocean
X Occasion	__ objective	X Original

Directions: Read each unedited sentence and underline the word that is written incorrectly. Write each sentence correctly on the line.

지도: 편집되지 않은 각 문장을 읽고 잘못 쓰여진 단어에 밑줄을굿습 니다. 각 문장을 줄에 올바르게 쓰십시오.

Model
At <u>One</u> o'clock, the Owens family went to Onega Bay.
<u>At one o'clock, the Owens family went to Onega Bay.</u>

1. Mr. <u>o'Connor</u> is planning an outstanding trip to the Orient.
<u>Mr. O'Connor is planning an outstanding trip to the Orient.</u>

2. Marie, Octavia and I are <u>Overjoyed</u> about our trip to Oktoberfest.
<u>Marie, Octavia and I are overjoyed about our trip to Oktoberfest.</u>

3. Mr. O'Keeffe gave the class a fact sheet about the <u>oregon</u> Trail.
<u>Mr. O'Keeffe gave the class a fact sheet about the Oregon Trail.</u>

4. In October, the official <u>olympic</u> Games tryouts will begin.
<u>In October, the official Olympic Games tryouts will begin.</u>

Classwork

Name: _____ Date: ___/___/_____ Score: _____

Lesson 16.1

Reading Words with the Letter P/p

✓ **Lesson Check Point**

Directions: Read each target word. Find the letter "p" and put a check (✓) in the column that identifies its position: beginning, within or end.
지도: 각 대상 단어를 읽으십시오. 문자"p"를 찾아 체크 표시(✓)위치를 식별하는 열에서 시작, 내부 또는 끝.

Target Words	Beginning (First Letter)	Within	End (Last Letter)
1. price	✓		
2. pest	✓		
3. plans	✓		
4. asleep			✓
5. concept		✓	

Directions: Read each sentence and underline the words that begin with the letter "p." Write all the underlined words in alphabetical order on the lines below.
지도: 각 문장을 읽고"p"로 시작하는 단어에 밑줄을 긋습니다. 아래 줄에 밑줄 친 단어를 알파벳 순서로 모두 쓰십시오.

6. The <u>pitcher</u> threw <u>powerful</u> fastballs.

7. Lydia is sending a <u>package</u> to <u>Panama</u>.

8. Gabby's <u>pageant</u> gown is white and <u>purple</u>.

9. The <u>police</u> officer is <u>patrolling</u> our college campus.

10. <u>People</u> in the courtroom said the <u>plaintiff</u> has a strong case.

package   pageant   Panama
patrolling   People   pitcher
plaintiff   police   powerful
                  purple

 Name: _____ Date:___/___/_____ Score:_____

Lesson 16.2

Reading Words with the "ph" Letter Combination

✓ Lesson Check Point

 Directions: Read each target word. Circle the word in the column that has the same "ph" sound(s) as the target word.
지도: 각 대상 단어를 읽으십시오. 대상 단어와 동일한 "ph" 소리를 가진 열의 단어에 동그라미를 치십시오.

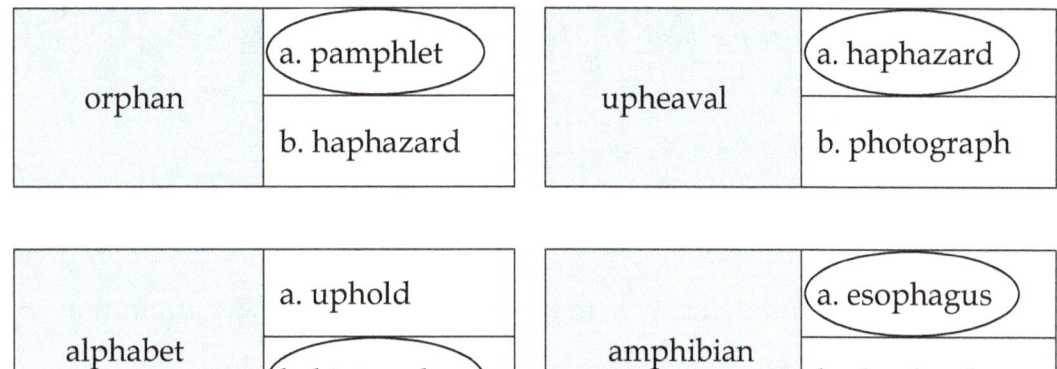

 Directions: Read each target word. Put a check (✓) under the correct column heading.
지도: 각 대상 단어를 읽으십시오. 올바른 열 제목 아래에 체크(✓)를 하십시오.

Target Words	"ph" has the /f/ sound as in the word phone	"ph" has the /p/ + /h/ sounds as in the word uphill
1. orphan	✓	
2. upheaval		✓
3. alphabet	✓	
4. amphibian	✓	

Classwork

Name: _____ Date:___/___/_____ Score:_____

Lesson 16.3

Reading Words with the "pr" Letter Combination

Dictionary Skills/ Vocabulary

✓ Lesson Check Point

Directions: Read each target word and its definition. Write the letter of the definition on the line of each target word. Use a dictionary or the Internet to check your answers.
지도: 각 대상 단어와 그 정의를 읽으십시오. 각 대상 단어의 행에 정의의 문자를 씁니다. 사전이나 인터넷을 사용하여 답을 확인하십시오.

Target Words	Definitions

1. _b_ praised   a. an educator/instructor at a university or college

2. _c_ predators   b. to have expressed words of admiration or approval

3. _d_ president   c. animals that kill and eat other animals for survival

4. _a_ professor   d. an elected or appointed leader of a country

5. _e_ program   e. an organized business that provides activities

Directions: Read each sentence and write the target word that correctly completes the sentence.
지도: 각 대상 단어를 읽으십시오. 올바른 열 제목 아래에체크(✓)를 하 십시오.

6. The great white whales and lions are alpha ____predators____.

7. Dr. Pringle is a _____professor_____ at Pratt University.

8. The _____president_____ was elected for a four-year term.

9. The teacher _____praised_____ her hardworking students.

10. My sister and I attend an after-school _____program_____.

Name: _____ Date: ___/___/_____ Score: _____

Lesson 16.4

Reading Words with the "pl" Letter Combination

Dictionary Skills/ Vocabulary

✓ Lesson Check Point

Directions: Read each target word and its definition. Write the target word on the line in front of its meaning. Use a dictionary or the Internet to check your answers.
지도: 각 대상 단어와 그 정의를 읽으십시오. 의미 앞 줄에 대상단어 를 쓰십시오. 사전이나 인터넷을 사용하여 답을 확인하십시오.

Target Word Box				
plaintiff	pleasure	plowing	plum	plush

1. <u>plowing</u>   the act of breaking up the land for farming
2. <u>plush</u>   a luxury item that is nice and expensive
3. <u>plaintiff</u> a person or group of people who file a lawsuit
4. <u>pleasure</u> an experience that is enjoyable or satisfying
5. <u>plum</u>   purple, smooth-skinned fruit that is very sweet

Directions: Read each sentence. Underline the word in the parentheses that correctly completes each sentence. Then, write the underlined word on the line.
지도: 각 문장을 읽으십시오. 각 문장을 올바르게 완성하는 괄호 안에 있는 단어에 밑줄을 긋습니다. 그런 다음 밑줄 친 단어를 줄에 쓰십시오.

6. The <u>plaintiff</u> filed a case at the courthouse. (pleasure, <u>plaintiff</u>)

7. The farmer is <u>plowing</u> the center of his field. (<u>plowing</u>, plush)

8. I spent a lot of money for my <u>plush</u> condo. (plum, <u>plush</u>)

9. I bought peaches and <u>plums</u> from the fruit store. (<u>plums</u>, pleasure)

10. I agree that it is a <u>pleasure</u> to work with children. (<u>pleasure</u>, plaintiff)

Learn To Read English With Directions In Korean

Classwork

 Name: _____ Date: ___/___/_____ Score: _____

Lesson 16.4

Reading Words with the "ple" Letter Combination

✓ **Lesson Check Point**

 Directions: Read each target word. Find the "ple" letter combination and put a check (✓) in the column that identifies its position: beginning, within or end.
지도: 각 대상 단어를 읽으십시오. "ple"문자 조합을 찾고위치를 식별하는 열에 체크(✓)를 하십시오: 시작, 내또는 끝.

Target Words	Beginning (First 3 Letters)	Within	End (Last 3 Letters)
1. participle			✓
2. multiple			✓
3. displeased		✓	
4. simple			✓
5. plentiful	✓		

 Directions: Read each target word. Put a check (✓) in the "yes" column if the "ple" letter combination has the /p/ + /ə/ + /l/ sounds. Put a check (✓) in the "no" column if the "ple" letter combination does not have the /p/ + /ə/ + /l/ sounds.
지도: 각 대상 단어를 읽으십시오. "ple" 문자 조합에/p/ + /ə/ + /l/ 소리가 있는 경우"yes" 열에 체크(✓)를 하십시오. "ple" 문자 조합에/p/ + /ə/ + /l/소리가 없으면"no" 열에 체크(✓)를 하십시오.

Target Words	Yes	No
6. participle	✓	
7. multiple	✓	
8. displeased		✓
9. simple	✓	
10. plentiful		✓

Name: _____ Date: ___/___/_____ Score: _____

Lesson 16.5

Reading Words with a Silent Letter "p"

✓ Lesson Check Point

 Directions: Read the target words in the word box. Write the words that have a silent letter "p" in the first column. Write the words that do not have a silent letter "p" in the second column.

지도: 단어 상자에 있는 대상 단어를 읽으십시오. 첫 번째 열에 묵음 문자 "p"가 있는 단어를 쓰십시오. 두 번째 열에 묵음 문자 "p"가 없는 단어를 쓰십시오.

Target Word Box				
apple	receipt	sleep	compose	slippery
suppose	point	puppy	hopping	raspberry
tips	sample	corps	predict	play
plot	psychic	cupboard	stamps	surprise

Letter "p" is silent	Letter "p" has the /p/ sound
corps	plot
apple	tips
receipt	play
slippery	sleep
puppy	point
psychic	predict
raspberry	sample
cupboard	stamps
suppose	surprise
hopping	compose

Classwork

Name: _____ Date: ___/___/_____ Score: _____

The Reading Challenge

Lesson 16.6

Reading Multisyllable Words

 Lesson Check Point

 Directions: Read and divide each target word into syllables. Write each word and place a hyphen (-) between the syllables in the second column. Write the number of syllables in the third column. Use a dictionary or the Internet to check your answers.

지도: 각 대상 단어를 읽고 음절로 나눕니다. 각 단어를 쓰고 두 번째 열의 음절 사이에 하이픈(-)을 넣습니다. 세 번째 열에 음절 수를 쓰십시오. 사전이나 인터넷을 사용하여 답을 확인하십시오.

Target Words	Words Divided into Syllables	Number of Syllables
1. people	peo-ple	2
2. plural	plu-ral	2
3. powder	pow-der	2
4. privatized	pri-va-tized	3
5. platform	plat-form	2
6. politeness	po-lite-ness	3
7. plastic	plas-tic	2
8. persistence	per-sis-tence	3
9. parsley	pars-ley	2
10. peanut	pea-nut	2

Name: _____ Date: ___/___/_____ Score: _____

The Reading Challenge

Lesson 16.6

Reading Multisyllable Words

✓ Lesson Check Point

Directions: Read each target word. Circle the word in the row that is divided correctly into syllables. Use a dictionary or the Internet to check your answers.

지도: 각 대상 단어를 읽으십시오. 음절로 올바르게 나누어진 행에 있는 단어에 동그라미를 치십시오. 사전이나 인터넷을 사용하여 답을 확인하십시오.

Model

| paragraph | a. par-a-graph ⭕ | b. pa-ra-graph | c. par-ag-raph |

1. period	a. per-i-od	b. pe-ri-od ⭕	c. pe-r-iod
2. pyramid	a. pyr-a-mid ⭕	b. py-ra-mid	c. pyr-am-id
3. personal	a. per-son-al ⭕	b. pers-on-al	c. per-so-nal
4. parakeet	a. pa-ra-keet	b. par-a-keet ⭕	c. pa-rak-eet
5. punctual	a. pun-ctu-al	b. punc-t-ual	c. punc-tu-al ⭕
6. Panama	a. Pan-am-a	b. Pan-a-ma ⭕	c. Pa-na-ma
7. perigee	a. pe-rig-ee	b. per-i-gee ⭕	c. per-ig-ee
8. peculiar	a. pec-u-liar	b. pe-cul-iar	c. pe-cu-liar ⭕

Classwork

 Name: _____ Date: ___/___/_____ Score: _____

Lesson 16.7

Reading and Writing

Proper and Common Nouns and Adjectives

✓ Lesson Check Point

 Directions: Read the words in the word box. Put an (X) on the line next to each word that is written incorrectly. Remember that all proper nouns and proper adjectives are capitalized. Use a dictionary or the Internet to check your answers.

지도: 단어 상자에 있는 단어를 읽으십시오. 잘못 쓰여진 각 단어 옆의 줄에 (X)를 표시하십시오. 모든 고유 명사와 고유 형용사는 대문자임을 기억하십시오. 사전이나 인터넷을 사용하여 답을 확인하십시오.

Word Box					
__	Poland	X	philippine	__	place
__	passport	__	Peruvian	X	panama
X	Penguin	__	people	X	Passenger
__	pharmacist	X	pennsylvania	X	Poodle

 Directions: Read each unedited sentence and underline the word that is written incorrectly. Write each sentence correctly on the line.

지도: 편집되지 않은 각 문장을 읽고 잘못 쓰여진 단어에 밑줄을긋습 니다. 각 문장을 줄에 올바르게 쓰십시오.

Model
The poem, "<u>puddles</u>," was written by Patrick Parker.
<u>The poem, "Puddles," was written by Patrick Parker.</u>

1. The <u>panama</u> Canal is a powerful structure.
<u>The Panama Canal is a powerful structure.</u>

2. The City of <u>philadelphia</u> is located in Pennsylvania.
<u>The City of Philadelphia is located in Pennsylvania.</u>

3. The <u>peruvian</u> coast bordering the Pacific Ocean is a desert strip.
<u>The Peruvian coast bordering the Pacific Ocean is a desert strip.</u>

4. <u>perry</u> the Platypus is the star of the hit show "Phineas and Ferb."
<u>Perry the Platypus is the star of the hit show "Phineas and Ferb."</u>

 Name: _____ Date: ___/___/_____ Score: _____

Lesson 17.1

Reading Words with the Letter Q/q

✓ Lesson Check Point

 Directions: Read each target word. Find the letter "q" and put a check (✓) in the column that identifies its position: beginning, within or end.
지도: 각 대상 단어를 읽으십시오. 문자"q"를 찾아 체크 표시(✓)위치를 식별하는 열에서 시작, 내부 또는 끝.

Target Words	Beginning (First Letter)	Within	End (Last Letter)
1. question	✓		
2. squabbled		✓	
3. quotation	✓		
4. Iraq			✓
5. consequent		✓	

 Directions: Read each sentence and underline the words that begin with the letter "q." Write all the underlined words in alphabetical order on the lines below.
지도: 각 문장을 읽고"q"로 시작하는 단어에 밑줄을 긋습니다. 아래 줄에 밑줄 친 단어를 알파벳 순서로 모두 쓰십시오.

6. <u>Quincy</u> and his family are from <u>Quebec</u>, Canada.

7. The new <u>quilts</u> are made with high <u>quality</u> fabrics.

8. My sister, <u>Queenisha</u>, sleeps on a <u>queen-sized</u> bed.

9. All the children in the <u>Quinn</u> family have four <u>quarters</u>.

10. All the candidates are highly <u>qualified</u> for the job at <u>Quick</u> Inc.

qualified _____   quality _____   quarters _____
Quebec _____   Queenisha _____   queen-sized _____
Quick _____   quilts _____   Quincy _____
                    Quinn _____

Classwork

 Name: _____ Date: ___/___/_____ Score: _____

Lesson 17.2

Reading Words with the Letter "q" and "qu" Letter Combination

✓ **Lesson Check Point**

 Directions: Read each target word. Circle the word in the column that has the same "q" or "qu" sound(s) as the target word.
지도: 각 대상 단어를 읽으십시오. 대상 단어와 동일한 "q" 또는 "qu" 소리가 있는 열의 단어에 동그라미를 치십시오.

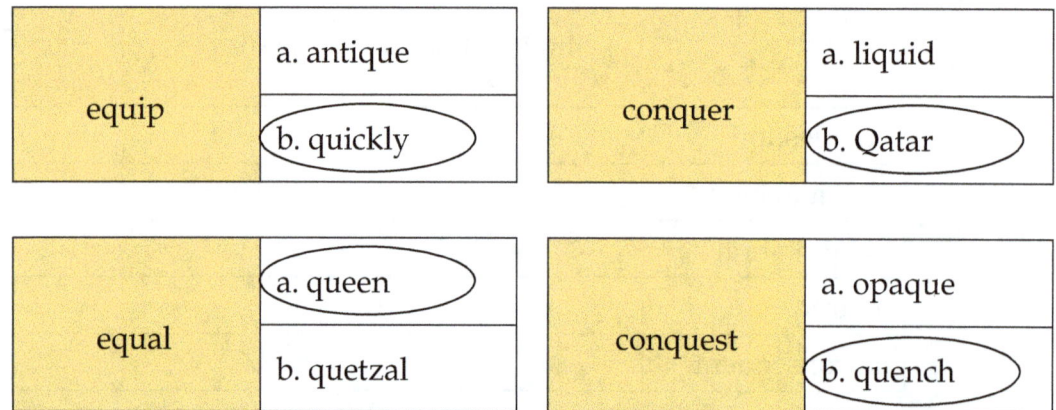

 Directions: Read each target word. Put a check (✓) under the correct column heading.
지도: 각 대상 단어를 읽으십시오. 올바른 열 제목 아래에 체크(✓)를 하십시오.

Target Words	"qu" has the /k/ sound as in the word <u>plaque</u>	"qu" has the /k/ + /w/ sounds as in the word <u>queen</u>
1. equip		✓
2. conquer	✓	
3. equal		✓
4. conquest		✓

Learn To Read English With Directions In Korean

 Name: _____ Date: ___/___/_____ Score: _____

Lesson 17.2

Reading Words with the "qu" Letter Combination

✓ Lesson Check Point

 Directions: Read each target word. Circle the word in the column that has the same "qu" sound(s) as the target word.
지도: 각 대상 단어를 읽으십시오. 대상 단어와 동일한 "qu" 소리가 있는 열의 단어에 동그라미를 치십시오.

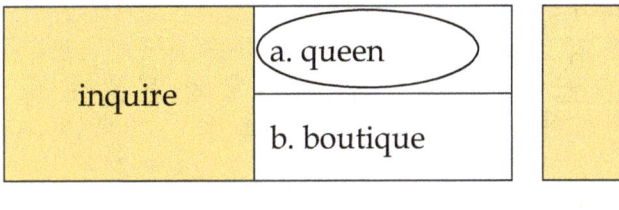

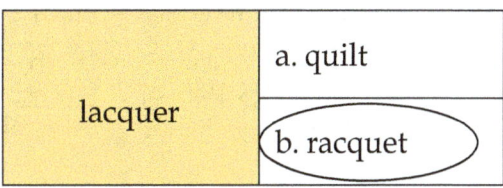

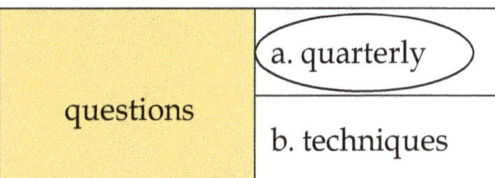

 Directions: Read each target word. Put a check (✓) under the correct column heading.
지도: 각 대상 단어를 읽으십시오. 올바른 열 제목 아래에 체크(✓)를 하십시오.

Target Words	"qu" has the /k/ + /w/ sounds as in the word <u>queen</u>	"qu" has the /k/ sound as in the word <u>plaque</u>	"qu" is silent as in the word <u>racquet</u>
1. inquire	✓		
2. lacquer			✓
3. technique		✓	
4. questions	✓		

Classwork

 Name: _____ Date: ___/___/_____ Score: _____

The Reading Challenge

Lesson 17.3

Reading Multisyllable Words

✓ Lesson Check Point

 Directions: Read and divide each target word into syllables. Write each word and place a hyphen (-) between the syllables in the second column. Write the number of syllables in the third column. Use a dictionary or the Internet to check your answers.

지도: 각 대상 단어를 읽고 음절로 나눕니다. 각 단어를 쓰고 두 번째 열의 음절 사이에 하이픈(-)을 넣습니다. 세 번째 열에 음절 수를 쓰십시오. 사전이나 인터넷을 사용하여 답을 확인하십시오.

Target Words	Words Divided into Syllables	Number of Syllables
1. quarantine	quar-an-tine	3
2. quintet	quin-tet	2
3. quiver	quiv-er	2
4. quota	quo-ta	2
5. query	que-ry	2
6. quartet	quar-tet	2
7. quantities	quan-ti-ties	3
8. qualified	qual-i-fied	3
9. quadruple	quad-ru-ple	3
10. quietness	qui-et-ness	3

Name: _____ Date: ___/___/_____ Score: _____

The Reading Challenge

Lesson 17.3

Reading Multisyllable Words

✓ Lesson Check Point

 Directions: Read each target word. Circle the word in the row that is divided correctly into syllables. Use a dictionary or the Internet to check your answers.

지도: 각 대상 단어를 읽으십시오. 음절로 올바르게 나누어진 행에 있는 단어에 동그라미를 치십시오. 사전이나 인터넷을 사용하여 답을 확인하십시오.

Model

| quarter | a. quart-er | (b. quar-ter) | c. qu-arter |

1. quantum	(a. quan-tum)	b. quant-um	c. qua-ntum
2. qualify	(a. qual-i-fy)	b. qua-li-fy	c. qua-lif-y
3. quiver	a. qui-ver	(b. quiv-er)	c. qu-iver
4. question	(a. ques-tion)	b. quest-ion	c. que-stion
5. quotient	a. quot-ient	b. qu-otient	(c. quo-tient)
6. quota	a. qu-ota	(b. quo-ta)	c. quot-a
7. Quebec	a. Qu-ebec	(b. Que-bec)	c. Queb-ec
8. quietude	(a. qui-e-tude)	b. quiet-ude	c. quie-tu-de

Classwork

 Name: _____ Date: ___/___/_____ Score: _____

Lesson 17.4

Reading and Writing

Proper and Common Nouns and Adjectives

✓ Lesson Check Point

 Directions: Read the words in the word box. Put an (X) on the line next to each word that is written incorrectly. Remember that all proper nouns and proper adjectives are capitalized. Use a dictionary or the Internet to check your answers.

지도: 단어 상자에 있는 단어를 읽으십시오. 잘못 쓰여진 각 단어 옆의 줄에 (X)를 표시하십시오. 모든 고유 명사와 고유 형용사는 대문자임을 기억하십시오. 사전이나 인터넷을 사용하여 답을 확인하십시오.

Word Box					
__	quarrel	X	quebec	__	Quakers
X	Quotient	__	Qatar	__	questionable
X	Quotes	__	quickly	X	queen Anne
X	Quiver	X	Quiche	__	Quincy

 Directions: Read each unedited sentence and underline the word that is written incorrectly. Write each sentence correctly on the line.

지도: 편집되지 않은 각 문장을 읽고 잘못 쓰여진 단어에 밑줄을긋습 니다. 각 문장을 줄에 올바르게 쓰십시오.

Model
The <u>queen</u> of England is very quiet.
<u>The Queen of England is very quiet.</u>

1. According to my <u>Quartz</u> watch, it is a <u>Quarter</u> after two.
<u>According to my Quartz watch, it is a quarter after two.</u>

2. My good friends, Mr. and Mrs. Quinn, are <u>quakers</u>.
<u>My good friends, Mr. and Mrs. Quinn, are Quakers.</u>

3. The queen is going to visit <u>quezon</u> City in the Philippines.
<u>The queen is going to visit Quezon City in the Philippines.</u>

4. After reading the article, I asked a <u>Question</u> about Queen Elizabeth.
<u>After reading the article, I asked a question about Queen Elizabeth.</u>

Name: _____ Date: ___/___/_____ Score: _____

Lesson 18.1

Reading Words with the Letter R/r

✓ Lesson Check Point

 Directions: Read each target word. Find the letter "r" and put a check (✓) in the column that identifies its position: beginning, within or end.
지도: 각 대상 단어를 읽으십시오. 문자"r"을 찾아 체크 표시(✓)위치를 식별하는 열에서 시작, 내부 또는 끝.

Target Words	Beginning (First Letter)	Within	End (Last Letter)
1. cashier			✓
2. recent	✓		
3. folder			✓
4. grape		✓	
5. runaway	✓		

 Directions: Read each sentence and underline the words that begin with the letter "r." Write all the underlined words in alphabetical order on the lines below.
지도: 각 문장을 읽고 문자"r"로 시작하는 단어에 밑줄을 긋습니다. 아래 줄에 밑줄 친 단어를 알파벳 순서로 모두 쓰십시오.

6. At <u>recess</u>, Brianna and I <u>ran</u> quickly on the track.

7. The green <u>rowboat</u> is floating along the Nile <u>River</u>.

8. Brian <u>rode</u> his bike along the base of the <u>Rocky</u> Mountains.

9. The <u>residents</u> have the new Long Island <u>Railroad</u> schedule.

10. We can preserve our planet by <u>recycling</u> and <u>reusing</u> items.

<u>Railroad</u>   <u>ran</u>   <u>recess</u>
<u>recycling</u>   <u>residents</u>   <u>reusing</u>
<u>River</u>   <u>Rocky</u>   <u>rode</u>
                     <u>rowboat</u>

Classwork

Name: _____ Date: ___/___/_____ Score: _____

Lesson 18.2

Reading Words with the Letter "r" Combinations:
"br," "cr," "dr," "fr," "gr," "pr" and "tr"

✓ Lesson Check Point

Directions: Read the target words in the word box. Identify the words with the following letter combinations: "br," "cr," "dr," "fr," "gr," "pr" and "tr." Write the target word on the line that correctly completes each sentence.

지도: 단어 상자에 있는 대상 단어를 읽으십시오. "br," "cr," "dr," "fr," "gr," "pr" 및 "tr" 문자 조합으로 단어를 식별합니다. 각 문장을 올바르게 완성하는 행에 목표 단어를 쓰십시오.

Target Word Box			
friends	traveling	bread	groom
principal		cruise	drifting
brochure		program	trucks

1. The _____cruise_____ brochure is on the brass table.

2. Francis and Brad are best _____friends_____.

3. The new _____principal_____ is our school's leader.

4. Yesterday, I saw logs _____drifting_____ along the riverbank.

5. The two loaves of _____bread_____ are fresh out of the oven.

6. The train is _____traveling_____ from New York to Chicago.

7. The college admission _____brochure_____ is very informative.

8. My social service _____program_____ distributes food to needy families.

9. Testa's electric _____trucks_____ travel up to 100 miles without recharging.

10. The bride and _____groom_____ received lots of expensive wedding presents.

Name: _____ Date: ___/___/_____ Score: _____

The Reading Challenge

Lesson 18.3

Reading Multisyllable Words

✓ **Lesson Check Point**

Directions: Read and divide each target word into syllables. Write each word and place a hyphen (-) between the syllables in the second column. Write the number of syllables in the third column. Use a dictionary or the Internet to check your answers.

지도: 각 대상 단어를 읽고 음절로 나눕니다. 각 단어를 쓰고 두 번째 열의 음절 사이에 하이픈(-)을 넣습니다. 세 번째 열에 음절 수를 쓰십시오. 사전이나 인터넷을 사용하여 답을 확인하십시오.

Target Words	Words Divided into Syllables	Number of Syllables
1. reviewing	re-view-ing	3
2. rigorously	rig-or-ous-ly	4
3. rapidly	rap-id-ly	3
4. ready	read-y	2
5. rocky	rock-y	2
6. rather	rath-er	2
7. reading	read-ing	2
8. rapture	rap-ture	2
9. reflection	re-flec-tion	3
10. reporting	re-port-ing	3

Classwork

Name: _____ Date: ___/___/_____ Score: _____

The Reading Challenge

Lesson 18.3

Reading Multisyllable Words

✓ **Lesson Check Point**

Directions: Read each target word. Circle the word in the row that is divided correctly into syllables. Use a dictionary or the Internet to check your answers.

지도: 각 대상 단어를 읽으십시오. 음절로 올바르게 나누어진 행에 있는 단어에 동그라미를 치십시오. 사전이나 인터넷을 사용하여 답을 확인하십시오.

Model

runaway	a. ru-na-way	b. run-a-way ⭕	c. run-aw-ay

1. robotics	a. ro-bot-ics ⭕	b. rob-ot-ics	c. ro-bo-tics

2. radius	a. ra-di-us ⭕	b. rad-i-us	c. ra-diu-s
3. radical	a. rad-i-cal ⭕	b. ra-dic-al	c. ra-di-cal

4. reception	a. re-cept-ion	b. rec-ep-tion	c. re-cep-tion ⭕

5. royalist	a. ro-yal-ist	b. roy-a-list	c. roy-al-ist ⭕

6. reconcile	a. re-con-cile	b. rec-on-cile ⭕	c. rec-onc-ile

7. recliner	a. rec-lin-er	b. re-cli-ner	c. re-clin-er ⭕

8. refresher	a. re-fresh-er ⭕	b. ref-res-her	c. ref-resh-er

Learn To Read English With Directions In Korean   Copyrighted Material

Name: _____ Date: ___/___/_____ Score: _____

Lesson 18.4

Reading and Writing

Proper and Common Nouns and Adjectives

✓ Lesson Check Point

 Directions: Read the words in the word box. Put an (X) on the line next to each word that is written incorrectly. Remember that all proper nouns and proper adjectives are capitalized. Use a dictionary or the Internet to check your answers.

지도: 단어 상자에 있는 단어를 읽으십시오. 잘못 쓰여진 각 단어 옆의 줄에 (X)를 표시하십시오. 모든 고유 명사와 고유 형용사는 대문자임을 기억하십시오. 사전이나 인터넷을 사용하여 답을 확인하십시오.

Word Box					
__	runner	X	Amazon river	X	Red CRoss
__	Richard	__	Ryan	__	rainforest
X	romanian	__	Richmond, VA	X	Railroad
X	The rockies	__	roaches	X	rome

 Directions: Read each unedited sentence and underline the word that is written incorrectly. Write each sentence correctly on the line.

지도: 편집되지 않은 각 문장을 읽고 잘못 쓰여진 단어에 밑줄을긋습 니다. 각 문장을 줄에 올바르게 쓰십시오.

Model
We saw two <u>Retired</u> racehorses at Richardson Ranch.
<u>We saw two retired racehorses at Richardson Ranch.</u>

1. Raphael said, "<u>russia</u> is the world's largest country."
<u>Raphael said, "Russia is the world's largest country."</u>

2. My friends, Rachel and Ricky, went to the Amazon <u>rainforest</u>.
<u>My friends, Rachel and Ricky, went to the Amazon Rainforest.</u>

3. Mr. Richards received the <u>rockefeller</u> Merit Award for Excellence.
<u>Mr. Richards received the Rockefeller Merit Award for Excellence.</u>

4. Do you know that Rose Robin <u>restaurant</u> serves the best ribs?
<u>Do you know that Rose Robin Restaurant serves the best ribs?</u>

Classwork

Name: _____ Date: ___/___/_____ Score: _____

Lesson 19.1

Reading Words with the Letter S/s

✓ **Lesson Check Point**

Directions: Read each target word. Find the letter "s" and put a check (✓) in the column that identifies its position: beginning, within or end.
지도: 각 대상 단어를 읽으십시오. 문자 "s"를 찾아 체크 표시(✓)위치를 식별하는 열에서 시작, 내부 또는 끝.

Target Words	Beginning (First Letter)	Within	End (Last Letter)
1. safety	✓		
2. matches			✓
3. runners			✓
4. shower	✓		
5. construct		✓	

Directions: Read each sentence and underline the words that begin with the letter "s." Write all the underlined words in alphabetical order on the lines below.
지도: 각 문장을 읽고 "s"로 시작하는 단어에 밑줄을 긋습니다. 아래 줄에 밑줄 친 단어를 알파벳 순서로 모두 쓰십시오.

6. Dexter ate a tasty <u>salami</u> <u>sandwich</u> for lunch.
7. My brother received two <u>scholarships</u> for <u>school</u>.
8. Melanie <u>said</u>, "My grandmother is a great <u>singer</u>."
9. Melissa is using <u>scissors</u> to cut ten <u>sheets</u> of paper.
10. Both Josiah and <u>Simone</u> are <u>seventy-six</u> years old.

said   salami   sandwich
scholarship   school   scissors
singer   seventy-six   sheets
                  Simone

 Name: _____   Date: ___/___/_____   Score: _____

Lesson 19.1

Reading Words with the Letter S/s

✓ **Lesson Check Point**

 Directions: Read each target word. Circle the word in the column that has the same "s" sound as the target word.
지도: 각 대상 단어를 읽으십시오. 대상 단어와 동일한 "s" 소리가 나는 열의 단어에 동그라미를 치십시오.

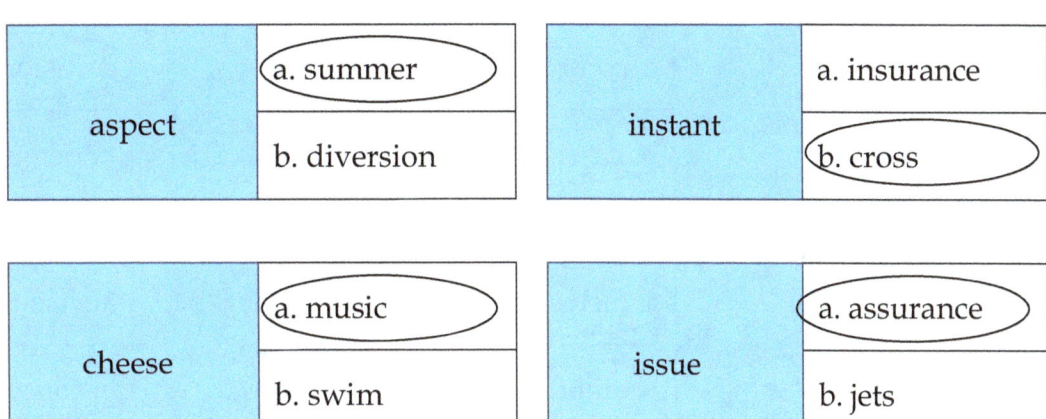

 Directions: Read each target word. Put a check (✓) under the correct column heading.
지도: 각 대상 단어를 읽으십시오. 올바른 열 제목 아래에 체크(✓)를 하십시오.

Target Words	"s" has the /s/ sound as in the word <u>sun</u>	"s" has the /sh/ sound as in the word <u>sugar</u>	"s" has the /z/ sound as in the word <u>his</u>	"s" has the /zh/ sound as in the word <u>vision</u>
1. aspect	✓			
2. instant	✓			
3. cheese			✓	
4. issue		✓		

Learn To Read English With Directions In Korean

Classwork

Name: _____ Date: ___/___/_____ Score: _____

Lesson 19.2

Reading Words with the "sion," "sial" & "scious" Suffixes

✓ **Lesson Check Point**

Directions: Read each target word. Circle the word in the column that has the same "sion," "sial" or "scious" sound as the target word.
지도: 각 대상 단어를 읽으십시오. 대상 단어와 동일한 "sion," "sial" 또는 "scious" 소리가 나는 열의 단어에 동그라미를 치십시오.

commission	a. controversial
	b. (passion) ◯

conversion	a. (fusion) ◯
	b. percussion

compulsion	a. (inclusion) ◯
	b. ambrosial

unconscious	a. vision
	b. (conscious) ◯

Directions: Read each target word. Put a check (✓) under the correct column heading.
지도: 각 대상 단어를 읽으십시오. 올바른 열 제목 아래에 체크(✓)를 하십시오.

Target Words	"sion" has the /sh/ + /ə/ + /n/ sounds as in the word <u>passion</u>	"sion" has the /zh/ + /ə/ + /n/ sounds as in the word <u>vision</u>	"scious" has the /sh/ + /ə/ + /s/ sounds as in the word <u>conscious</u>
1. commission	✓		
2. conversion		✓	
3. compulsion	✓		
4. unconscious			✓

 Name: _____ Date: ___/___/_____ Score: _____

Lesson 19.3

Reading Words with the "sch" Letter Combination

✓ **Lesson Check Point**

 Directions: Read each target word. Circle the word in the column that has the same "sch" sound(s) as the target word.
지도: 각 대상 단어를 읽으십시오. 대상 단어와 같은 "sch" 소리가 나는 열의 단어에 동그라미를 치십시오

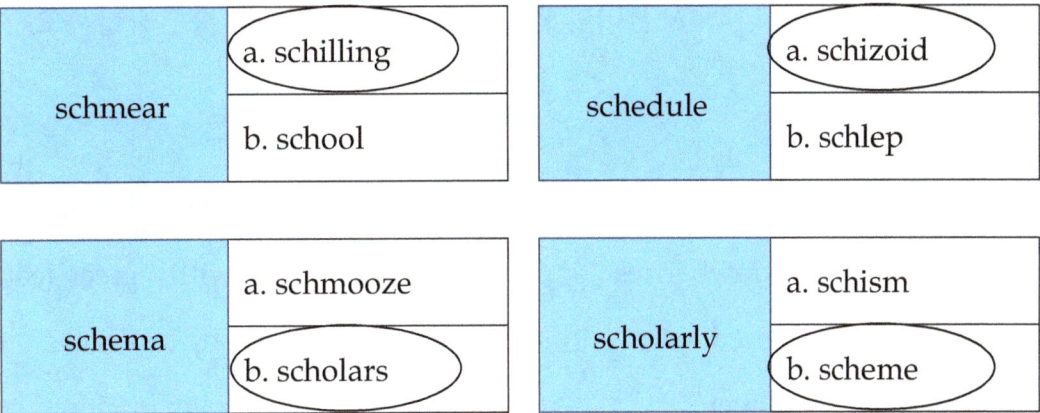

 Directions: Read each target word. Put a check (✓) under the correct column heading.
지도: 각 대상 단어를 읽으십시오. 올바른 열 제목 아래에 체크(✓)를 하십시오.

Target Words	"sch" has the /s/ + /k/ sounds as in the word school	"sch" has the /sh/ sound as in the word schilling
1. schmear		✓
2. schedule	✓	
3. schema	✓	
4. scholarly	✓	

Classwork

 Name: _____ Date:___/___/_____ Score:_____

Lesson 19.4

Reading Words with the "scr," "shr," "spr" & "str" Letter Combinations

Dictionary Skills/ Vocabulary

✓ Lesson Check Point

 Directions: Read each target word and its definition. Write the letter of the definition on the line of each target word. Use a dictionary or the Internet to check your answers.
지도: 각 대상 단어와 그 정의를 읽으십시오. 각 대상 단어의 행에 정의의 문자를 씁니다. 사전이나 인터넷을 사용하여 답을 확인하십시오.

Target Words	Definitions
1. _c_ scrub	a. a device used to sprinkle water on a lawn
2. _b_ strawberries	b. sweet, red berries with a green leaf on top
3. _e_ shredder	c. to clean something by brushing
4. _d_ street	d. a paved road in a town or city
5. _a_ sprinkler	e. a machine that cuts paper into small pieces

 Directions: Read each sentence. Underline the word in the parentheses that correctly completes each sentence. Then, write the underlined word on the line.
지도: 각 문장을 읽으십시오. 각 문장을 올바르게 완성하는 괄호 안에 있는 단어에 밑줄을 긋습니다. 그런 다음 밑줄 친 단어를 줄에 쓰십시오.

6. I will water my grass with a __sprinkler__ system. (street, <u>sprinkler</u>)

7. She will __scrub__ the dirty floor with a firm brush. (street, <u>scrub</u>)

8. Stan shreds documents with a __shredder__. (<u>shredder</u>, sprinkler)

9. The driver drove down the __street__ at a high speed. (<u>street</u>, scrub)

10. I enjoy __strawberries__ with my breakfast cereal. (shredder, <u>strawberries</u>)

Name: _____ Date:___/___/_____ Score:_____

Lesson 19.5

Reading Words with the "sl" & "sle" Letter Combinations

Dictionary Skills/ Vocabulary

✓ Lesson Check Point

Directions: Read each target word and its definition. Write the target word on the line in front of its meaning. Use a dictionary or the Internet to check your answers.

지도: 각 대상 단어와 그 정의를 읽으십시오. 의미 앞 줄에 대상단어 를 쓰십시오. 사전이나 인터넷을 사용하여 답을 확인하십시오.

Target Word Box				
sleeves	slippery	slope	sloth	sly

1. <u>slippery</u> causing to slip and/or slide
2. <u>sly</u> a characteristic of a tricky person
3. <u>sloth</u> a furry mammal that moves very slowly
4. <u>slopes</u> a falling or rising land surface
5. <u>sleeves</u> the parts of a garment that cover a person's arms

Directions: Read each sentence. Underline the word in the parentheses that correctly completes each sentence. Then, write the underlined word on the line.

지도: 각 문장을 읽으십시오. 각 문장을 올바르게 완성하는 괄호 안에 있는 단어에 밑줄을 긋습니다. 그런 다음 밑줄 친 단어를 줄에 쓰십시오.

6. In the woods, the tricky fox has a ___sly___ smile. (sloth, <u>sly</u>)

7. I could not hold the ___slippery___ starfish. (<u>slippery</u>, slopes)

8. The ___sloth___ is hanging on the tropical tree. (<u>sloth</u>, slippery)

9. Sam is wearing a shirt with short ___sleeves___. (sly, <u>sleeves</u>)

10. The ski ___slopes___ are covered with snow and ice. (<u>slopes</u>, sleeves)

Classwork

Name: _____ Date: ___/___/_____ Score: _____

Lesson 19.5

Reading Words with the "sle" Letter Combination

✓ Lesson Check Point

Directions: Read each target word. Find the "sle" letter combination and put a check (✓) in the column that identifies its position: beginning, within or end.

지도: 각 대상 단어를 읽으십시오. "sle" 문자 조합을 찾고위치를 식별하는 열에 체크(✓)를 하십시오: 시작, 내또는 끝.

Target Words	Beginning (First 3 Letters)	Within	End (Last 3 Letters)
1. sleet	✓		
2. sleeves	✓		
3. sleigh	✓		
4. tussle			✓
5. measles		✓	

Directions: Read each target word. Put a check (✓) in the "yes" column if the "sle" letter combination has the /s/ + /ə/ + /l/ or /z/ + /ə/ + /l/ sounds. Put a check (✓) in the "no" column if the "sle" letter combination does not have the /s/ + /ə/ + /l/ or /z/ + /ə/ + /l/ sounds.

지도: 각 대상 단어를 읽으십시오. "sle" 문자 조합에/s/ + /ə/ + /l/ 또는/z/ + /ə/ + /소리 가 있으면"yes" 열에 체크(✓)를 하십시오. "sle" 문자 조합에/s/ + /ə/ + /l/ 또는/z/ + /ə/ + /소리가 없으면"no" 열에 체크(✓)를 하십시오.

Target Words	Yes	No
6. sleet		✓
7. sleeves		✓
8. sleigh		✓
9. tussle	✓	
10. measles	✓	

Name: _____ Date: ___/___/_____ Score: _____

Lesson 19.6

Reading Words with the "sm" Letter Combination

✓ **Lesson Check Point**

 Directions: Read each target word. Circle the word in the column that has the same "sm" sounds as the target word.

지도: 각 대상 단어를 읽으십시오. 대상 단어와 동일한 "sm" 소리가 나는 열의 단어에 동그라미를 치십시오.

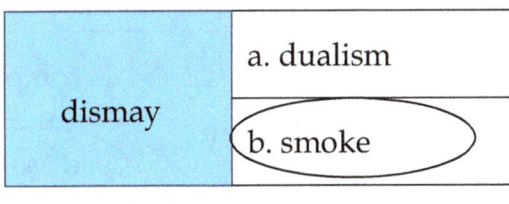
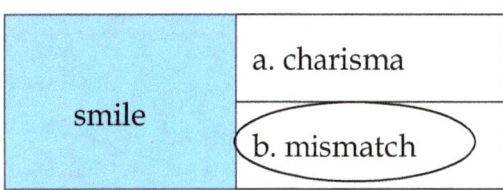
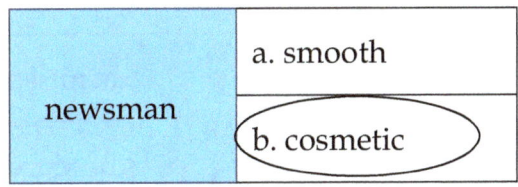
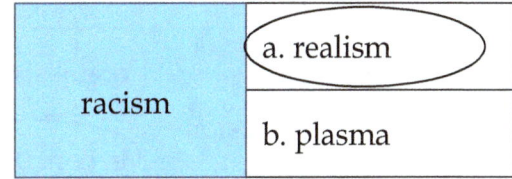

 Directions: Read each target word. Put a check (✓) under the correct column heading.

지도: 각 대상 단어를 읽으십시오. 올바른 열 제목 아래에 체크(✓)를 하십시오.

Target Words	"sm" has the /s/ + /m/ sounds as in the word smell	"sm" has the /z/ + /m/ sounds as in the word cosmic	"sm" has the /z/ + /ə/ + /m/ sounds as in the word autism
1. dismay	✓		
2. smile	✓		
3. newsman		✓	
4. racism			✓

Learn To Read English With Directions In Korean

Classwork

 Name: _____ Date: ___/___/_____ Score: _____

Lesson 19.7

Reading Words with the "ss" Letter Combination

✓ **Lesson Check Point**

 Directions: Read each target word. Circle the word in the column that has the same "ss" sound(s) as the target word.
지도: 각 대상 단어를 읽으십시오. 대상 단어와 동일한 "ss" 소리가 나는 열의 단어에 동그라미를 치십시오.

misshaped	a. dissolving
	b. dissatisfy ⃝

Missouri	a. compassion
	b. dissolve ⃝

expression	a. misstated
	b. concussion ⃝

mission	a. misspell
	b. aggression ⃝

 Directions: Read each target word. Put a check (✓) under the correct column heading.
지도: 각 대상 단어를 읽으십시오. 올바른 열 제목 아래에 체크(✓)를 하십시오.

Target Words	"ss" has the /sh/ sound as in the word <u>tissue</u>	"ss" has the /s/ + /s/ sounds as in the word <u>misspell</u>	"ss" has the /z/ sound as in the word <u>dissolve</u>
1. misshaped		✓	
2. Missouri			✓
3. expression	✓		
4. mission	✓		

Name: _____ Date: ___/___/_____ Score: _____

Lesson 19.8

Reading Words with a Silent Letter "s"

✓ Lesson Check Point

Directions: Read the target words in the word box. Write the words that have a silent letter "s" in the first column. Write the words that do not have a silent letter "s" in the second column.

지도: 단어 상자에 있는 대상 단어를 읽으십시오. 첫 번째 열에 묵음문자 "s"가 있는 단어를 씁니다. 두 번째 열에 묵음 문자"s"가 없는 단어를 쓰십시오.

Target Word Box				
class	horses	handsome	island	debris
aisle	passage	estate	assess	becomes
request	hotels	Arkansas	consider	aside
optimist	address	discover	embassy	isle

Letter "s" is silent	Letter "s" has the /s/, /z/ or /sh/ sound
isle	aside
aisle	estate
assess	hotels
class	becomes
debris	request
island	horses
address	consider
embassy	optimist
passage	discover
Arkansas	handsome

Classwork

 Name: _____ Date: ___/___/_____ Score: _____

The Reading Challenge

Lesson 19.9

Reading Multisyllable Words

✓ **Lesson Check Point**

 Directions: Read and divide each target word into syllables. Write each word and place a hyphen (-) between the syllables in the second column. Write the number of syllables in the third column. Use a dictionary or the Internet to check your answers.

지도: 각 대상 단어를 읽고 음절로 나눕니다. 각 단어를 쓰고 두 번째 열의 음절 사이에 하이픈(-)을 넣습니다. 세 번째 열에 음절 수를 쓰십시오. 사전이나 인터넷을 사용하여 답을 확인하십시오.

Target Words	Words Divided into Syllables	Number of Syllables
1. safety	safe-ty	2
2. senior	sen-ior	2
3. sampling	sam-pling	2
4. shampoo	sham-poo	2
5. seaport	sea-port	2
6. soldiers	sol-diers	2
7. satisfaction	sat-is-fac-tion	4
8. sequential	se-quen-tial	3
9. shadowing	shad-ow-ing	3
10. sisterhood	sis-ter-hood	3

Name: _____ Date: ___/___/_____ Score: _____

The Reading Challenge

Lesson 19.9

Reading Multisyllable Words

✓ Lesson Check Point

 Directions: Read each target word. Circle the word in the row that is divided correctly into syllables. Use a dictionary or the Internet to check your answers.

지도: 각 대상 단어를 읽으십시오. 음절로 올바르게 나누어진 행에 있는 단어에 동그라미를 치십시오. 사전이나 인터넷을 사용하여 답을 확인하십시오.

Model

| Saturday | a. Sa-tur-day | b. Sat-ur-day ⃝ | c. Sa-turd-ay |

1. seminar	a. sem-i-nar ⃝	b. se-mi-nar	c. se-min-ar
2. satisfy	a. sa-tis-fy	b. sa-tisf-y	c. sat-is-fy ⃝
3. seasonal	a. seas-on-al	b. sea-so-nal	c. sea-son-al ⃝
4. several	a. se-ver-al	b. sev-er-al ⃝	c. sev-e-ral
5. singular	a. sing-u-lar	b. sin-gu-lar ⃝	c. sin-gul-ar
6. semester	a. se-mest-er	b. sem-est-er	c. se-mes-ter ⃝
7. skeleton	a. skel-e-ton ⃝	b. ske-le-ton	c. ske-let-on
8. salary	a. sa-lar-y	b. sal-ar-y	c. sal-a-ry ⃝

Learn To Read English With Directions In Korean

Classwork

Name: _____ Date: ___/___/_____ Score: _____

Lesson 19.10

Reading and Writing

Proper and Common Nouns and Adjectives

✓ **Lesson Check Point**

 **Directions:** Read the words in the word box. Put an (X) on the line next to each word that is written incorrectly. Remember that all proper nouns and proper adjectives are capitalized. Use a dictionary or the Internet to check your answers.

지도: 단어 상자에 있는 단어를 읽으십시오. 잘못 쓰여진 각 단어 옆의 줄에 (X)를 표시하십시오. 모든 고유 명사와 고유 형용사는 대문자임을 기억하십시오. 사전이나 인터넷을 사용하여 답을 확인하십시오.

Word Box					
X	Sandbox	X	siberia	__	Samoa
X	Salon	__	shrimp	X	Dr. samuel
__	San Juan	__	sample	X	Sailor
__	seagull	X	senator Sam	__	seahorse

 Directions: Read each unedited sentence and underline the word that is written incorrectly. Write each sentence correctly on the line.

지도: 편집되지 않은 각 문장을 읽고 잘못 쓰여진 단어에 밑줄을 긋습 니다. 각 문장을 줄에 올바르게 쓰십시오.

Model
<u>sandy</u> is going to Salt Lake City on Sunday.
<u>Sandy is going to Salt Lake City on Sunday.</u>

1. On <u>saturday</u>, we are going sailing around South Bay.
<u>On Saturday, we are going sailing around South Bay.</u>

2. My <u>Siblings</u> received scholarships to Sidney School.
<u>My siblings received scholarships to Sidney School.</u>

3. On Sunday, I am going to have lunch with <u>sergeant</u> Smith.
<u>On Sunday, I am going to have lunch with Sergeant Smith.</u>

4. My grandparents, Samuel and Samantha, are <u>Senior</u> citizens.
<u>My grandparents, Samuel and Samantha, are senior citizens.</u>

Name: _____ Date:___/___/_____ Score:_____

Lesson 20.1

Reading Words with the Letter T/t

Directions: Read each target word. Find the letter "t" and put a check (✓) in the column that identifies its position: beginning, within or end.
지도: 각 대상 단어를 읽으십시오. 문자"t"를 찾아 체크 표시(✓)위치를 식별하는 열에서 시작, 내부 또는 끝.

Target Words	Beginning (First Letter)	Within	End (Last Letter)
1. reporter		✓	
2. teenager	✓		
3. merchant			✓
4. Tuesday	✓		
5. section		✓	

Directions: Read each sentence and underline the words that begin with the letter "t." Write all the underlined words in alphabetical order on the lines below.
지도: 각 문장을 읽고 문자"t"로 시작하는 단어에 밑줄을 긋습니다. 아래 줄에 밑줄 친 단어를 알파벳 순서로 모두 쓰십시오.

6. My teacher, Ms. Peters, does not like tarantulas.

7. My sister tossed her interactive toys everywhere.

8. At Thanksgiving dinner, Danny ate rice and turkey.

9. Terrence likes putting tartar sauce on his fish sandwiches.

10. An intense thunderstorm caused damage throughout our county.

tarantulas _____   tartar _____   teacher _____
Terrence _____   Thanksgiving _____ throughout _____
thunderstorm _____   tossed _____   toys _____
                        turkey _____

Classwork

 Name: _____ Date:___/___/_____ Score:_____

Lesson 20.2

Reading Words with the "thm" Letter Combination

✓ Lesson Check Point

 Directions: Read each target word. Circle the word in the column that has the same "thm" sound(s) as the target word.
지도: 각 대상 단어를 읽으십시오. 대상 단어와 동일한 "thm" 소리가 있는 열의 단어에 동그라미를 치십시오.

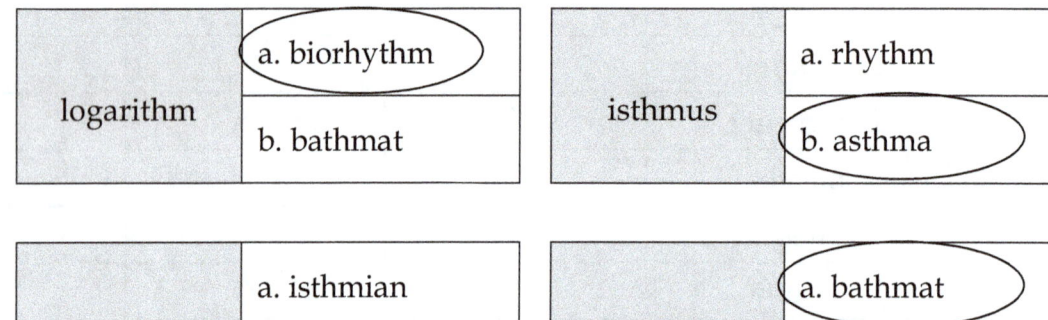

 Directions: Read each target word. Put a check (✓) under the correct column heading.
지도: 각 대상 단어를 읽으십시오. 올바른 열 제목 아래에 체크(✓)를 하십시오.

Target Words	"thm" has the /th/ + /ə/ + /m/ sounds as in the word <u>rhythm</u>	"thm" has the /th/ + /m/ sounds as in the word <u>bathmat</u>	"thm" silent "th" + /m/ sound as in the word <u>asthma</u>
1. logarithm	✓		
2. isthmus			✓
3. algorithm	✓		
4. birthmark		✓	

 Name: _____ Date: ___/___/_____ Score: _____

Lesson 20.3

Reading Words with the "tion," "tial" & "tious" Suffixes

✓ **Lesson Check Point**

 Directions: Read each target word. Circle the word in the column that has the same "tion," "tial" or "tious" sound as the target word.
지도: 각 대상 단어를 읽으십시오. 대상 단어와 같은 "tion," "tial" 또는 "tious" 소리가 나는 열의 단어에 동그라미를 치십시오.

distinction	(a. assumption)
	b. substantially

substantial	(a. confidential)
	b. celebration

infectious	(a. cautiously)
	b. animation

conditional	(a. admiration)
	b. bumptious

 Directions: Read each target word. Put a check (✓) under the correct column heading.
지도: 각 대상 단어를 읽으십시오. 올바른 열 제목 아래에 체크(✓)를하십시오.

Target Words	"tion" has the /sh/ +/ə/+/n/ sounds as in the word <u>education</u>	"tial" has the /sh/ +/ə/+/l/ sounds as in the word <u>partial</u>	"tious" has the /sh/ +/ə/+/s/ sounds as in the word <u>ambitious</u>
1. distinction	✓		
2. substantial		✓	
3. infectious			✓
4. conditional	✓		

Classwork

Name: _____ Date: ___/___/_____ Score: _____

Lesson 20.4

Reading Words with the "tr" Letter Combination

Dictionary Skills/ Vocabulary

✓ **Lesson Check Point**

Directions: Read each target word and its definition. Write the letter of the definition on the line of each target word. Use a dictionary or the Internet to check your answers.

지도: 각 대상 단어와 그 정의를 읽으십시오. 각 대상 단어의 행에 정의의 문자를 씁니다. 사전이나 인터넷을 사용하여 답을 확인하십시오.

Target Words	Definitions
1. _d_ tragic	a. a problematic situation, a conflict
2. _e_ trampled	b. to write words from one language to another
3. _c_ transfer	c. to move from one place to another
4. _b_ translate	d. a disastrous occurrence or event
5. _a_ trouble	e. the act of beating a surface down with one's feet

Directions: Read each sentence. Underline the word in the parentheses that correctly completes each sentence. Then, write the underlined word on the line.

지도: 각 문장을 읽으십시오. 각 문장을 올바르게 완성하는 괄호 안에 있는 단어에 밑줄을 긋습니다. 그런 다음 밑줄 친 단어를 줄에 쓰십시오.

6. I ____translated____ the report from English to Arabic. (<u>translated</u>, tragic)

7. He got in ____trouble____ for breaking the class rules. (<u>trouble</u>, transfer)

8. Tress cried when she read the story's __tragic__ ending. (<u>tragic</u>, trample)

9. Terrance will ____transfer____ to his connecting flight. (<u>transfer</u>, translate)

10. The horse ____trampled____ the crops in the field. (trouble, <u>trampled</u>)

Name: _____ Date: ___/___/_____ Score: _____

Lesson 20.5

Reading Words with the "tle" Letter Combination

✓ Lesson Check Point

 Directions: Read each target word. Find the "tle" letter combination and put a check (✓) in the column that identifies its position: beginning, within or end.
지도: 각 대상 단어를 읽으십시오. "tle" 문자 조합을 찾고위치를 식별하는 열에 체크(✓)를 하십시오: 시작, 내또는 끝.

Target Words	Beginning (First 3 Letters)	Within	End (Last 3 Letters)
1. hurtle			✓
2. cutlet		✓	
3. outlet		✓	
4. settle			✓
5. countless		✓	

 Directions: Read each target word. Put a check (✓) in the "yes" column if the "tle" letter combination has the /t/ + /ə/ + /l/ sounds. Put a check (✓) in the "no" column if the "tle" letter combination does not have the /t/ + /ə/ + /l/ sounds.
지도: 각 대상 단어를 읽으십시오. "tle" 문자 조합에/t/ + /ə/ + /l/소리가 있으면 "yes" 열에 체크(✓)를 하십시오. "tle" 문자 조합에/t/ + /ə/ + /l/ 소리가 없으면 "no" 열에 체크(✓)를 하십시오.

Target Words	Yes	No
6. hurtle	✓	
7. cutlet		✓
8. outlet		✓
9. settle	✓	
10. countless		✓

Classwork

 Name: _____ Date: ___/___/_____ Score: _____

Lesson 20.6

Reading Words with the Letter "t" Sounds

✓ Lesson Check Point

 Directions: Read each target word. Circle the word in the column that has the same "t" sound as the target word.
지도: 각 대상 단어를 읽으십시오. 대상 단어와 "t" 소리가 같은 열의 단어에 동그라미를 치십시오.

| mention | (a. ambition) |
| | b. righteous |

| culture | (a. picture) |
| | b. contact |

| electric | (a. connect) |
| | b. action |

| actual | (a. denture) |
| | b. expect |

 Directions: Read each target word. Put a check (✓) under the correct column heading.
지도: 각 대상 단어를 읽으십시오. 올바른 열 제목 아래에 체크(✓)를 하십시오.

Target Words	"t" has the /t/ sound as in the word <u>multiply</u>	"t" has the /ch/ sound as in the word <u>picture</u>	"t" has the /sh/ sound as in the word <u>position</u>
1. mention			✓
2. culture		✓	
3. electric	✓		
4. actual		✓	

Name: _____   Date: ___/___/_____   Score: _____

Lesson 20.7

Reading Words with a Silent Letter "t"

✓ **Lesson Check Point**

 Directions: Read the target words in the word box. Write the words that have a silent letter "t" in the first column. Write the words that do not have a silent letter "t" in the second column.

지도: 단어 상자에 있는 대상 단어를 읽으십시오. 첫 번째 열에 묵음문자 "t"가 있는 단어를 쓰십시오. 두 번째 열에 묵음 문자"t"가 없는 단어를 쓰십시오.

Target Word Box				
continue	itch	crochet	entrance	totally
pottery	curtain	kitchen	heart	factory
clothes	defeat	denote	listening	dieting
castle	postman	sitting	mortgage	snitch

Letter "t" is silent

- itch
- kitchen
- castle
- clothes
- snitch
- sitting
- pottery
- crochet
- listening
- mortgage

Letter "t" has the /t/ sound

- heart
- denote
- defeat
- curtain
- totally
- factory
- entrance
- dieting
- continue
- postman

Classwork

 Name: _____ Date: ___/___/_____ Score: _____

The Reading Challenge

Lesson 20.8

Reading Multisyllable Words

✓ Lesson Check Point

 Directions: Read and divide each target word into syllables. Write each word and place a hyphen (-) between the syllables in the second column. Write the number of syllables in the third column. Use a dictionary or the Internet to check your answers.

지도: 각 대상 단어를 읽고 음절로 나눕니다. 각 단어를 쓰고 두 번째 열의 음절 사이에 하이픈(-)을 넣습니다. 세 번째 열에 음절 수를 쓰십시오. 사전이나 인터넷을 사용하여 답을 확인하십시오.

Target Words	Words Divided into Syllables	Number of Syllables
1. traveling	trav-el-ing	3
2. tiny	ti-ny	2
3. treasure	treas-ure	2
4. textbooks	text-books	2
5. tonight	to-night	2
6. timbering	tim-ber-ing	3
7. tweezers	tweez-ers	2
8. turquoise	tur-quoise	2
9. transplanting	trans-plant-ing	3
10. title	ti-tle	2

Name: _____ Date:___/___/_____ Score:_____

The Reading Challenge

Lesson 20.8

Reading Multisyllable Words

✓ **Lesson Check Point**

 Directions: Read each target word. Circle the word in the row that is divided correctly into syllables. Use a dictionary or the Internet to check your answers.

지도: 각 대상 단어를 읽으십시오. 음절로 올바르게 나누어진 행에 있는 단어에 동그라미를 치십시오. 사전이나 인터넷을 사용하여 답을 확인하십시오.

Model

| telephone | a. te-lep-hone | b. tel-e-phone ✓ | c. te-le-phone |

1. teenager	a. teen-ag-er ✓	b. teen-a-ger	c. teena-g-er
2. taxicab	a. ta-xic-ab	b. tax-ic-ab	c. tax-i-cab ✓
3. technical	a. te-chnic-al	b. tech-nic-al	c. tech-ni-cal ✓
4. triangle	a. tri-ang-le	b. tri-an-gle ✓	c. tria-n-gle
5. testify	a. tes-ti-fy ✓	b. te-stif-y	c. tes-tif-y
6. temperate	a. temp-er-ate	b. tem-pe-rate	c. tem-per-ate ✓
7. typical	a. ty-pi-cal	b. ty-pic-al	c. typ-i-cal ✓
8. translated	a. trans-lat-ed ✓	b. transl-a-ted	c. tran-slat-ed

Classwork

 Name: _____ Date:___/___/_____ Score:_____

Lesson 20.9

Reading and Writing

Proper and Common Nouns and Adjectives

✓ Lesson Check Point

 Directions: Read the words in the word box. Put an (X) on the line next to each word that is written incorrectly. Remember that all proper nouns and proper adjectives are capitalized. Use a dictionary or the Internet to check your answers.

지도: 단어 상자에 있는 단어를 읽으십시오. 잘못 쓰여진 각 단어 옆의 줄에 (X)를 표시하십시오. 모든 고유 명사와 고유 형용사는 대문자임을 기억하십시오. 사전이나 인터넷을 사용하여 답을 확인하십시오.

Word Box					
X	taiwan	X	thursday	__	thousand
__	Togo	X	Today	__	Tonga
__	thunder	__	Tokyo	X	tunisia
X	Twins	__	target	X	Tomato

 Directions: Read each unedited sentence and underline the word that is written incorrectly. Write each sentence correctly on the line.

지도: 편집되지 않은 각 문장을 읽고 잘못 쓰여진 단어에 밑줄을긋습 니다. 각 문장을 줄에 올바르게 쓰십시오.

Model
On <u>thursday</u>, a tornado destroyed my hometown.
<u>On Thursday, a tornado destroyed my hometown.</u>

1. I ate tasty <u>thai</u> food at Lemongrass Thailand Restaurant.
<u>I ate tasty Thai food at Lemongrass Thailand Restaurant.</u>

2. My dentist, Dr. Tracks, <u>Takes</u> good care of my teeth.
<u>My dentist, Dr. Tracks, takes good care of my teeth.</u>

3. In <u>tanzania</u>, the townspeople have tremendous hearts.
<u>In Tanzania, the townspeople have tremendous hearts.</u>

4. I will travel to the beautiful twin islands of Trinidad and <u>tobago</u>.
<u>I will travel to the beautiful twin islands of Trinidad and Tobago.</u>

Name: _____ Date: ___/___/_____ Score: _____

Lesson 21.1

Reading Words with the Letter U/u

✓ **Lesson Check Point**

 Directions: Read each target word. Find the letter "u" and put a check (✓) in the column that identifies its position: beginning, within or end.
지도: 각 대상 단어를 읽으십시오. 문자 "u"를 찾아 체크 표시(✓)위치를 식별하는 열에서 시작, 내부 또는 끝.

Target Words	Beginning (First Letter)	Within	End (Last Letter)
1. under	✓		
2. menu			✓
3. success		✓	
4. you			✓
5. university	✓		

 Directions: Read each target word. Read the words in the row and circle the word that has a different vowel "u" sound.
지도: 각 대상 단어를 읽으십시오. 줄에 있는 단어를 읽고 모음 "u" 소리가 다른 단어에 동그라미를 치세요. 다른 단어에 동그라미를 치세요.

Target Words				
6. swum	mud	(June)	tug	sub
7. chum	(thru)	bum	cut	hum
8. snub	nut	bud	(tube)	bun
9. thug	pun	cub	nun	(juke)
10. funny	(burst)	makeup	snuff	tux

Classwork

 Name: _____ Date:___/___/_____ Score:_____

Lesson 21.2

Reading Words with the Short Vowel "u" Sound

✓ Lesson Check Point

 **Directions:** Read the words in the four boxes. Circle two words with the short vowel /ŭ/ sound. The anchor word for the short vowel /ŭ/ sound is <u>up</u>.

지도: 네 개의 상자에 있는 단어를 읽으십시오. 짧은 모음 /ŭ/ 소리로 두 단어에 동그라미를 치십시오. 단모음 /ŭ/ 소리의 기준어는 up입니다.

fume	(buck)	(bump)	rust	suck	null
June	(dull)	crude	brute	rule	truce

chute	(lush)	(drunk)	mute	dune	flute
used	(punch)	fuse	(plush)	(duck)	buff

 Directions: Read the words in the four boxes. Circle two words that rhyme. Rhyming words have the same ending sound, such as <u>just</u> and <u>must</u>.

지도: 네 개의 상자에 있는 단어를 읽으십시오. 해당하는 두 단어에 동그라미 표시운. 운율이 있는 단어는 just 및 must와 같이 끝 소리가 같습니다.

tuba	(dump)	(luck)	gush	grub	(rush)
(lump)	drug	(tuck)	flu	(hush)	use

stub	(rust)	cute	slug	super	(much)
tune	(dust)	(brush)	(crush)	smug	(such)

Name: _____ Date: ___/___/_____ Score: _____

Lesson 21.2

Reading & Writing Words with the Short Vowel "u" Sound

✓ **Lesson Check Point**

Directions: Read each sentence and underline three words with the short vowel /ŭ/ sound. Then, write the underlined words on the lines below. The anchor word for the short vowel /ŭ/ sound is up.

지도: 각 문장을 읽고 세 단어에 짧은 모음 /ŭ/ 소리에 밑줄을 긋습니다. 그런 다음 밑줄 친 단어를 아래 줄에 쓰십시오. 단모음 /ŭ/ 소리의 기준 어는 up입니다.

Model

Ulysses, the <u>drummer</u>, <u>jumps</u> when he plays the <u>drums</u>.

drummer	jumps	drums

1. As Luke <u>trudged</u> in, he got <u>mud</u> on the <u>rug</u>.

trudged	mud	rug

2. The oatmeal in the <u>cup</u> is usually not <u>lumpy</u> and <u>mushy</u>.

cup	lumpy	mushy

3. The groomer <u>brushed</u> the <u>puppy's</u> fur with a soft <u>brush</u>.

brushed	puppy's	brush

4. In June, I was <u>lucky</u> to see the <u>ducks</u> and <u>cubs</u> at the zoo.

lucky	ducks	cubs

5. The <u>club's</u> members sat on the <u>rug</u> and ate blueberry <u>muffins</u>.

club's	rug	muffins

Classwork

 Name: _____ Date: ___/___/_____ Score: _____

Lesson 21.3

Reading Words with the Long Vowel "u" Sound

✓ Lesson Check Point

 Directions: Read the words in the four boxes. Circle two words with the long vowel /y͞oo/ or /͞oo/ sound. The anchor word for the long vowel /y͞oo/ and /͞oo/ sounds is <u>tube</u>.

지도: 네 개의 상자에 있는 단어를 읽으십시오. 장모음/y͞oo/ 또는/͞oo/소리 로 두 단어에 동그라미를 치십시오. 장모음의 앵커 단어/y͞oo/ 및/͞oo/ 소리는 tube입니다.

guard	(June)	(brute)	junk	yucky	(dilute)
biscuit	(use)	bunch	(volume)	guest	(reduce)

stump	gulp	must	(prune)	sunken	(salute)
(nude)	(accuse)	(confuse)	quiet	lungs	(include)

 Directions: Read the words in the four boxes. Circle two words that rhyme. Rhyming words have the same ending sound, such as <u>rule</u> and <u>mule</u>.

지도: 네 개의 상자에 있는 단어를 읽으십시오. 해당하는 두 단어에동그 라미 표시운. 운율이 있는 단어는 rule 및 mule과 같이 끝 소리가같습 니다.

dump	(cruel)	dusk	lumpy	(June)	duckling
Just	(fuel)	(glue)	(blue)	lucky	(tune)

(mute)	Dutch	sung	(rude)	munch	rushing
(flute)	pumps	(crude)	bumper	(excuse)	(refuse)

Learn To Read English With Directions In Korean

Name: _____   Date: ___/___/_____   Score: _____

Lesson 21.3

Reading & Writing Words with the Long Vowel "u" Sound

✓ **Lesson Check Point**

Directions: Read each sentence and underline three words with the long vowel /y$\overline{oo}$/ or /$\overline{oo}$/ sound. Then, write the underlined words on the lines below. The anchor word for the long vowel /y$\overline{oo}$/ and /$\overline{oo}$/ sounds is tube.

지도: 각 문장을 읽고 긴 단어로 세 단어에 밑줄을 긋습니다. 모음 /y$\overline{oo}$/ 또는 /$\overline{oo}$/ 소리. 그런 다음 밑줄 친 단어를 아래 줄에 쓰십시오. 장모음 /y$\overline{oo}$/ 및 /$\overline{oo}$/ 소리의 앵커 워드는 tube입니다.

Model

Bruce is going to play the tuba and drums in Uganda.

Bruce _____ tuba _____ Uganda _____

1. At lunch, Lucy enjoys eating juicy fruits.

   Lucy _____ juicy _____ fruits _____

2. The students' blue uniforms are dull and unattractive.

   students' _____ blue _____ uniforms _____

3. My aunt used flowers to produce a fragrant perfume.

   used _____ produce _____ perfume _____

4. In June, the club's rules gradually changed for the better.

   June _____ rules _____ gradually _____

5. Mr. Gus Underhill refused to accept the students' excuses.

   refused _____ students' _____ excuses _____

Classwork

Name: _____ Date: ___/___/_____ Score: _____

Review Lessons 21.2 & 21.3

Reading Short Vowel and Long Vowel Words

Directions: Read the target words in the word box. In the first column, write the words that have the short vowel /ŭ/ sound, as in the word <u>up</u>. In the second column, write the words that have the long vowel /yōō/ or /ōō/ sound, as in the word <u>tube</u>.

지도: 단어 상자에 있는 대상 단어를 읽으십시오. 첫 번째 열에는 up 단어와 같이 단모음 /ŭ/ 소리가 나는 단어를 씁니다. 두 번째 칸에는 장모음 /yōō/ 또는 /ōō/ 소리, 단어 tube에서와 같이.

Target Word Box				
lucky	bunch	consume	hunter	rung
using	dull	bumpers	accuse	truce
computer	tofu	lungs	commute	jumping
rushing	debut	music	dusty	uniform

Letter "u" has the /ŭ/ sound as in the word <u>up</u>

- dull
- rung
- lungs
- lucky
- dusty
- bunch
- hunter
- jumping
- rushing
- bumpers

Letter "u" has the /yōō/ or /ōō/ sound as in the word <u>tube</u>

- tofu
- truce
- music
- debut
- using
- accuse
- uniform
- consume
- commute
- computer

 Name: _____ Date: ___/___/_____ Score: _____

Lesson 21.4

Reading Words with Letter "u" Vowel Pairs

✓ **Lesson Check Point**

 Directions: Read each target word. Circle the word in the column that has the same vowel "ua," "ue" or "ui" sound(s) as the target word.
지도: 각 대상 단어를 읽으십시오. 대상 단어와 동일한 모음 "ua," "ue" 또는 "ui" 소리를 갖는 열의 단어에 동그라미를 치십시오.

fruits	(a. clue)
	b. dual

avenue	a. suite
	(b. juicy)

perpetual	(a. gradual)
	b. recruit

built	a. ritual
	(b. building)

 Directions: Read each target word. Put a check (✓) under the correct column heading.
지도: 각 대상 단어를 읽으십시오. 올바른 열 제목 아래에 체크(✓)를 하십시오.

Target Words	Words have the long "u" sound as in the word <u>blue</u>	Words do not have the long "u" sound
1. builds		✓
2. affluent	✓	
3. factual	✓	
4. suites		✓

Classwork

 Name: _____ Date: ___/___/_____ Score: _____

Lesson 21.5

Reading Words with the Final Letter "u"

✓ Lesson Check Point

 Directions: Read each target word. Find the letter "u" and put a check (✓) in the column that identifies its position within the syllable.
지도: 각 대상 단어를 읽으십시오. 문자"u"를 찾아 체크 표시(✓)음절 내에서 위치를 식별하는 열에서.

Target Words	"u" is at the end of a one syllable word	"u" is at the end of the first syllable	"u" is at the end of a multi-syllable word
1. July		✓	
2. you	✓		
3. impromptu			✓
4. Utah		✓	
5. uniform		✓	

 Directions: Read each target word. Put a check (✓) under the correct column heading.
지도: 각 대상 단어를 읽으십시오. 올바른 열 제목 아래에 체크(✓)를 하십시오.

Target Words	"u" has the /ŭ/ sound as in the word <u>tub</u>	"u" has the /yōō/ sound as in the word <u>tube</u>	"u" has the /ə/ sound as in the word <u>circus</u>	"u" is silent as in the word <u>build</u>
6. vague				✓
7. radius			✓	
8. clue		✓		
9. drums	✓			
10. survive			✓	

 Name: _____ Date: ___/___/_____ Score: _____

Lesson 21.6

Reading Letter "u" Words with the Schwa Vowel Sound

✓ Lesson Check Point

 Directions: Read each target word. Circle the word in the column that has the same "u" sound as the target word.
지도: 각 대상 단어를 읽으십시오. 대상 단어와 "u" 소리가 같은 열의 단어에 동그라미를 치십시오.

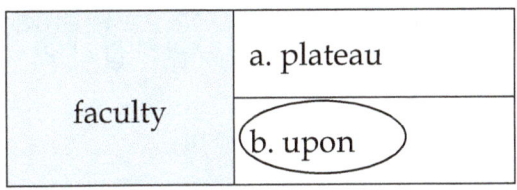
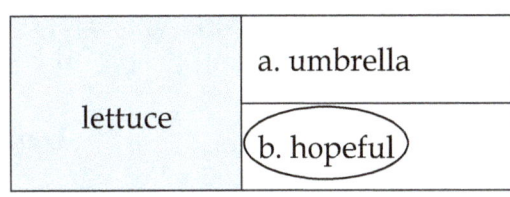
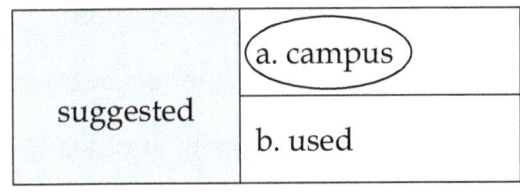
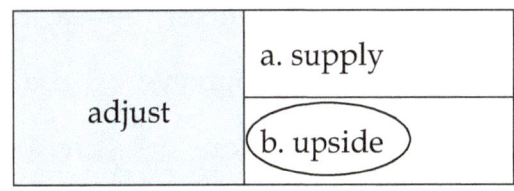

 Directions: Read each sentence and underline the letter "u" word that has the schwa vowel /ə/ sound. The anchor word for the letter "u" schwa vowel sound is campus.
지도: 각 문장을 읽고 슈와 모음 /ə/ 소리가 있는 문자 "u" 단어에 밑줄을 긋습니다. 문자 "u" 슈와 모음 소리의 앵커 단어는 campus입니다.

1. The umpire is not very <u>popular</u>.

2. Some of my students are very <u>playful</u>.

3. Hugo has nice <u>pictures</u> and gifts from Guyana.

4. In January, Eugene will visit <u>Portugal</u> and Uganda.

5. The <u>Museum</u> of Urban Studies is close to Pace University.

6. During class, I tend to <u>focus</u> on the bilingual presentations.

Classwork

 Name: _____ Date: ___/___/_____ Score: _____

Lesson 21.7

Reading Words with the "ur" Letter Combination

Dictionary Skills/ Vocabulary

✓ Lesson Check Point

 **Directions:** Read each target word and its definition. Write the letter of the definition on the line of each target word. Use a dictionary or the Internet to check your answers.
지도: 각 대상 단어와 그 정의를 읽으십시오. 각 대상 단어의 행에 정의의 문자를 씁니다. 사전이나 인터넷을 사용하여 답을 확인하십시오.

Target Words	Definitions
1. _b_ purse	a. the possessive form of the word, you
2. _c_ journey	b. a small bag used to carry money and items
3. _a_ Your	c. a trip; to go from one place to another
4. _e_ Failure	d. to have felt extreme sadness or sorrow
5. _d_ mourned	e. act of not succeeding

 Directions: Read each sentence and write the target word on the line that correctly completes the sentence.
지도: 각 문장을 읽고 다음과 같은 목표 단어를 쓰십시오. 장을 올바르게 완성합니다.

6. My teacher shouted, "__Failure__ in school is unacceptable."

7. Jimmy _____mourned_____ the loss of his pet goldfish.

8. Grandma carries keys and money in her ____purse____.

9. ____Your____ brother is going to join the basketball team.

10. The characters are on a dangerous __journey__ in the woods.

Name: _____ Date: ___/___/_____ Score: _____

Lesson 21.8

Reading Words with a Silent Letter "u"

✓ **Lesson Check Point**

Directions: Read the target words in the word box. Write the words that have a silent letter "u" in the first column. Write the words that do not have a silent letter "u" in the second column.

지도: 단어 상자에 있는 대상 단어를 읽으십시오. 첫 번째 열에 묵음문자 "u"가 있는 단어를 쓰십시오. 두 번째 열에 묵음 문자"u"가 없는 단어를 쓰십시오.

Target Word Box				
fatigue	continuum	circuit	laughing	Guinea
guiding	avenue	Tuesday	rulers	attitude
unison	under	annual	guessing	visual
impromptu	building	tongues	biscuit	shoulder

Letter "u" is silent	Letter "u" has a letter "u" sound
fatigue	unison
circuit	avenue
laughing	Tuesday
Guinea	rulers
guiding	attitude
guessing	under
building	annual
biscuit	visual
shoulder	impromptu
tongues	continuum

Classwork

 Name: _____ Date: ___/___/_____ Score: _____

Unit Review - U/u

Reading Words with Vowel "u" Sounds: /ŭ/, /o͞o/, /ə/ & Silent

✓ **Lesson Check Point**

 Directions: Read each target word. Circle the word in the column that has the same "u" sound as the target word.

지도: 각 대상 단어를 읽으십시오. 대상 단어와 "u" 소리가 같은 열의 단어에 동그라미를 치십시오.

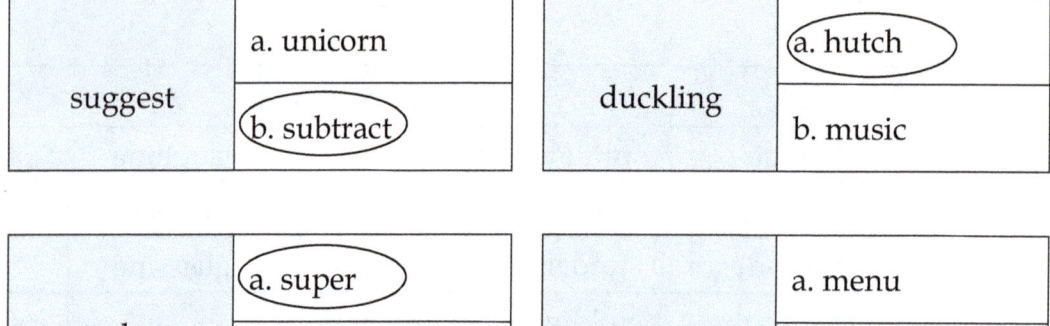

 Directions: Read each target word. Put a check (✓) under the correct column heading.

지도: 각 대상 단어를 읽으십시오. 올바른 열 제목 아래에 체크(✓)를 하십시오.

Target Words	"u" has the /ŭ/ sound as in the word **tub**	"u" has the /o͞o/ sound as in the word **tube**	"u" has the /ə/ sound as in the word **circus**	"u" is silent as in the word **build**
1. suggest			✓	
2. duckling	✓			
3. student		✓		
4. tongue				✓

Name: _____ Date: ___/___/_____ Score: _____

The Reading Challenge

Lesson 21.9

Reading Multisyllable Words

✓ **Lesson Check Point**

 Directions: Read and divide each target word into syllables. Write each word and place a hyphen (-) between the syllables in the second column. Write the number of syllables in the third column. Use a dictionary or the Internet to check your answers.

지도: 각 대상 단어를 읽고 음절로 나눕니다. 각 단어를 쓰고 두 번째 열의 음절 사이에 하이픈(-)을 넣습니다. 세 번째 열에 음절 수를 쓰십시오. 사전이나 인터넷을 사용하여 답을 확인하십시오.

Target Words	Words Divided into Syllables	Number of Syllables
1. luncheon	lunch-eon	2
2. bunches	bunch-es	2
3. duckling	duck-ling	2
4. crushing	crush-ing	2
5. sugary	sug-ar-y	3
6. pulpit	pul-pit	2
7. bumper	bump-er	2
8. intruding	in-trud-ing	3
9. denouncing	de-nounc-ing	3
10. capsulate	cap-su-late	3

Classwork

Name: _____ Date:___/___/_____ Score:_____

The Reading Challenge

Lesson 21.9

Reading Multisyllable Words

✓ **Lesson Check Point**

Directions: Read each target word. Circle the word in the row that is divided correctly into syllables. Use a dictionary or the Internet to check your answers.

지도: 각 대상 단어를 읽으십시오. 음절로 올바르게 나누어진 행에 있는 단어에 동그라미를 치십시오. 사전이나 인터넷을 사용하여 답을 확인하십시오.

Model

| visualize | a. vis-ua-lize | (b. vi-su-al-ize) | c. vis-u-a-lize |

| 1. habitual | (a. ha-bit-u-al) | b. ha-bit-ual | c. hab-it-ual |

| 2. avenue | (a. av-e-nue) | b. ave-nu-e | c. a-ve-nue |

| 3. diluting | a. dil-u-ting | (b. di-lut-ing) | c. di-lu-ting |

| 4. amusing | a. a-mu-sing | (b. a-mus-ing) | c. am-u-sing |

| 5. confusion | (a. con-fu-sion) | b. con-fus-ion | c. conf-u-sion |

| 6. saluting | (a. sa-lut-ing) | b. sal-u-ting | c. sa-lu-ting |

| 7. fortunate | a. fort-u-nate | b. for-tun-ate | (c. for-tu-nate) |

| 8. truancy | a. tru-anc-y | b. tru-a-ncy | (c. tru-an-cy) |

Name: _____ Date: ___/___/_____ Score: _____

Lesson 21.10

Reading and Writing

Proper and Common Nouns and Adjectives

Directions: Read the words in the word box. Put an (X) on the line next to each word that is written incorrectly. Remember that all proper nouns and proper adjectives are capitalized. Use a dictionary or the Internet to check your answers.

지도: 단어 상자에 있는 단어를 읽으십시오. 잘못 쓰여진 각 단어 옆의 줄에 (X)를 표시하십시오. 모든 고유 명사와 고유 형용사는 대문자임을 기억하십시오. 사전이나 인터넷을 사용하여 답을 확인하십시오.

Word Box					
X	University	X	ukraine	__	URL
__	USSR	X	ubangi	__	upbeat
X	Universal	__	umbrella	__	Uncle
X	Ultra	__	Uruguay	X	Uncovered

Directions: Read each unedited sentence and underline the word that is written incorrectly. Write each sentence correctly on the line.

지도: 편집되지 않은 각 문장을 읽고 잘못 쓰여진 단어에 밑줄을긋습 니다. 각 문장을 줄에 올바르게 쓰십시오.

Model
Mrs. Ubangi usually has union meetings at a local <u>University</u>.
<u>Mrs. Ubangi usually has union meetings at a local university.</u>

1. We are studying the planet Uranus in Mrs. <u>ubet's</u> class.
<u>We are studying the planet Uranus in Mrs. Ubet's class.</u>

2. Professor Utrecht said, "The <u>united</u> Nations is very influential."
<u>Professor Utrecht said, "The United Nations is very influential."</u>

3. In 1971, <u>uzbekistan</u> became independent from the U.S.S.R.
<u>In 1971, Uzbekistan became independent from the U.S.S.R.</u>

4. I found information about two universities in <u>upper</u> Canada.
<u>I found information about two universities in Upper Canada.</u>

Classwork

 Name: _____ Date: ___/___/_____ Score: _____

Lesson 22.1

Reading Words with the Letter V/v

✓ **Lesson Check Point**

 Directions: Read each target word. Find the letter "v" and put a check (✓) in the column that identifies its position: beginning, within or end.
지도: 각 대상 단어를 읽으십시오. 문자"v"를 찾아 체크 표시(✓)위치를 식별하는 열에서 시작, 내부 또는 끝.

Target Words	Beginning (First Letter)	Within	End (Last Letter)
1. visitor	✓		
2. travel		✓	
3. veterans	✓		
4. silver		✓	
5. Yugoslav			✓

 Directions: Read each sentence and underline the words that begin with the letter "v." Write all the underlined words in alphabetical order on the lines below.
지도: 각 문장을 읽고"v"로 시작하는 단어에 밑줄을 긋습니다. 아래 줄에 밑줄 친 단어를 알파벳 순서로 모두 쓰십시오.

6. My guitar case has a <u>valuable</u> <u>velvet</u> lining.

7. Samantha's <u>vintage</u> dress is <u>violet</u> and white.

8. Our <u>vice</u> president has a <u>vibrant</u> personality.

9. The character in the <u>video</u> game <u>vanished</u> into thin air.

10. Joshua plays <u>volleyball</u> for his school's team, The <u>Vikings</u>.

valuable	vanished	velvet
vibrant	vice	video
Vikings	vintage	violet
	volleyball	

Name: _____   Date:___/___/_____   Score:_____

The Reading Challenge

Lesson 22.2

Reading Multisyllable Words

✓ **Lesson Check Point**

 Directions: Read and divide each target word into syllables. Write each word and place a hyphen (-) between the syllables in the second column. Write the number of syllables in the third column. Use a dictionary or the Internet to check your answers.

지도: 각 대상 단어를 읽고 음절로 나눕니다. 각 단어를 쓰고 두 번째 열의 음절 사이에 하이픈(-)을 넣습니다. 세 번째 열에 음절 수를 쓰십시오. 사전이나 인터넷을 사용하여 답을 확인하십시오.

Target Words	Words Divided into Syllables	Number of Syllables
1. visionary	vi-sion-ar-y	4
2. vocalized	vo-cal-ized	3
3. vantage	van-tage	2
4. visiting	vis-it-ing	3
5. volume	vol-ume	2
6. verdict	ver-dict	2
7. vanishing	van-ish-ing	3
8. victorious	vic-to-ri-ous	4
9. vineyard	vine-yard	2
10. various	var-i-ous	3

Classwork

 Name: _____   Date:___/___/_____   Score:_____

The Reading Challenge

Lesson 22.2

Reading Multisyllable Words

✓ **Lesson Check Point**

 Directions: Read each target word. Circle the word in the row that is divided correctly into syllables. Use a dictionary or the Internet to check your answers.

지도: 각 대상 단어를 읽으십시오. 음절로 올바르게 나누어진 행에 있는 단어에 동그라미를 치십시오. 사전이나 인터넷을 사용하여 답을 확인하십시오.

Model

volcano	a. vo-lcan-o	b. vol-can-o	(c. vol-ca-no)

1. victory	a. vic-tor-y	(b. vic-to-ry)	c. vi-ctor-y
2. varsity	a. var-sit-y	b. va-rsi-ty	(c. var-si-ty)
3. visual	a. vis-u-al	(b. vi-su-al)	c. visu-a-l
4. vacation	a. va-cat-ion	b. vac-a-tion	(c. va-ca-tion)
5. volunteer	(a. vol-un-teer)	b. vo-lun-teer	c. vol-u-nteer
6. vitamin	a. vit-a-min	b. vi-tam-in	(c. vi-ta-min)
7. vehement	a. ve-hem-ent	b. veh-e-ment	(c. ve-he-ment)
8. vehicle	(a. ve-hi-cle)	b. veh-i-cle	c. ve-hicl-e

Learn To Read English With Directions In Korean   Copyrighted Material

Name: _____ Date: ___/___/_____ Score: _____

Lesson 22.3

Reading and Writing

Proper and Common Nouns and Adjectives

✓ Lesson Check Point

 Directions: Read the words in the word box. Put an (X) on the line next to each word that is written incorrectly. Remember that all proper nouns and proper adjectives are capitalized. Use a dictionary or the Internet to check your answers.

지도: 단어 상자에 있는 단어를 읽으십시오. 잘못 쓰여진 각 단어 옆의 줄에 (X)를 표시하십시오. 모든 고유 명사와 고유 형용사는 대문자임을 기억하십시오. 사전이나 인터넷을 사용하여 답을 확인하십시오.

Word Box					
__	vision	X	vienna	X	vikings
X	Las vegas	__	Vietnam	__	velvet
X	Village	__	vehicle	__	Virginia
X	Volume	__	VIP	X	Vice president

 Directions: Read each unedited sentence and underline the word that is written incorrectly. Write each sentence correctly on the line.

지도: 편집되지 않은 각 문장을 읽고 잘못 쓰여진 단어에 밑줄을긋습 니다. 각 문장을 줄에 올바르게 쓰십시오.

Model
In the fall, the leaves in <u>vermont</u> have vibrant colors.
<u>In the fall, the leaves in Vermont have vibrant colors.</u>

1. <u>valerie</u> is attending Valor Vocational School.
<u>Valerie is attending Valor Vocational School.</u>

2. Vince voted to go to the British <u>virgin</u> Islands.
<u>Vince voted to go to the British Virgin Islands.</u>

3. Washington's troops were victorious at <u>valley</u> Forge.
<u>Washington's troops were victorious at Valley Forge.</u>

4. This summer, I am going on <u>Vacation</u> to Victoria Falls.
<u>This summer, I am going on vacation to Victoria Falls.</u>

Classwork

Name: _____ Date: ___/___/_____ Score: _____

Lesson 23.1

Reading Words with the Letter W/w

✓ **Lesson Check Point**

Directions: Read each target word. Find the letter "w" and put a check (✓) in the column that identifies its position: beginning, within or end.
지도: 각 대상 단어를 읽으십시오. 문자"w"를 찾아 체크 표시(✓)위치를 식별하는 열에서 시작, 내부 또는 끝.

Target Words	Beginning (First Letter)	Within	End (Last Letter)
1. bowling		✓	
2. arrow			✓
3. western	✓		
4. bookworm		✓	
5. shadow			✓

Directions: Read each sentence and underline the words that begin with the letter "w." Write all the underlined words in alphabetical order on the lines below.
지도: 각 문장을 읽고"w"로 시작하는 단어에 밑줄을 긋습니다. 아래 줄에 밑줄 친 단어를 알파벳 순서로 모두 쓰십시오.

6. The <u>wildcats</u> have very long <u>whiskers</u>.

7. The tourists are <u>walking</u> along the <u>waterfront</u>.

8. The <u>wilderness</u> is home to <u>wolves</u> and eagles.

9. There are beautiful <u>waterfalls</u> in the <u>West</u> Indies.

10. My <u>wife</u> placed the clothes in the new <u>washing</u> machine.

walking	washing	waterfalls
waterfront	West	whiskers
wife	wildcats	wilderness
	wolves	

 Name: _____ Date: ___/___/_____ Score: _____

Lesson 23.2

Reading Words with a Vowel before the Letter "w"

✓ **Lesson Check Point**

 Directions: Read each target word. Circle the word in the column that has the same "aw," "ew" or "ow" sound as the target word.
지도: 각 대상 단어를 읽으십시오. 대상 단어와 같은 "aw," "ew" 또는 "ow" 소리가 나는 열의 단어에 동그라미를 치십시오.

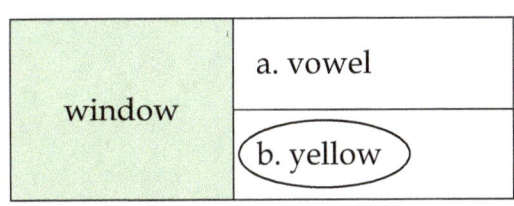
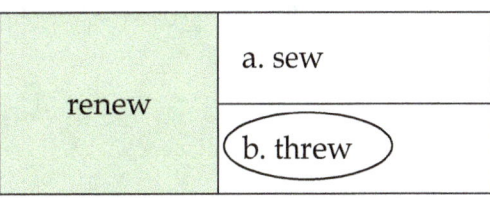
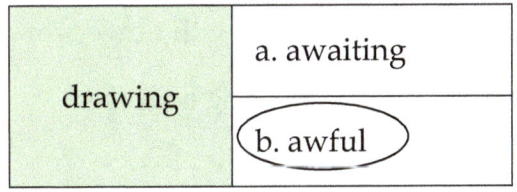
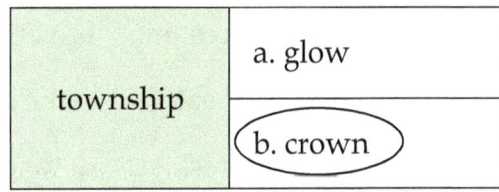

 Directions: Read each target word. Put a check (✓) under the correct column heading.
지도: 각 대상 단어를 읽으십시오. 올바른 열 제목 아래에 체크(✓)를 하십시오.

Target Words	Underlined letters have /o͞o/ sound as in the word <u>few</u>	Underlined letters have /ô/ sound as in the word <u>law</u>	Underlined letters have /ō/ sound as in the word <u>sew</u>	Underlined letters have /ou/ sound as in the word <u>cow</u>
1. wind<u>ow</u>			✓	
2. ren<u>ew</u>	✓			
3. dr<u>aw</u>ing		✓		
4. t<u>ow</u>nship				✓

Classwork

Name: _____ Date: ___/___/_____ Score: _____

Lesson 23.3

Reading Words with a Silent "w" and "wr" Letter Combination

Dictionary Skills/ Vocabulary

✓ Lesson Check Point

Directions: Read each target word and its definition. Write the letter of the definition on the line of each target word. Use a dictionary or the Internet to check your answers
지도: 각 대상 단어를 읽으십시오. 문자"w"를 찾아 체크 표시(✓)위치를 식별하는 열에서 시작, 내부 또는 끝.

Target Words	Definitions
1. _d_ wrap	a. to have destroyed something with intense force
2. _e_ wrestling	b. a circular decoration made with flowers or evergreens
3. _b_ wreath	c. the act of arguing or debating a topic
4. _a_ wrecked	d. to fold in a fitted covering
5. _c_ wrangling	e. a physical sport

Directions: Read each sentence. Underline the word in the parentheses that correctly completes each sentence. Then, write the underlined word on the line.
지도: 각 문장을 읽고"w"로 시작하는 단어에 밑줄을 긋습니다. 아래 줄에 밑줄 친 단어를 알파벳 순서로 모두 쓰십시오.

6. Wendy placed a beautiful __wreath__ on the door. (wrestling, <u>wreath</u>)

7. His house was __wrecked__ by the tornado. (wrangling, <u>wrecked</u>)

8. The wrestler has a __wrestling__ match tonight. (<u>wrestling</u>, wrap)

9. The mothers will __wrap__ their babies in warm blankets. (<u>wrap</u>, wreath)

10. He was __wrangling__ with his teacher over an unfair grade. (<u>wrangling</u>, wrap)

 Name: _____ Date:___/___/_____ Score:_____

Lesson 23.3

Reading Words with a Silent Letter "w"

✓ Lesson Check Point

 Directions: Read the target words in the word box. Write the words that have a silent letter "w" in the first column. Write the words that do not have a silent letter "w" in the second column.

지도: 단어 상자에 있는 대상 단어를 읽으십시오. 첫 번째 열에 묵음문자 "w"가 있는 단어를 쓰십시오. 두 번째 열에 묵음 문자"w"가 없는 단어를 쓰십시오.

Target Word Box				
sword	tomorrow	below	dwell	disown
winner	bandwidth	eastward	two	freewill
afterward	answer	farewell	firewall	writing
wrap	doorway	wreck	wrongly	went

Letter "w" is silent

two
wrap
below
disown
wreck
sword
answer
writing
wrongly
tomorrow

Letter "w" has the /w/ sound

went
dwell
winner
eastward
freewill
afterward
farewell
firewall
doorway
bandwidth

Classwork

 Name: _____ Date: ___/___/_____ Score: _____

The Reading Challenge

Lesson 23.4

Reading Multisyllable Words

✓ **Lesson Check Point**

Directions: Read and divide each target word into syllables. Write each word and place a hyphen (-) between the syllables in the second column. Write the number of syllables in the third column. Use a dictionary or the Internet to check your answers.

지도: 각 대상 단어를 읽고 음절로 나눕니다. 각 단어를 쓰고 두 번째 열의 음절 사이에 하이픈(-)을 넣습니다. 세 번째 열에 음절 수를 쓰십시오. 사전이나 인터넷을 사용하여 답을 확인하십시오.

Target Words	Words Divided into Syllables	Number of Syllables
1. waistband	waist-band	2
2. woman	wom-an	2
3. whistle	whis-tle	2
4. western	west-ern	2
5. wondering	won-der-ing	3
6. washing	wash-ing	2
7. writer	writ-er	2
8. worthless	worth-less	2
9. willful	will-ful	2
10. waterfall	wa-ter-fall	3

Name: _____ Date: ___/___/_____ Score: _____

The Reading Challenge

Lesson 23.4

Reading Multisyllable Words

✓ **Lesson Check Point**

 Directions: Read each target word. Circle the word in the row that is divided correctly into syllables. Use a dictionary or the Internet to check your answers.
지도: 각 대상 단어를 읽으십시오. 음절로 올바르게 나누어진 행에 있는 단어에 동그라미를 치십시오. 사전이나 인터넷을 사용하여 답을 확인하십시오.

Model

| wonderful | a. wo-nder-ful | (b. won-der-ful) | c. won-derf-ul |

1. waterbed	(a. wa-ter-bed)	b. wa-terb-ed	c. wat-er-bed
2. wandering	a. wand-er-ing	b. wand-e-ring	(c. wan-der-ing)
3. Wyoming	(a. Wy-o-ming)	b. Wy-om-ing	c. Wyo-mi-ng
4. whenever	a. whe-nev-er	(b. when-ev-er)	c. wh-ene-ver
5. withdrawal	a. withdr-aw-al	(b. with-draw-al)	c. with-dra-wal
6. watermark	a. wat-er-mark	b. wa-term-ark	(c. wa-ter-mark)
7. workable	a. wor-ka-ble	b. wor-kab-le	(c. work-a-ble)
8. weekender	a. wee-kend-er	(b. week-end-er)	c. week-en-der

Classwork

Name: _____ Date:___/___/_____ Score:_____

Lesson 23.5

Reading and Writing

Proper and Common Nouns and Adjectives

✓ **Lesson Check Point**

Directions: Read the words in the word box. Put an (X) on the line next to each word that is written incorrectly. Remember that all proper nouns and proper adjectives are capitalized. Use a dictionary or the Internet to check your answers.

지도: 단어 상자에 있는 단어를 읽으십시오. 잘못 쓰여진 각 단어 옆의 줄에 (X)를 표시하십시오. 모든 고유 명사와 고유 형용사는 대문자임을 기억하십시오. 사전이나 인터넷을 사용하여 답을 확인하십시오.

Word Box					
X	wakefield, NY	__	wrappers	__	whiplash
X	Wealth	X	wisconsin	__	West Virginia
__	Washington	X	Wheelchair	X	white House
__	waterfall	__	Wake Island	X	Workforce

Directions: Read each unedited sentence and underline the word that is written incorrectly. Write each sentence correctly on the line.

지도: 편집되지 않은 각 문장을 읽고 잘못 쓰여진 단어에 밑줄을 긋습 니다. 각 문장을 줄에 올바르게 쓰십시오.

Model

We walked along the winding path that led to the <u>Waterfalls</u>.
We walked along the winding path that led to the waterfalls.

1. The <u>Warden</u> works for the Wisconsin Prison System.
   The warden works for the Wisconsin Prison System.

2. The waterfalls in the <u>west</u> Indies are breathtaking.
   The waterfalls in the West Indies are breathtaking.

3. The new <u>Waitress</u> is from Washington, D.C.
   The new waitress is from Washington, D.C.

4. The woodpeckers made their homes in <u>wilmington</u>.
   The woodpeckers made their homes in Wilmington.

Name: _____ Date: ___/___/_____ Score: _____

Lesson 24.1

Reading Words with the Letter X/x

✓ Lesson Check Point

Directions: Read each target word. Find the letter "x" and put a check (✓) in the column that identifies its position: beginning, within or end.
지도: 각 대상 단어를 읽으십시오. 문자"x"를 찾아 체크 표시(✓)위치를 식별하는 열에서 시작, 내부 또는 끝.

Target Words	Beginning (First Letter)	Within	End (Last Letter)
1. sixty		✓	
2. oxen		✓	
3. prefix			✓
4. x-ray	✓		
5. wax			✓

Directions: Read each sentence and underline the words that begin with the letter "x." Write all the underlined words in alphabetical order on the lines below.
지도: 각 문장을 읽고 문자"x"로 시작하는 단어에 밑줄을 긋습니다. 아래 줄에 밑줄 친 단어를 알파벳 순서로 모두 쓰십시오.

6. <u>Xaria</u> has to go to the hospital for chest <u>x-rays</u>.

7. <u>Xavier</u> enjoys playing the <u>xylophone</u> at concerts.

8. <u>Xianna</u> used the <u>Xerox</u> machine to make photocopies.

9. <u>Xander</u> said, "<u>Xiamen</u> is an island of Southeast China."

10. I have worked for <u>Xola's</u> company for <u>x</u> number of years.

x _____	Xander _____	Xaria _____
Xavier _____	Xerox _____	Xiamen _____
Xianna _____	Xola's _____	x-rays _____
	xylophone _____	

Classwork

 Name: _____ Date: _____/ ___/ _____ Score: _____

Lesson 24.1

Reading Words with the Letter X/x

✓ **Lesson Check Point**

 Directions: Read each target word. Circle the word in the column that has the same "x" sound(s) as the target word.
지도: 각 대상 단어를 읽으십시오. 대상 단어와 동일한 "x" 소리가 있는 열의 단어에 동그라미를 치십시오.

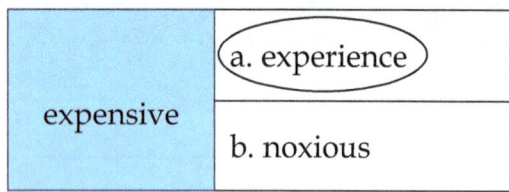

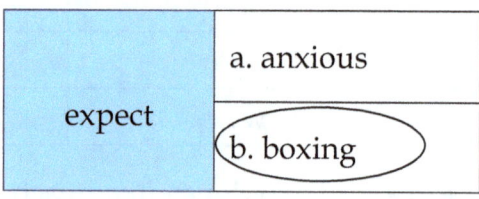

 Directions: Read each target word. Put a check (✓) under the correct column heading.
지도: 각 대상 단어를 읽으십시오. 올바른 열 제목 아래에 체크(✓)를하십시오.

Target Words	"x" has the /k/ + /s/ sounds as in the word <u>box</u>	"x" has the /z/ sound as in the word <u>xylophone</u>	"x" has the /g/ + /z/ sounds as in the word <u>exhibit</u>	"x" has the /k/ + /sh/ sounds as in the word <u>anxious</u>
1. expect	✓			
2. complexion				✓
3. Xanadu		✓		
4. expensive	✓			

Name: _____ Date: ___/___/_____ Score: _____

The Reading Challenge

Lesson 24.2

Reading Multisyllable Words

✓ **Lesson Check Point**

 Directions: Read and divide each target word into syllables. Write each word and place a hyphen (-) between the syllables in the second column. Write the number of syllables in the third column. Use a dictionary or the Internet to check your answers.

지도: 각 대상 단어를 읽고 음절로 나눕니다. 각 단어를 쓰고 두 번째 열의 음절 사이에 하이픈(-)을 넣습니다. 세 번째 열에 음절 수를 쓰십시오. 사전이나 인터넷을 사용하여 답을 확인하십시오.

Target Words	Words Divided into Syllables	Number of Syllables
1. boxer	box-er	2
2. prefix	pre-fix	2
3. saxophone	sax-o-phone	3
4. complexion	com-plex-ion	3
5. index	in-dex	2
6. textual	tex-tu-al	3
7. sixteen	six-teen	2
8. perplexing	per-plex-ing	3
9. taxicab	tax-i-cab	3
10. oxygen	ox-y-gen	3

Classwork

Name: _____ Date: ___/___/_____ Score: _____

The Reading Challenge

Lesson 24.2

Reading Multisyllable Words

✓ **Lesson Check Point**

Directions: Read each target word. Circle the word in the row that is divided correctly into syllables. Use a dictionary or the Internet to check your answers.

지도: 각 대상 단어를 읽으십시오. 음절로 올바르게 나누어진 행에 있는 단어에 동그라미를 치십시오. 사전이나 인터넷을 사용하여 답을 확인하십시오.

Model

oxidized	(a. ox-i-dized)	b. oxi-d-ized	c. o-xi-dized
1. paradox	a. pa-rad-ox	b. par-ad-ox	(c. par-a-dox)
2. explorer	(a. ex-plor-er)	b. exp-lo-rer	c. expl-or-er
3. taxable	a. ta-xa-ble	(b. tax-a-ble)	c. ta-xab-le
4. existence	a. exi-ste-nce	(b. ex-is-tence)	c. ex-i-stence
5. hexagon	a. he-xa-gon	b. he-xag-on	(c. hex-a-gon)
6. exciting	(a. ex-cit-ing)	b. exc-i-ting	c. exc-it-ing
7. lexical	a. le-xic-al	b. le-xi-cal	(c. lex-i-cal)
8. expanding	a. ex-pan-ding	(b. ex-pand-ing)	c. exp-and-ing

Unit X Lesson 24.2

Name: _____ Date: ___/___/_____ Score: _____

Lesson 24.3

Reading and Writing

Proper and Common Nouns and Adjectives

✓ Lesson Check Point

Directions: Read the words in the word box. Put an (X) on the line next to each word that is written incorrectly. Remember that all proper nouns and proper adjectives are capitalized. Use a dictionary or the Internet to check your answers.

지도: 단어 상자에 있는 단어를 읽으십시오. 잘못 쓰여진 각 단어 옆의 줄에 (X)를 표시하십시오. 모든 고유 명사와 고유 형용사는 대문자임을 기억하십시오. 사전이나 인터넷을 사용하여 답을 확인하십시오.

Word Box					
X	xerox Inc.	__	xylems	X	King xerxes I
__	xanthium	__	xenon	X	Xylophone
__	xylene	__	Xiang	X	Xanthic acid
X	X-ray	X	xavier	__	xebec

Directions: Read each unedited sentence and underline the word that is written incorrectly. Write each sentence correctly on the line.

지도: 편집되지 않은 각 문장을 읽고 잘못 쓰여진 단어에 밑줄을 긋습 니다. 각 문장을 줄에 올바르게 쓰십시오.

Model
Xia said, "The population of <u>xankandi</u> is 33,000 people."
<u>Xia said, "The population of Xankandi is 33,000 people."</u>

1. Xia is reading about <u>xanthus</u>, the ancient City of Lycia.
<u>Xia is reading about Xanthus, the ancient City of Lycia.</u>

2. Mr. and Mrs. Xem visited the Chinese province of <u>xuzhou</u>.
<u>Mr. and Mrs. Xem visited the Chinese province of Xuzhou.</u>

3. My friend, <u>xavier</u>, is scheduled to have an x-ray at six o'clock.
<u>My friend, Xavier, is scheduled to have an x-ray at six o'clock.</u>

4. My dentist, Dr. Xu, applied a local anesthetic, <u>Xylocaine</u>, to my gums.
<u>My dentist, Dr. Xu, applied a local anesthetic, xylocaine, to my gums.</u>

Classwork

 Name: _____ Date:___/___/_____ Score:_____

Lesson 25.1

Reading Words with the Letter Y/y

✓ Lesson Check Point

 Directions: Read each target word. Find the letter "y" and put a check (✓) in the column that identifies its position: beginning, within or end.
지도: 각 대상 단어를 읽으십시오. 문자"y"를 찾아 체크 표시(✓)위치를 식별하는 열에서 시작, 내부 또는 끝.

Target Words	Beginning (First Letter)	Within	End (Last Letter)
1. galaxy			✓
2. yellow	✓		
3. hyperactive		✓	
4. strawberry			✓
5. younger	✓		

 Directions: Read each sentence and underline the words that begin with the letter "y." Write all the underlined words in alphabetical order on the lines below.
지도: 각 대상 단어를 읽으십시오. 문자"y를 찾아 체크 표시(✓)위치를식별 하는 열에서 시작, 내부 또는 끝.

6. <u>Yesterday</u>, I had a relaxing <u>yoga</u> class.

7. <u>Yolanda</u> and Nancy enjoyed my <u>yodeling</u> contest.

8. In <u>Yorktown</u>, I saw a pair of oxen <u>yoked</u> together.

9. The <u>yellow</u> car stopped at the triangular <u>yield</u> sign.

10. Mr. <u>Young</u> lives close to <u>Yellowstone</u> National Park.

yellow	Yellowstone	Yesterday
yield	yodeling	yoga
yoked	Yolanda	Yorktown
	Young	

Name: _____ Date: ___/___/_____ Score: _____

Lesson 25.1

Reading Words with the Letter Y/y

✓ Lesson Check Point

Directions: Read each target word. Circle the word in the row that has a different "y" sound than the target word.
지도: 각 대상 단어를 읽으십시오. 목표 단어와 다른 "y" 소리가 나는 행의 단어에 동그라미를 치십시오.

Target Words				
1. yours	young	(candy)	year	yield
2. lyric	(myself)	gymnast	cylinders	symbols
3. Polynesia	sibyl	vinyl	(younger)	polymer
4. community	energy	baby	penny	(pyramid)
5. young	(money)	yours	yes	youth

Directions: Read the words in the four boxes. Circle two words that have the same "y" sound.
지도: 네 개의 상자에 있는 단어를 읽으십시오. "y" 소리가 같은 두 단어에 동그라미를 치십시오.

young	(belly)
reply	(city)

cylinder	(yesterday)
cycles	(yahoo)

(very)	apply
your	(jelly)

(happy)	(shiny)
ratify	years

penny	July
(syringe)	(vinyl)

(plywood)	baby
cylinder	(identify)

Classwork

 Name: _____ Date: ___/___/_____ Score: _____

Lesson 25.2

Reading Words with a Vowel before the Letter "y"

✓ **Lesson Check Point**

 Directions: Read each target word. Circle the word in the column that has the same "y" sound as the target word.

지도: 각 대상 단어를 읽으십시오. 목표 단어와 같은 "y" 소리가 나는 열의 단어에 동그라미를 치십시오.

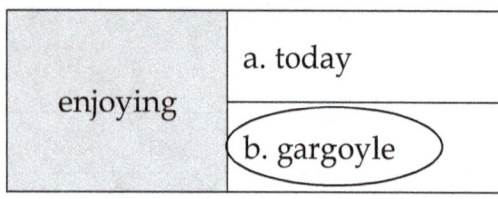
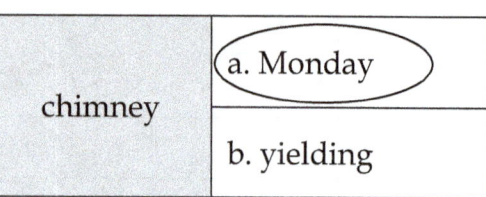
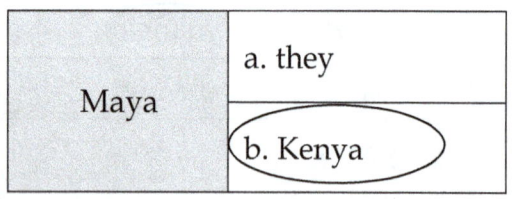
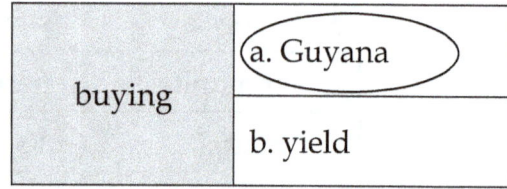

 Directions: Read each target word. Put a check (✓) under the correct column heading.

지도: 각 대상 단어를 읽으십시오. 올바른 열 제목 아래에 체크(✓)를 하십시오.

Target Words	"y" has the /y/ sound as in the word <u>yes</u>	"oy" has the /oi/ sound as in the word <u>boy</u>	"y" has the /ī/ sound as in the word <u>by</u>	"y" is silent as in the word <u>day</u>
1. enjoying		✓		
2. chimney				✓
3. Maya	✓			
4. buying			✓	

Name: _____ Date: ___/___/_____ Score: _____

Lesson 25.3

Reading Words with the "cy" Letter Combination

✓ **Lesson Check Point**

Directions: Read each target word. Find the "cy" letter combination and put a check (✓) in the column to identify its position in the word: beginning, within or end.
지도: 각 대상 단어를 읽으십시오. "cy" 문자 조합을 찾고 열에 체크(✓)를 넣어 단어에서 시작, 안에 또는 끝의 위치를 식별합니다.

Target Words	Beginning (First 2 Letters)	Within	End (Last 2 Letters)
1. Nancy			✓
2. bicyclist		✓	
3. cymbal	✓		
4. regency			✓
5. cytoplasm	✓		

Directions: Read each target word. Put a check (✓) under the correct column heading.
지도: 각 대상 단어를 읽으십시오. 올바른 열 제목 아래에 체크(✓)를 하십시오.

Target Words	"cy" has the /s/ + /ĭ/ sounds as in the word <u>cylinder</u>	"cy" has the /s/ + /ī/ sounds as in the word <u>cycle</u>	"cy" has the /s/ + /ē/ sounds as in the word <u>agency</u>
6. Nancy			✓
7. bicyclist	✓		
8. cymbal	✓		
9. regency			✓
10. cytoplasm		✓	

Classwork

 Name: _____ Date: ___/___/_____ Score: _____

Lesson 25.4

Reading Words with the Final Letter "y"

✓ Lesson Check Point

 Directions: Read each target word. Find the letter "y" and put a check (✓) in the column that identifies its position within the word.
지도: 각 대상 단어를 읽으십시오. 문자"y"를 찾아 체크 표시(✓)단어내에서의 위치를 식별하는 열에서.

Target Words	"y" is at the end of a one syllable word	"y" is at the end of the first syllable	"y" is at the end of a multi-syllable word
1. myself		✓	
2. community			✓
3. cry	✓		
4. discovery			✓
5. tycoon		✓	

 Directions: Read each target word. Put a check (✓) under the correct column heading.
지도: 각 대상 단어를 읽으십시오. 올바른 열 제목 아래에 체크(✓)를하십시오.

Target Words	"y" has the /ē/ sound as in the word <u>agency</u>	"y" has the /ī/ sound as in the word <u>flying</u>
6. myself		✓
7. community	✓	
8. cry		✓
9. discovery	✓	
10. tycoon		✓

Name: _____ Date: ___/___/_____ Score: _____

Lesson 25.5

Reading Words with the "yr" Letter Combination

✓ Lesson Check Point

 Directions: Read each target word. Circle the word in the column that has the same "yr" sounds as the target word.
지도: 각 대상 단어를 읽으십시오. 목표 단어와 같은 "yr" 소리가 나는 열의 단어에 동그라미를 치십시오.

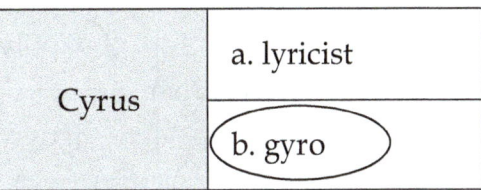

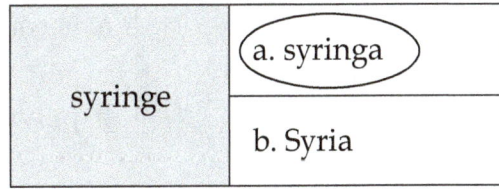

 Directions: Read each target word. Put a check (✓) under the correct column heading.
지도: 각 대상 단어를 읽으십시오. 올바른 열 제목 아래에 체크(✓)를 하십시오.

Target Words	"yr" has the /û/ + /r/ sounds as in the word myrtle	"yr" has the /ĭ/ + /r/ sounds as in the word pyramid	"yr" has the /ī/ + /r/ sounds as in the word gyro	"yr" has the /ə/ + /r/ sounds as in the word martyr
1. myrrh	✓			
2. Cyrus			✓	
3. myriad		✓		
4. syringe				✓

Learn To Read English With Directions In Korean   239

Classwork

Name: _____ Date: ___/___/_____ Score: _____

Lesson 25.6

Reading Letter "y" Words with the Schwa Vowel Sound

✓ Lesson Check Point

Directions: Read each target word. Circle the word in the column that has the same "y" sound as the target word.
지도: 각 대상 단어를 읽으십시오. 대상 단어와"y" 소리가 같은 열의단어에 동그라미를 치십시오.

Polynesian	(a. polyvinyl)
	b. pyramid

sibyl	a. mandatory
	(b. vinyl)

nicely	(a. vacancy)
	b. polymerize

Pennsylvania	(a. polymer)
	b. younger

Directions: Read each target word. Put a check (✓) under the correct column heading.
지도: 각 대상 단어를 읽으십시오. 올바른 열 제목 아래에 체크(✓)를하십시오.

Target Words	"y" has the /ə/ sound as in the word <u>syringe</u>	"y" does not have the /ə/ sound
1. Polynesian	✓	
2. sibyl	✓	
3. nicely		✓
4. Pennsylvania	✓	

Name: _____ Date: ___/___/_____ Score: _____

Lesson 25.7

Reading Words with a Silent Letter "y"

✓ Lesson Check Point

 Directions: Read the target words in the word box. Write the words that have a silent letter "y" in the first column. Write the words that do not have a silent letter "y" in the second column.
지도: 단어 상자에 있는 대상 단어를 읽으십시오. 첫 번째 열에 묵음문자 "y"가 있는 단어를 쓰십시오. 두 번째 열에 묵음 문자"y"가 없는 단어를 쓰십시오.

Target Word Box				
prey	mayor	yes	payday	playing
yeast	jeopardy	donkey	midday	yellow
abundantly	yogurt	friendly	safely	always
layer	chewy	youth	prayer	today

Letter "y" is silent

prey
mayor
payday
playing
donkey
midday
always
layer
prayer
today

Letter "y" has the /y/ or /ē/ sound

yes
yeast
chewy
yellow
youth
yogurt
friendly
safely
jeopardy
abundantly

Classwork

 Name: _____ Date:___/___/_____ Score:_____

The Reading Challenge

Lesson 25.8

Reading Multisyllable Words

✓ **Lesson Check Point**

Directions: Read and divide each target word into syllables. Write each word and place a hyphen (-) between the syllables in the second column. Write the number of syllables in the third column. Use a dictionary or the Internet to check your answers.

지도: 각 대상 단어를 읽고 음절로 나눕니다. 각 단어를 쓰고 두 번째 열의 음절 사이에 하이픈(-)을 넣습니다. 세 번째 열에 음절 수를 쓰십시오. 사전이나 인터넷을 사용하여 답을 확인하십시오.

Target Words	Words Divided into Syllables	Number of Syllables
1. yourself	your-self	2
2. Yemenite	Yem-en-ite	3
3. Yorktown	York-town	2
4. yoga	yo-ga	2
5. yonder	yon-der	2
6. Yankee	Yan-kee	2
7. yardstick	yard-stick	2
8. yearly	year-ly	2
9. yodeling	yo-del-ing	3
10. youthfulness	youth-ful-ness	3

Name: _____ Date: ____/____/____ Score: _____

The Reading Challenge

Lesson 25.8

Reading Multisyllable Words

✓ **Lesson Check Point**

 Directions: Read each target word. Circle the word in the row that is divided correctly into syllables. Use a dictionary or the Internet to check your answers.
지도: 각 대상 단어를 읽으십시오. 음절로 올바르게 나누어진 행에 있는 단어에 동그라미를 치십시오. 사전이나 인터넷을 사용하여 답을 확인하십시오.

Model

yesterday	a. ye-ster-day	b. yest-er-day	c. yes-ter-day ⭕

1. Yucatán	a. Yuc-a-tán	b. Yu-ca-tán ⭕	c. Yu-cat-án
2. yarmulke	a. yar-mul-ke ⭕	b. yar-mulk-e	c. yarm-u-lke
3. yodeling	a. yod-e-ling	b. yo-de-ling	c. yo-del-ing ⭕
4. youthful	a. youthf-ul	b. youth-ful ⭕	c. you-thful
5. Yoruba	a. Yo-ru-ba ⭕	b. Yor-u-ba	c. Yo-rub-a
6. Yankee	a. Yank-ee	b. Ya-nk-ee	c. Yan-kee ⭕
7. yielding	a. yield-ing ⭕	b. yiel-di-ng	c. yieldi-ng
8. younger	a. you-nger	b. youn-ger	c. young-er ⭕

Classwork

Name: _____ Date: ____/__/____ Score: _____

Lesson 25.9

Reading and Writing

Proper and Common Nouns and Adjectives

Directions: Read the words in the word box. Put an (X) on the line next to each word that is written incorrectly. Remember that all proper nouns and proper adjectives are capitalized. Use a dictionary or the Internet to check your answers.

지도: 단어 상자에 있는 단어를 읽으십시오. 잘못 쓰여진 각 단어 옆의 줄에 (X)를 표시하십시오. 모든 고유 명사와 고유 형용사는 대문자임을 기억하십시오. 사전이나 인터넷을 사용하여 답을 확인하십시오.

Word Box					
__	Yemen	X	yokosuka	__	yachting
__	yellow	__	Yankees	X	Yogurt
X	Young	__	yardage	__	yesterday
X	yoruba	X	Yourself	X	yorktown

Directions: Read each unedited sentence and underline the word that is written incorrectly. Write each sentence correctly on the line.

지도: 편집되지 않은 각 문장을 읽고 잘못 쓰여진 단어에 밑줄을 긋습 니다. 각 문장을 줄에 올바르게 쓰십시오.

Model
Is the New York <u>yankees</u> your favorite baseball team?
<u>Is the New York Yankees your favorite baseball team?</u>

1. Yolanda's friend loves to eat <u>yoplait</u> yogurt.
   <u>Yolanda's friend loves to eat Yoplait yogurt.</u>

2. All the signs in <u>yorktown</u> are painted yellow.
   <u>All the signs in Yorktown are painted yellow.</u>

3. Last year, the <u>young</u> family visited Yosemite National Park.
   <u>Last year, the Young family visited Yosemite National Park.</u>

4. <u>yesterday</u>, Yusef plotted the y-axis and the x-axis on graph paper.
   <u>Yesterday, Yusef plotted the y-axis and the x-axis on graph paper.</u>

 Name: _____ Date: ___/___/_____ Score: _____

Lesson 26.1

Reading Words with the Letter Z/z

✓ Lesson Check Point

 Directions: Read each target word. Find the letter "z" and put a check (✓) in the column that identifies its position: beginning, within or end.
지도: 각 대상 단어를 읽으십시오. 문자"z"를 찾아 체크 표시(✓)위치를 식별하는 열에서 시작, 내부 또는 끝.

Target Words	Beginning (First Letter)	Within	End (Last Letter)
1. blizzard		✓	
2. topaz			✓
3. Tanzania		✓	
4. zebra	✓		
5. zookeeper	✓		

 Directions: Read each sentence and underline the words that begin with the letter "z." Write all the underlined words in alphabetical order on the lines below.
지도: 각 문장을 읽고"z"로 시작하는 단어에 밑줄을 긋습니다. 아래 줄에 밑줄 친 단어를 알파벳 순서로 모두 쓰십시오.

6. Samira <u>zipped</u> up her <u>zebra</u> costume.

7. Danny wants to work at the <u>zoo</u> as a trained <u>zoologist</u>.

8. The two <u>zoom</u> lenses on <u>Zianna's</u> camera are very expensive.

9. In New <u>Zealand</u>, Abdulla wore his shirt with a <u>zigzag</u> design.

10. Valeria is studying the rich cultures of <u>Zambia</u> and <u>Zimbabwe</u>.

Zambia _____   Zealand _____   zebra _____

Zianna's _____   zigzag _____   Zimbabwe _____

zipped _____   zoo _____   zoologist _____

         zoom _____

Classwork

 Name: _____ Date: ___/___/_____ Score: _____

Lesson 26.1

Reading Words with the Letter Z/z

✓ Lesson Check Point

 Directions: Read each target word. Circle the word in the column that has the same "z" sound as the target word.
지도: 각 대상 단어를 읽으십시오. 대상 단어와 "z" 소리가 같은 열의 단어에 동그라미를 치십시오.

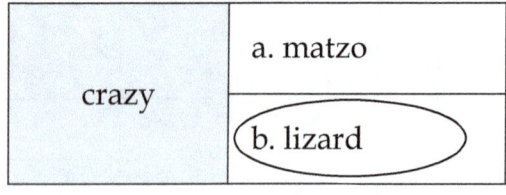

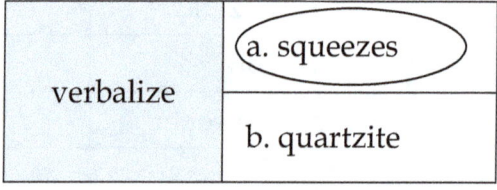

 Directions: Read each target word. Put a check (✓) under the correct column heading.
지도: 각 대상 단어를 읽으십시오. 올바른 열 제목 아래에 체크(✓)를 하십시오.

Target Words	"z" has the /z/ sound as in the word <u>zipper</u>	"z" has the /s/ sound as in the word <u>quartz</u>
1. crazy	✓	
2. normalize	✓	
3. Lutz		✓
4. verbalize	✓	

Name: _____ Date:____/____/_____ Score: _____

Lesson 26.2

Reading Words with a Silent Letter "z"

✓ Lesson Check Point

 Directions: Read the target words in the word box. Write the words that have a silent letter "z" in the first column. Write the words that do not have a silent letter "z" in the second column.

지도: 단어 상자에 있는 대상 단어를 읽으십시오. 첫 번째 열에 묵음 문자 "z"가 있는 단어를 쓰십시오. 두 번째 열에 묵음 문자"z"가 없는 단어를쓰십시오.

Target Word Box				
fizzle	sizzler	Brazil	analyze	capitalize
agonize	dozen	dizziness	amazing	gizzard
cadenza	blazing	puzzling	economize	blizzard
sizzles	fuzz	centralize	drizzling	puzzle

Letter "z" is silent	Letter "z" has the /z/ or /s/ sound
fuzz	Brazil
sizzler	analyze
puzzle	capitalize
gizzard	agonize
fizzle	dozen
blizzard	amazing
sizzles	cadenza
puzzling	blazing
dizziness	economize
drizzling	centralize

Classwork

 Name: _____ Date:___/___/_____ Score:_____

The Reading Challenge

Lesson 26.3

Reading Multisyllable Words

✓ **Lesson Check Point**

 Directions: Read and divide each target word into syllables. Write each word and place a hyphen (-) between the syllables in the second column. Write the number of syllables in the third column. Use a dictionary or the Internet to check your answers.

지도: 각 대상 단어를 읽고 음절로 나눕니다. 각 단어를 쓰고 두 번째 열의 음절 사이에 하이픈(-)을 넣습니다. 세 번째 열에 음절 수를 쓰십시오. 사전이나 인터넷을 사용하여 답을 확인하십시오.

Target Words	Words Divided into Syllables	Number of Syllables
1. Zaire	Za-ire	2
2. zealot	zeal-ot	2
3. zodiac	zo-di-ac	3
4. zigzag	zig-zag	2
5. Zulu	Zu-lu	2
6. zeniths	ze-niths	2
7. zany	za-ny	2
8. zinger	zing-er	2
9. zestfulness	zest-ful-ness	3
10. Zambia	Zam-bi-a	3

Name: _____ Date: ___/___/_____ Score: _____

The Reading Challenge

Lesson 26.3

Reading Multisyllable Words

✓ **Lesson Check Point**

 Directions: Read each target word. Circle the word in the row that is divided correctly into syllables. Use a dictionary or the Internet to check your answers.

지도: 각 대상 단어를 읽으십시오. 음절로 올바르게 나누어진 행에 있는 단어에 동그라미를 치십시오. 사전이나 인터넷을 사용하여 답을 확인하십시오.

Model

| zoology | a. zo-ol-o-gy (circled) | b. zoo-lo-gy | c. zool-o-gy |

1. Zealand	a. Zea-land (circled)	b. Zeal-an-d	c. Zeal-and
2. Zimbabwe	a. Zimb-ab-we	b. Zim-bab-we (circled)	c. Zim-ba-bwe
3. zodiac	a. zo-di-a-c	b. zod-ia-c	c. zo-di-ac (circled)
4. zoologist	a. zo-ol-o-gist (circled)	b. zoo-log-ist	c. zoo-lo-gist
5. zeroing	a. ze-roi-ng	b. zer-o-ing	c. ze-ro-ing (circled)
6. zonal	a. zo-nal	b. zon-al (circled)	c. zo-n-al
7. Zambia	a. Za-mbi-a	b. Zam-bi-a (circled)	c. Zamb-i-a
8. zestful	a. ze-stf-ul	b. ze-stful	c. zest-ful (circled)

Classwork

 Name: _____ Date: ___/___/_____ Score: _____

Lesson 26.4

Reading and Writing

Proper and Common Nouns and Adjectives

✓ Lesson Check Point

 Directions: Read the words in the word box. Put an (X) on the line next to each word that is written incorrectly. Remember that all proper nouns and proper adjectives are capitalized. Use a dictionary or the Internet to check your answers.

지도: 단어 상자에 있는 단어를 읽으십시오. 잘못 쓰여진 각 단어 옆의 줄에 (X)를 표시하십시오. 모든 고유 명사와 고유 형용사는 대문자임을 기억하십시오. 사전이나 인터넷을 사용하여 답을 확인하십시오.

Word Box					
X	Zillion	_	zippers	_	Zealand
_	Zambia	X	Zookeeper	_	Zululand
X	zurich	_	zealous	X	Zoom lens
_	Zeus	X	zanzibar	X	Zoology

 Directions: Read each unedited sentence and underline the word that is written incorrectly. Write each sentence correctly on the line.

지도: 편집되지 않은 각 문장을 읽고 잘못 쓰여진 단어에 밑줄을 긋습 니다. 각 문장을 줄에 올바르게 쓰십시오.

Model
The steep path zigzags through the <u>zagros</u> Mountains.
<u>The steep path zigzags through the Zagros Mountains.</u>

1. Zoey lives in the Eastern Time <u>zone</u>.
   <u>Zoey lives in the Eastern Time Zone.</u>

2. At noon, the <u>Zebras</u> at the Bronx Zoo were sleeping.
   <u>At noon, the zebras at the Bronx Zoo were sleeping.</u>

3. My school, Zesty Academy, has <u>Zero</u> tolerance for bullying.
   <u>My school, Zesty Academy, has zero tolerance for bullying.</u>

4. Mr. Zinger's new movie is a <u>Zillion</u> times better than his first one.
   <u>Mr. Zinger's new movie is a zillion times better than his first one.</u>

Name: _____ Date: ___/___/_____ Score: _____

Appendix 1.0

Introduction of the Letter A/a

✓ **Lesson Check Point**

 Directions: Circle the correct letter "a" pair: uppercase and lowercase letters.
지도: 올바른 문자 "a" 쌍에 동그라미를 치십시오: 대문자와 소문자.

Ao (Aa) aE Au iA

 Directions: The uppercase letter "A" is in the first column. Look at the four letters in the row and circle the lowercase letter that matches the uppercase letter "A."
지도: 대문자 "A"는 첫 번째 열에 있습니다. 행의 네 글자를 보고 대문자 "A"와 일치하는 소문자에 동그라미를 치십시오.

A	o	e	u	(a)
A	(a)	c	z	x
A	e	w	(a)	c
A	o	(a)	c	u

 Directions: The lowercase letter "a" is in the first column. Look at the four letters in the row and circle the uppercase letter that matches the lowercase letter "a."
지도: 소문자 "a"는 첫 번째 열에 있습니다. 행의 네 글자를 보고 소문자 "a"와 일치하는 대문자에 동그라미를 치세요.

a	Z	(A)	V	W
a	V	C	(A)	Z
a	D	O	W	(A)
a	(A)	H	V	Q

Learn To Read English With Directions In Korean

Classwork

 Name: _____ Date: ____/____/_____ Score: _____

Appendix 2.0

Introduction of the Letter B/b

✓ **Lesson Check Point**

 Directions: Circle the correct letter "b" pair: uppercase and lowercase letters.
지도: 올바른 문자"b" 쌍에 동그라미를 치십시오: 대문자와 소문자.

    Bd   (Bb)   bF   Db   Bk

 Directions: The uppercase letter "B" is in the first column. Look at the four letters in the row and circle the lowercase letter that matches the uppercase letter "B."
지도: 대문자"B"는 첫 번째 열에 있습니다. 행의 네 글자를 보고 대문자 "B"와 일치하는 소문자에 동그라미를 치십시오.

B	b	f	q	d
B	g	b	d	h
B	f	p	d	b
B	h	b	p	k

 Directions: The lowercase letter "b" is in the first column. Look at the four letters in the row and circle the uppercase letter that matches the lowercase letter "b."
지도: 소문자"b"는 첫 번째 열에 있습니다. 행의 네 글자를 보고 소문자 "b"와 일치하는 대문자에 동그라미를 치세요.

b	F	D	B	G
b	Q	P	D	B
b	P	B	F	M
b	H	R	Q	B

Name: _____ Date: ___/___/_____ Score: _____

Appendix 2.0

Letter Recognition B/b

Uppercase and Lowercase Letter

✓ **Lesson Check Point**

Directions: Read each target word. Read the words in the row and circle the word that begins with a different letter.

지도: 각 대상 단어를 읽으십시오. 행에 있는 단어를 읽고 다른 문자로시작하는 단어에 동그라미를 치십시오.

Target Words				
1. boy	bin	bean	(fat)	buns
2. buzz	balloon	(house)	bandit	blood
3. both	bandage	brick	(queen)	bang
4. bubbles	(drip)	bank	bag	break
5. because	(puppet)	ballot	baggage	black

Directions: Read the words in the four boxes. Circle two words that start with the uppercase and lowercase letter "b."

지도: 네 개의 상자에 있는 단어를 읽으십시오. 대문자와 소문자 "b"로 시작하는 두 단어에 동그라미를 치십시오.

(bin)	win		(Bit)	sit		Bake	Make
tin	(Bin)		Hit	(bit)		(bake)	dare

(bat)	(Bat)		Float	oat		Wet	(Best)
hat	Sat		(Boat)	(boat)		date	(best)

253

Classwork

 Name: _____ Date: ___/___/_____ Score: _____

Appendix 3.0

Introduction of the Letter C/c

✓ **Lesson Check Point**

 Directions: Circle the correct letter "c" pair: uppercase and lowercase letters.
지도: 올바른 문자"c" 쌍에 동그라미를 치십시오: 대문자와 소문자.

(Cc)   Kc   Co   Oc   cS

 Directions: The uppercase letter "C" is in the first column. Look at the four letters in the row and circle the lowercase letter that matches the uppercase letter "C."
지도: 대문자"C"는 첫 번째 열에 있습니다. 행의 네 글자를 보고 대문자 "C"와 일치하는 소문자에 동그라미를 치십시오.

C	o	(c)	u	g
C	v	a	r	(c)
C	(c)	g	d	o
C	q	(c)	p	k

 Directions: The lowercase letter "c" is in the first column. Look at the four letters in the row and circle the uppercase letter that matches the lowercase letter "c."
지도: 소문자"c"는 첫 번째 열에 있습니다. 행의 네 글자를 보고 소문자 "c"와 일치하는 대문자에 동그라미를 치세요.

c	Q	O	(C)	G
c	(C)	T	Q	M
c	D	B	H	(C)
c	(C)	K	J	D

 Name: _____ Date: ___/___/_____ Score: _____

Appendix 3.0

Letter Recognition C/c

Uppercase and Lowercase Letter

✓ **Lesson Check Point**

 Directions: Read each target word. Read the words in the row and circle the word that begins with a different letter.
지도: 각 대상 단어를 읽으십시오. 행에 있는 단어를 읽고 다른 문자로시작하는 단어에 동그라미를 치십시오.

Target Words				
1. clip	cool	came	(poll)	color
2. cart	caramel	(open)	capture	clump
3. cent	cell	(queen)	choice	chap
4. curtain	chat	center	(goat)	city
5. church	chocolate	(engage)	chair	civic

 Directions: Read the words in the four boxes. Circle two words that start with the uppercase and lowercase letter "c."
지도: 네 개의 상자에 있는 단어를 읽으십시오. 대문자와 소문자"c"로 시작하는 두 단어에 동그라미를 치십시오.

book	(Camel)		(comb)	Octopus		(Cake)	keep
Brook	(clue)		(Cook)	Kite		Goat	(capital)

(Cat)	Queen		Grow	(cute)		(come)	home
(cow)	open		(Cab)	float		Tom	(Candy)

Learn To Read English With Directions In Korean

Classwork

 Name: _____ Date: ___/___/_____ Score: _____

Appendix 4.0

Introduction of the Letter D/d

✓ **Lesson Check Point**

 Directions: Circle the correct letter "d" pair: uppercase and lowercase letters.
지도: 올바른 문자"d" 쌍에 동그라미를 치십시오: 대문자와 소문자.

Db　　　Df　　　(Dd)　　　Bd　　　Op

 Directions: The uppercase letter "D" is in the first column. Look at the four letters in the row and circle the lowercase letter that matches the uppercase letter "D."
지도: 대문자"D"는 첫 번째 열에 있습니다. 행의 네 글자를 보고 대문자 "D"와 일치하는 소문자에 동그라미를 치십시오.

D	p	(d)	t	b
D	h	y	(d)	t
D	l	t	b	(d)
D	t	(d)	k	f

 Directions: The lowercase letter "d" is in the first column. Look at the four letters in the row and circle the uppercase letter that matches the lowercase letter "d."
지도: 소문자"d"는 첫 번째 열에 있습니다. 행의 네 글자를 보고 소문자 "d"와 일치하는 대문자에 동그라미를 치세요.

d	B	Q	(D)	F
d	K	(D)	P	B
d	B	T	(D)	K
d	(D)	F	B	P

Name: _____ Date: ___/___/_____ Score: _____

Appendix 4.0

Letter Recognition D/d

Uppercase and Lowercase Letter

✓ Lesson Check Point

Directions: Read each target word. Read the words in the row and circle the word that begins with a different letter.
지도: 각 대상 단어를 읽으십시오. 행에 있는 단어를 읽고 다른 문자로시작하는 단어에 동그라미를 치십시오.

Target Words				
1. dad	day	(box)	drive	duck
2. deep	(pull)	drum	dove	dull
3. dwell	doll	dawn	dock	(peace)
4. dryer	do	dense	(queen)	dash
5. drink	(both)	den	down	deer

Directions: Read the words in the four boxes. Circle two words that start with the uppercase and lowercase letter "d."
지도: 네 개의 상자에 있는 단어를 읽으십시오. 대문자와 소문자"d"로 시작하는 두 단어에 동그라미를 치십시오.

(date)	late	(Ditch)	Queen	Bell	Quite
open	(Draw)	(dock)	boat	(Deal)	(doll)

Quick	(dream)	Back	(dome)	Race	(drive)
quack	(Dawn)	belt	(Drip)	(Dog)	Quill

Classwork

 Name: _____ Date: ___/___/_____ Score: _____

Appendix 5.0

Introduction of the Letter E/e

✓ **Lesson Check Point**

 Directions: Circle the correct letter "e" pair: uppercase and lowercase letters.
지도: 올바른 문자"e" 쌍에 동그라미를 치십시오: 대문자와 소문자.

eF　　　　Ex　　　　fE　　　　(eE)　　　　Ae

 Directions: The uppercase letter "E" is in the first column. Look at the four letters in the row and circle the lowercase letter that matches the uppercase letter "E."
지도: 대문자"E"는 첫 번째 열에 있습니다. 행의 네 글자를 보고 대문자 "E"와 일치하는 소문자에 동그라미를 치십시오.

E	r	(e)	f	a
E	c	a	w	(e)
E	(e)	c	x	r
E	z	s	(e)	a

 Directions: The lowercase letter "e" is in the first column. Look at the four letters in the row and circle the uppercase letter that matches the lowercase letter "e."
지도: 소문자"e"는 첫 번째 열에 있습니다. 행의 네 글자를 보고 소문자 "e"와 일치하는 대문자에 동그라미를 치세요.

e	D	(E)	R	F
e	G	H	T	(E)
e	(E)	F	V	D
e	F	(E)	S	X

Name: _____ Date: ___/___/_____ Score: _____

Appendix 6.0

Introduction of the Letter F/f

✓ **Lesson Check Point**

 Directions: Circle the correct letter "f" pair: uppercase and lowercase letters.
지도: 올바른 문자"f" 쌍에 동그라미를 치십시오: 대문자와 소문자.

    fE   Fh   (fF)   Ef   Tf

 Directions: The uppercase letter "F" is in the first column. Look at the four letters in the row and circle the lowercase letter that matches the uppercase letter "F."
지도: 대문자"F"는 첫 번째 열에 있습니다. 행의 네 글자를 보고 대문자 "F"와 일치하는 소문자에 동그라미를 치십시오.

F	l	t	k	(f)
F	j	l	(f)	m
F	t	(f)	b	h
F	(f)	l	t	h

 Directions: The lowercase letter "f" is in the first column. Look at the four letters in the row and circle the uppercase letter that matches the lowercase letter "f."
지도: 소문자"f"는 첫 번째 열에 있습니다. 행의 네 글자를 보고 소문자 "f"와 일치하는 대문자에 동그라미를 치세요.

f	(F)	E	K	H
f	L	(F)	J	E
f	E	K	H	(F)
f	H	(F)	D	B

Classwork

 Name: _____ Date: ___/___/_____ Score: _____

Appendix 6.0

Letter Recognition F/f

Uppercase and Lowercase Letter

✓ **Lesson Check Point**

 Directions: Read each target word. Read the words in the row and circle the word that begins with a different letter.

지도: 각 대상 단어를 읽으십시오. 행에 있는 단어를 읽고 다른 문자로시작하는 단어에 동그라미를 치십시오.

Target Words				
1. face	force	fault	(house)	form
2. fire	(pizza)	fizz	friend	flow
3. fork	frisk	(quiet)	fourth	fall
4. flirt	(love)	from	fast	fur
5. full	fright	flash	firm	(boys)

 Directions: Read the words in the four boxes. Circle two words that start with the uppercase and lowercase letter "f."

지도: 네 개의 상자에 있는 단어를 읽으십시오. 대문자와 소문자"f"로 시작하는 두 단어에 동그라미를 치십시오.

(Field)	flake	both	(Fig)	(fame)	teach
Years	take	(fond)	Hours	(Fist)	Laugh

book	Drip	(Flank)	tea	happens	(fee)
(fight)	(Few)	Pup	(fair)	Dreams	(Float)

Name: _____ Date:___/___/_____ Score:_____

Appendix 7.0

Introduction of the Letter G/g

✓ **Lesson Check Point**

 Directions: Circle the correct letter "g" pair: uppercase and lowercase letters.
지도: 올바른 문자"g" 쌍에 동그라미를 치십시오: 대문자와 소문자.

    yG   Gj   gJ   (Gg)   gO

 Directions: The uppercase letter "G" is in the first column. Look at the four letters in the row and circle the lowercase letter that matches the uppercase letter "G."
지도: 대문자"G"는 첫 번째 열에 있습니다. 행의 네 글자를 보고 대문자 "G"와 일치하는 소문자에 동그라미를 치십시오.

G	p	q	y	(g)
G	j	y	(g)	p
G	(g)	j	y	q
G	j	(g)	q	y

 Directions: The lowercase letter "g" is in the first column. Look at the four letters in the row and circle the uppercase letter that matches the lowercase letter "g."
지도: 소문자"g"는 첫 번째 열에 있습니다. 행의 네 글자를 보고 소문자 "g"와 일치하는 대문자에 동그라미를 치세요.

g	Q	O	J	(G)
g	U	(G)	O	J
g	Q	K	C	(G)
g	(G)	Q	P	O

Unit G
Appendix 7.0

Classwork

 Name: _____ Date: ___/___/_____ Score: _____

Appendix 7.0

Letter Recognition G/g

Uppercase and Lowercase Letter

✓ **Lesson Check Point**

 Directions: Read each target word. Read the words in the row and circle the word that begins with a different letter.

지도: 각 대상 단어를 읽으십시오. 행에 있는 단어를 읽고 다른 문자로시작하는 단어에 동그라미를 치십시오.

Target Words				
1. gel	guest	garb	(jeep)	gown
2. grant	(pet)	goal	guard	gulp
3. game	grief	grant	(queen)	go
4. goat	glove	(ball)	glaze	grown
5. gold	(jump)	glide	gray	ghost

 Directions: Read the words in the four boxes. Circle two words that start with the uppercase and lowercase letter "g."

지도: 네 개의 상자에 있는 단어를 읽으십시오. 대문자와 소문자"g"로 시작하는 두 단어에 동그라미를 치십시오.

(gold)	open		(ground)	Down		Once	June
Queen	(Greece)		(Gulf)	jump		(Graph)	(game)

Ooze	(Gone)		year	(Grub)		(Glee)	(gram)
(greed)	jeep		Dock	(glare)		joke	Day

Learn To Read English With Directions In Korean

Name: _____ Date: ___/___/_____ Score: _____

Appendix 8.0

Introduction of the Letter H/h

✓ **Lesson Check Point**

 Directions: Circle the correct letter "h" pair: uppercase and lowercase letters.
지도: 올바른 문자"h" 쌍에 동그라미를 치십시오: 대문자와 소문자.

    Hf   (hH)   Ht   hB   Hb

 Directions: The uppercase letter "H" is in the first column. Look at the four letters in the row and circle the lowercase letter that matches the uppercase letter "H."
지도: 대문자"H"는 첫 번째 열에 있습니다. 행의 네 글자를 보고 대문자 "H"와 일치하는 소문자에 동그라미를 치십시오.

H	(h)	f	t	b
H	m	(h)	f	t
H	l	k	(h)	f
H	b	t	d	(h)

 Directions: The lowercase letter "h" is in the first column. Look at the four letters in the row and circle the uppercase letter that matches the lowercase letter "h."
지도: 소문자"h"는 첫 번째 열에 있습니다. 행의 네 글자를 보고 소문자 "h"와 일치하는 대문자에 동그라미를 치세요.

h	T	F	U	(H)
h	(H)	J	F	M
h	E	M	C	(H)
h	D	(H)	B	T

Classwork

Name: _____ Date: ___/___/_____ Score: _____

Appendix 8.0

Letter Recognition H/h

Uppercase and Lowercase Letter

✓ Lesson Check Point

Directions: Read each target word. Read the words in the row and circle the word that begins with a different letter.

지도: 각 대상 단어를 읽으십시오. 행에 있는 단어를 읽고 다른 문자로 시작하는 단어에 동그라미를 치십시오.

Target Words				
1. home	hat	(land)	heart	hill
2. head	horse	heat	hulk	(boat)
3. hatch	heel	(down)	harm	here
4. heir	hold	high	host	(love)
5. hint	half	hitch	(team)	hemp

Directions: Read the words in the four boxes. Circle two words that start with the uppercase and lowercase letter "h."

지도: 네 개의 상자에 있는 단어를 읽으십시오. 대문자와 소문자 "h"로 시작하는 두 단어에 동그라미를 치십시오.

tune	love	(Hole)	bless	flame	(Hint)
(help)	(Hold)	pole	(hiss)	blink	(hence)

(hook)	(Heel)	(Hit)	kind	dress	(hope)
trees	peel	(hood)	look	(Here)	from

 Name: _____ Date: ___/___/_____ Score: _____

Appendix 9.0

Introduction of the Letter I/i

✓ **Lesson Check Point**

 Directions: Circle the correct letter "i" pair: uppercase and lowercase letters.
지도: 올바른 문자"i" 쌍에 동그라미를 치십시오: 대문자와 소문자.

Ji　　　Ti　　　(Ii)　　　jI　　　Il

 Directions: The uppercase letter "I" is in the first column. Look at the four letters in the row and circle the lowercase letter that matches the uppercase letter "I."
지도: 대문자"I"는 첫 번째 열에 있습니다. 행의 네 글자를 보고 대문자 "I"와 일치하는 소문자에 동그라미를 치십시오.

I	j	(i)	t	u
I	q	g	j	(i)
I	(i)	t	g	l
I	l	t	(i)	h

 Directions: The lowercase letter "i" is in the first column. Look at the four letters in the row and circle the uppercase letter that matches the lowercase letter "i."
지도: 소문자"i"는 첫 번째 열에 있습니다. 행의 네 글자를 보고 소문자 "i"와 일치하는 대문자에 동그라미를 치세요.

i	(I)	T	J	L
i	K	G	H	(I)
i	Y	L	(I)	T
i	J	(I)	Y	K

Learn To Read English With Directions In Korean

Classwork

 Name: _____ Date: ___/___/_____ Score: _____

Appendix 10.0

Introduction of the Letter J/j

✓ Lesson Check Point

 Directions: Circle the correct letter "j" pair: uppercase and lowercase letters.
지도: 올바른 문자 "j" 쌍에 동그라미를 치십시오: 대문자와 소문자.

Gj   Ji   (jJ)   JI   Pj

 Directions: The uppercase letter "J" is in the first column. Look at the four letters in the row and circle the lowercase letter that matches the uppercase letter "J."
지도: 대문자 "J"는 첫 번째 열에 있습니다. 행의 네 글자를 보고 대문자 "J"와 일치하는 소문자에 동그라미를 치십시오.

J	p	(j)	n	q
J	(j)	q	y	k
J	b	c	(j)	v
J	y	h	c	(j)

 Directions: The lowercase letter "j" is in the first column. Look at the four letters in the row and circle the uppercase letter that matches the lowercase letter "j."
지도: 소문자 "j"는 첫 번째 열에 있습니다. 행의 네 글자를 보고 소문자 "j"와 일치하는 대문자에 동그라미를 치세요.

j	B	Q	(J)	G
j	G	V	F	(J)
j	(J)	U	C	O
j	Q	H	(J)	T

Name: _____ Date: ___/___/_____ Score: _____

Appendix 10.0

Letter Recognition J/j

Uppercase and Lowercase Letter

✓ Lesson Check Point

 Directions: Read each target word. Read the words in the row and circle the word that begins with a different letter.

지도: 각 대상 단어를 읽으십시오. 행에 있는 단어를 읽고 다른 문자로 시작하는 단어에 동그라미를 치십시오.

Target Words				
1. jaw	just	(house)	Jim	jumbo
2. jolt	(bunny)	jelly	juice	joy
3. junk	job	jam	(yearly)	jump
4. jet	(giggles)	joke	June	joint
5. just	jigsaw	(puppy)	journal	Jack

 Directions: Read the words in the four boxes. Circle two words that start with the uppercase and lowercase letter "j."

지도: 네 개의 상자에 있는 단어를 읽으십시오. 대문자와 소문자"j"로 시작하는 두 단어에 동그라미를 치십시오.

quest	(journey)
yarn	(Join)

(Jacket)	boat
gold	(just)

pie	you
(juicy)	(Jelly)

(Jumbo)	(jail)
good	yes

(junk)	great
(Job)	queen

youth	(Jungle)
(jealous)	guest

Classwork

 Name: _____ Date: ___/___/_____ Score: _____

Appendix 11.0

Introduction of the Letter K/k

✓ Lesson Check Point

 Directions: Circle the correct letter "k" pair: uppercase and lowercase letters.
지도: 올바른 문자 "k" 쌍에 동그라미를 치십시오: 대문자와 소문자.

Bk   (Kk)   kL   Mk   Kl

 Directions: The uppercase letter "K" is in the first column. Look at the four letters in the row and circle the lowercase letter that matches the uppercase letter "K."
지도: 대문자 "K"는 첫 번째 열에 있습니다. 행의 네 글자를 보고 대문자 "K"와 일치하는 소문자에 동그라미를 치십시오.

K	p	h	(k)	q
K	(k)	f	b	l
K	f	b	d	(k)
K	h	(k)	p	l

 Directions: The lowercase letter "k" is in the first column. Look at the four letters in the row and circle the uppercase letter that matches the lowercase letter "k."
지도: 소문자 "k"는 첫 번째 열에 있습니다. 행의 네 글자를 보고 소문자 "k"와 일치하는 대문자에 동그라미를 치세요.

k	B	(K)	N	L
k	(K)	P	L	B
k	B	X	(K)	C
k	P	G	L	(K)

Name: _____   Date: ___/__/____   Score: _____

Appendix 11.0

Letter Recognition K/k

Uppercase and Lowercase Letter

✓ Lesson Check Point

Directions: Read each target word. Read the words in the row and circle the word that begins with a different letter.
지도: 각 대상 단어를 읽으십시오. 행에 있는 단어를 읽고 다른 문자로시작하는 단어에 동그라미를 치십시오.

Target Words				
1. keep	kale	kedge	(heal)	knoll
2. kick	(laugh)	knot	kid	ketch
3. knight	karts	(home)	kept	kick
4. know	kill	(bald)	kind	keel
5. keys	(down)	knock	keg	knob

Directions: Read the words in the four boxes. Circle two words that start with the uppercase and lowercase letter "k."
지도: 네 개의 상자에 있는 단어를 읽으십시오. 대문자와 소문자 "k"로 시작하는 두 단어에 동그라미를 치십시오.

light	house
(Kale)	(keep)

From	(Keen)
Right	(kick)

(key)	blue
low	(Kept)

(Knock)	Bold
(kid)	laugh

Rose	(kind)
(Knit)	bay

(know)	(Karts)
West	team

Learn To Read English With Directions In Korean   269   Copyrighted Material

Classwork

 Name: _____ Date: ___/___/_____ Score: _____

Appendix 12.0

Introduction of the Letter L/l

✓ Lesson Check Point

 Directions: Circle the correct letter "l" pair: uppercase and lowercase letters.
지도: 올바른 문자"l" 쌍에 동그라미를 치십시오: 대문자와 소문자.

    Lb   Kl   (lL)   lH   lJ

 Directions: The uppercase letter "L" is in the first column. Look at the four letters in the row and circle the lowercase letter that matches the uppercase letter "L."
지도: 대문자"L"는 첫 번째 열에 있습니다. 행의 네 글자를 보고 대문자 "L"와 일치하는 소문자에 동그라미를 치십시오.

L	h	(l)	f	b
L	(l)	k	y	p
L	f	b	(l)	d
L	h	b	k	(l)

 Directions: The lowercase letter "l" is in the first column. Look at the four letters in the row and circle the uppercase letter that matches the lowercase letter "l."
지도: 소문자"l"는 첫 번째 열에 있습니다. 행의 네 글자를 보고 소문자 "l"와 일치하는 대문자에 동그라미를 치세요.

l	B	K	(L)	D
l	H	F	K	(L)
l	(L)	H	C	P
l	D	(L)	V	H

Name: _____   Date: ___/___/_____   Score: _____

Appendix 12.0

Letter Recognition L/l

Uppercase and Lowercase Letter

✓ Lesson Check Point

 Directions: Read each target word. Read the words in the row and circle the word that begins with a different letter.
지도: 각 대상 단어를 읽으십시오. 행에 있는 단어를 읽고 다른 문자로 시작하는 단어에 동그라미를 치십시오.

Target Words				
1. love	lace	(home)	low	lent
2. load	(tree)	laugh	lid	loaf
3. last	lip	lease	lapse	(mail)
4. learn	(hope)	lark	least	lungs
5. large	limbs	life	lamps	(boats)

 Directions: Read the words in the four boxes. Circle two words that start with the uppercase and lowercase letter "l."
지도: 네 개의 상자에 있는 단어를 읽으십시오. 대문자와 소문자 "l"로 시작하는 두 단어에 동그라미를 치십시오.

| teach | found |
| (lake) | (Leave) |

| branch | (League) |
| touch | (loud) |

| (leech) | Trees |
| dreams | (Lamb) |

| (Lounge) | (leash) |
| Bold | keeps |

| Young | (Lean) |
| (lame) | drawn |

| (lime) | Friends |
| (Lawn) | deep |

Learn To Read English With Directions In Korean   271   Copyrighted Material

Classwork

 Name: _____   Date:___/___/_____   Score:_____

Appendix 13.0

Introduction of the Letter M/m

✓ Lesson Check Point

 Directions: Circle the correct letter "m" pair: uppercase and lowercase letters.
지도: 올바른 문자"m" 쌍에 동그라미를 치십시오: 대문자와 소문자.

    Mn   Nm   Um   (Mm)   Mw

 Directions: The uppercase letter "M" is in the first column. Look at the four letters in the row and circle the lowercase letter that matches the uppercase letter "M."
지도: 대문자"M"는 첫 번째 열에 있습니다. 행의 네 글자를 보고 대문자 "M"와 일치하는 소문자에 동그라미를 치십시오.

M	(m)	n	v	w
M	v	(m)	w	s
M	n	x	p	(m)
M	(m)	v	n	j

 Directions: The lowercase letter "m" is in the first column. Look at the four letters in the row and circle the uppercase letter that matches the lowercase letter "m."
지도: 소문자"m"는 첫 번째 열에 있습니다. 행의 네 글자를 보고 소문자 "m"와 일치하는 대문자에 동그라미를 치세요.

m	N	V	Z	(M)
m	K	(M)	N	U
m	W	V	(M)	X
m	N	(M)	V	W

Name: _____ Date:___/___/_____ Score:_____

Appendix 13.0

Letter Recognition M/m

Uppercase and Lowercase Letter

✓ Lesson Check Point

Directions: Read each target word. Read the words in the row and circle the word that begins with a different letter.
지도: 각 대상 단어를 읽으십시오. 행에 있는 단어를 읽고 다른 문자로시작하는 단어에 동그라미를 치십시오.

Target Words				
1. maid	(nose)	mud	mock	mince
2. moon	make	mixed	(used)	mouth
3. mint	(went)	moist	map	musk
4. meal	meat	(need)	mole	Maine
5. must	mix	mail	moan	(under)

Directions: Read the words in the four boxes. Circle two words that start with the uppercase and lowercase letter "m."
지도: 네 개의 상자에 있는 단어를 읽으십시오. 대문자와 소문자"m"로 시작하는 두 단어에 동그라미를 치십시오.

none	(Made)
wind	(mood)

nod	vase
(Miss)	mean

night	(Mouse)
(might)	wage

(mold)	(Much)
Whose	Noun

(mild)	noise
watch	(Mane)

(mumps)	voice
(Moat)	nail

Learn To Read English With Directions In Korean

Classwork

 Name: _____ Date: ___/___/_____ Score: _____

Appendix 14.0

Introduction of the Letter N/n

✓ **Lesson Check Point**

 Directions: Circle the correct letter "n" pair: uppercase and lowercase letters.
지도: 올바른 문자"n" 쌍에 동그라미를 치십시오: 대문자와 소문자.

    nM   (nN)   wN   Nu   Wn

 Directions: The uppercase letter "N" is in the first column. Look at the four letters in the row and circle the lowercase letter that matches the uppercase letter "N."
지도: 대문자"N"는 첫 번째 열에 있습니다. 행의 네 글자를 보고 대문자 "N"와 일치하는 소문자에 동그라미를 치십시오.

N	w	m	(n)	v
N	(n)	v	w	x
N	m	b	(n)	w
N	v	(n)	c	x

 Directions: The lowercase letter "n" is in the first column. Look at the four letters in the row and circle the uppercase letter that matches the lowercase letter "n."
지도: 소문자"n"는 첫 번째 열에 있습니다. 행의 네 글자를 보고 소문자 "n"와 일치하는 대문자에 동그라미를 치세요.

n	S	M	(N)	X
n	C	V	M	(N)
n	(N)	M	Z	V
n	M	(N)	X	W

Name: _____ Date:__/__/_____ Score:_____

Appendix 14.0

Letter Recognition N/n

Uppercase and Lowercase Letter

✓ Lesson Check Point

 Directions: Read each target word. Read the words in the row and circle the word that begins with a different letter.
지도: 각 대상 단어를 읽으십시오. 행에 있는 단어를 읽고 다른 문자로시작하는 단어에 동그라미를 치십시오.

Target Words				
1. neck	nine	news	(milk)	next
2. noon	(used)	neat	notch	niche
3. name	nice	note	(wrong)	nip
4. numb	none	new	nod	(male)
5. notice	nerve	(unto)	nuke	Nile

 Directions: Read the words in the four boxes. Circle two words that start with the uppercase and lowercase letter "n."
지도: 네 개의 상자에 있는 단어를 읽으십시오. 대문자와 소문자 "n"로 시작하는 두 단어에 동그라미를 치십시오.

Mail	van
(Nile)	(nail)

(Noise)	under
wine	(noon)

flag	(Nine)
miss	(nice)

(Noun)	(note)
word	Mouth

(night)	mind
(Next)	set

(news)	win
united	(Nod)

Classwork

 Name: _____ Date:___/___/_____ Score: _____

Appendix 15.0

Introduction of the Letter O/o

✓ **Lesson Check Point**

 Directions: Circle the correct letter "o" pair: uppercase and lowercase letters.
지도: 올바른 문자"o" 쌍에 동그라미를 치십시오: 대문자와 소문자.

    Oc   (oO)   uO   pO   qO

 Directions: The uppercase letter "O" is in the first column. Look at the four letters in the row and circle the lowercase letter that matches the uppercase letter "O."
지도: 대문자"O"는 첫 번째 열에 있습니다. 행의 네 글자를 보고 대문자 "O"와 일치하는 소문자에 동그라미를 치십시오.

O	s	p	g	(o)
O	c	(o)	b	j
O	q	d	c	(o)
O	(o)	g	q	h

 Directions: The lowercase letter "o" is in the first column. Look at the four letters in the row and circle the uppercase letter that matches the lowercase letter "o."
지도: 소문자"o"는 첫 번째 열에 있습니다. 행의 네 글자를 보고 소문자 "o"와 일치하는 대문자에 동그라미를 치세요.

o	Q	C	G	(O)
o	(O)	D	U	R
o	C	B	(O)	D
o	G	(O)	C	E

Name: _____ Date:___/___/_____ Score:_____

Appendix 16.0

Introduction of the Letter P/p

✓ **Lesson Check Point**

 Directions: Circle the correct letter "p" pair: uppercase and lowercase letters.
지도: 올바른 문자"p" 쌍에 동그라미를 치십시오: 대문자와 소문자.

(Pp)　　　　Bp　　　　Dp　　　　Pg　　　　Fp

 Directions: The uppercase letter "P" is in the first column. Look at the four letters in the row and circle the lowercase letter that matches the uppercase letter "P."
지도: 대문자"P"는 첫 번째 열에 있습니다. 행의 네 글자를 보고 대문자 "P"와 일치하는 소문자에 동그라미를 치십시오.

P	(p)	q	b	d
P	b	f	(p)	q
P	h	(p)	b	f
P	q	d	s	(p)

 Directions: The lowercase letter "p" is in the first column. Look at the four letters in the row and circle the uppercase letter that matches the lowercase letter "p."
지도: 소문자"p"는 첫 번째 열에 있습니다. 행의 네 글자를 보고 소문자 "p"와 일치하는 대문자에 동그라미를 치세요.

p	Q	(P)	B	F
p	H	B	D	(P)
p	F	(P)	S	D
p	(P)	F	D	B

Learn To Read English With Directions In Korean

Classwork

 Name: _____ Date: ___/___/_____ Score: _____

Appendix 16.0

Letter Recognition P/p

Uppercase and Lowercase Letter

✓ **Lesson Check Point**

 Directions: Read each target word. Read the words in the row and circle the word that begins with a different letter.
지도: 각 대상 단어를 읽으십시오. 행에 있는 단어를 읽고 다른 문자로 시작하는 단어에 동그라미를 치십시오.

Target Words				
1. pitch	pack	(grow)	pound	purse
2. plots	(bind)	plush	proud	plight
3. peace	plate	page	(quest)	prowl
4. pale	(good)	plant	poor	pull
5. punch	prude	(quick)	pike	pool

 Directions: Read the words in the four boxes. Circle two words that start with the uppercase and lowercase letter "p."
지도: 네 개의 상자에 있는 단어를 읽으십시오. 대문자와 소문자 "p"로 시작하는 두 단어에 동그라미를 치십시오.

(Praise)	quaint		(point)	(Prince)		grew	(purse)
youth	(phase)		quart	group		(Prime)	quiet

(Pink)	quick		jump	quite		young	(peach)
(place)	jam		(Paid)	(peace)		guess	(Port)

Name: _____ Date: ___/___/_____ Score: _____

Appendix 17.0

Introduction of the Letter Q/q

✓ **Lesson Check Point**

 Directions: Circle the correct letter "q" pair: uppercase and lowercase letters.
지도: 올바른 문자"q" 쌍에 동그라미를 치십시오: 대문자와 소문자.

Qd　　　　Gq　　　　Oq　　　　(qQ)　　　　Qp

 Directions: The uppercase letter "Q" is in the first column. Look at the four letters in the row and circle the lowercase letter that matches the uppercase letter "Q."
지도: 대문자"Q"는 첫 번째 열에 있습니다. 행의 네 글자를 보고 대문자 "Q"와 일치하는 소문자에 동그라미를 치십시오.

Q	g	h	p	(q)
Q	(q)	j	y	b
Q	p	(q)	b	d
Q	y	p	(q)	b

 Directions: The lowercase letter "q" is in the first column. Look at the four letters in the row and circle the uppercase letter that matches the lowercase letter "q."
지도: 소문자"q"는 첫 번째 열에 있습니다. 행의 네 글자를 보고 소문자 "q"와 일치하는 대문자에 동그라미를 치세요.

q	D	O	(Q)	P
q	(Q)	A	D	O
q	O	C	G	(Q)
q	G	(Q)	C	O

Learn To Read English With Directions In Korean

Classwork

Name: _____ Date: ___/___/_____ Score: _____

Appendix 17.0

Letter Recognition Q/q

Uppercase and Lowercase Letter

✓ Lesson Check Point

Directions: Read each target word. Read the words in the row and circle the word that begins with a different letter.

지도: 각 대상 단어를 읽으십시오. 행에 있는 단어를 읽고 다른 문자로시작하는 단어에 동그라미를 치십시오.

Target Words				
1. quack	quaint	quick	(please)	quiz
2. quilt	(guess)	quip	quire	quote
3. quirt	quirk	(young)	quit	quartz
4. quench	quite	quiet	(jump)	quince
5. quake	quota	quail	quest	(guest)

Directions: Read the words in the four boxes. Circle two words that start with the uppercase and lowercase letter "q."

지도: 네 개의 상자에 있는 단어를 읽으십시오. 대문자와 소문자"q"로 시작하는 두 단어에 동그라미를 치십시오.

pajamas	(Qualm)		jacket	peanut		joint	(quicken)
(quality)	Orchid		(quarrel)	(Quarter)		oxygen	(Quartz)

(quest)	jumper		(quote)	(Quotient)		(quick)	painter
(Quiver)	yours		picture	Ocean		young	(Quebec)

Learn To Read English With Directions In Korean

Name: _____ Date: ___/___/_____ Score: _____

Appendix 18.0

Introduction of the Letter R/r

✓ **Lesson Check Point**

 Directions: Circle the correct letter "r" pair: uppercase and lowercase letters.
지도: 올바른 문자"r" 쌍에 동그라미를 치십시오: 대문자와 소문자.

Rz   (rR)   jR   rE   Fr

 Directions: The uppercase letter "R" is in the first column. Look at the four letters in the row and circle the lowercase letter that matches the uppercase letter "R."
지도: 대문자"R"는 첫 번째 열에 있습니다. 행의 네 글자를 보고 대문자 "R"와 일치하는 소문자에 동그라미를 치십시오.

R	x	ⓡ	v	u
R	ⓡ	x	z	c
R	b	h	c	ⓡ
R	n	z	ⓡ	s

 Directions: The lowercase letter "r" is in the first column. Look at the four letters in the row and circle the uppercase letter that matches the lowercase letter "r."
지도: 소문자"r"는 첫 번째 열에 있습니다. 행의 네 글자를 보고 소문자 "r"와 일치하는 대문자에 동그라미를 치세요.

r	Y	U	Ⓡ	Z
r	Ⓡ	H	C	M
r	U	N	F	Ⓡ
r	M	Ⓡ	D	O

Learn To Read English With Directions In Korean

Classwork

Name: _____ Date: ___/___/_____ Score: _____

Appendix 18.0

Letter Recognition R/r

Uppercase and Lowercase Letter

✓ Lesson Check Point

Directions: Read each target word. Read the words in the row and circle the word that begins with a different letter.

지도: 각 대상 단어를 읽으십시오. 행에 있는 단어를 읽고 다른 문자로시 작하는 단어에 동그라미를 치십시오.

Target Words				
1. race	roach	reel	(match)	rains
2. rode	(nurse)	range	roam	rule
3. rinse	ranch	(mouse)	robe	reed
4. raise	rend	rock	rank	(cease)
5. ripping	(cards)	read	rack	rope

Directions: Read the words in the four boxes. Circle two words that start with the uppercase and lowercase letter "r."

지도: 네 개의 상자에 있는 단어를 읽으십시오. 대문자와 소문자 "r"로 시작하는 두 단어에 동그라미를 치십시오.

(rate)	moose		(rob)	(Rave)		Part	(Roar)
Piece	(Rice)		nose	mother		mouse	(rhythm)

Pat	maple		team	Price		dream	(Room)
(roost)	(Rat)		(rope)	(Rich)		(ramp)	neck

Name: _____   Date: ___/___/_____   Score: _____

Appendix 19.0

Introduction of the Letter S/s

✓ **Lesson Check Point**

 Directions: Circle the correct letter "s" pair: uppercase and lowercase letters.
지도: 올바른 문자"s" 쌍에 동그라미를 치십시오: 대문자와 소문자.

    sA   sB   Zs   Cs   (sS)

 Directions: The uppercase letter "S" is in the first column. Look at the four letters in the row and circle the lowercase letter that matches the uppercase letter "S."
지도: 대문자"S"는 첫 번째 열에 있습니다. 행의 네 글자를 보고 대문자 "S"와 일치하는 소문자에 동그라미를 치십시오.

S	c	o	d	(s)
S	(s)	c	u	o
S	o	a	(s)	c
S	u	(s)	c	o

 Directions: The lowercase letter "s" is in the first column. Look at the four letters in the row and circle the uppercase letter that matches the lowercase letter "s."
지도: 소문자"s"는 첫 번째 열에 있습니다. 행의 네 글자를 보고 소문자 "s"와 일치하는 대문자에 동그라미를 치세요.

s	G	(S)	O	C
s	Q	C	U	(S)
s	(S)	U	O	C
s	Z	Q	(S)	V

Classwork

 Name: _____ Date:___/___/_____ Score: _____

Appendix 19.0

Letter Recognition S/s

Uppercase and Lowercase Letter

✓ Lesson Check Point

 Directions: Read each target word. Read the words in the row and circle the word that begins with a different letter.
지도: 각 대상 단어를 읽으십시오. 행에 있는 단어를 읽고 다른 문자로시작하는 단어에 동그라미를 치십시오.

Target Words				
1. smart	soft	(chart)	smith	shop
2. sail	(opens)	saw	skit	soil
3. skill	smooth	shoot	seat	(van)
4. source	soup	side	(zero)	sight
5. sky	snooze	(cake)	short	smell

 Directions: Read the words in the four boxes. Circle two words that start with the uppercase and lowercase letter "s."
지도: 네 개의 상자에 있는 단어를 읽으십시오. 대문자와 소문자"s"로 시작하는 두 단어에 동그라미를 치십시오.

zero	(Six)		(Shield)	cup		(shame)	(Said)
(shore)	cone		(sink)	zoo		zap	clean

Cross	(slurp)		none	child		camp	(song)
(Shine)	win		(soap)	(Snail)		zebra	(Shake)

Learn To Read English With Directions In Korean

Name: _____ Date:___/___/_____ Score:_____

Appendix 20.0

Introduction of the Letter T/t

✓ **Lesson Check Point**

 Directions: Circle the correct letter "t" pair: uppercase and lowercase letters.
지도: 올바른 문자"s" 쌍에 동그라미를 치십시오: 대문자와 소문자.

    Tf   tE   (Tt)   tF   iT

 Directions: The uppercase letter "T" is in the first column. Look at the four letters in the row and circle the lowercase letter that matches the uppercase letter "T."
지도: 대문자"T"는 첫 번째 열에 있습니다. 행의 네 글자를 보고 대문자 "T"와 일치하는 소문자에 동그라미를 치십시오.

T	(t)	h	f	d
T	b	f	(t)	h
T	l	(t)	b	f
T	h	d	b	(t)

 Directions: The lowercase letter "t" is in the first column. Look at the four letters in the row and circle the uppercase letter that matches the lowercase letter "t."
지도: 소문자"t"는 첫 번째 열에 있습니다. 행의 네 글자를 보고 소문자 "t"와 일치하는 대문자에 동그라미를 치세요.

t	F	(T)	H	E
t	(T)	B	E	F
t	H	B	(T)	Y
t	R	F	S	(T)

Learn To Read English With Directions In Korean

Classwork

 Name: _____ Date: ___/___/_____ Score: _____

Appendix 20.0

Letter Recognition T/t

Uppercase and Lowercase Letter

✓ Lesson Check Point

 Directions: Read each target word. Read the words in the row and circle the word that begins with a different letter.

지도: 각 대상 단어를 읽으십시오. 행에 있는 단어를 읽고 다른 문자로시작하는 단어에 동그라미를 치십시오.

Target Words				
1. twin	that	(day)	trust	talk
2. tooth	tight	team	top	(face)
3. tempt	(key)	time	trash	tweed
4. torch	though	their	temp	(live)
5. treat	thick	twice	(herd)	thief

 Directions: Read the words in the four boxes. Circle two words that start with the uppercase and lowercase letter "t."

지도: 네 개의 상자에 있는 단어를 읽으십시오. 대문자와 소문자"t"로 시작하는 두 단어에 동그라미를 치십시오.

Floor	(Trade)
(tear)	draw

horses	(toil)
lunch	(Track)

(tease)	keep
(Toll)	load

(Text)	Pie
(troop)	Joy

Egg	lone
(theme)	(Trip)

(taste)	pants
beach	(Think)

Learn To Read English With Directions In Korean

Name: _____ Date: ___/___/_____ Score: _____

Appendix 21.0

Introduction of the Letter U/u

✓ **Lesson Check Point**

 Directions: Circle the correct letter "u" pair: uppercase and lowercase letters.
지도: 올바른 문자"u" 쌍에 동그라미를 치십시오: 대문자와 소문자.。

   Yu   Gu   Uv   Au

 Directions: The uppercase letter "U" is in the first column. Look at the four letters in the row and circle the lowercase letter that matches the uppercase letter "U."
지도: 대문자"U"는 첫 번째 열에 있습니다. 행의 네 글자를 보고 대문자 "U"와 일치하는 소문자에 동그라미를 치십시오.

U	u	v	c	y
U	h	x	u	z
U	j	b	v	u
U	s	u	g	a

 Directions: The lowercase letter "u" is in the first column. Look at the four letters in the row and circle the uppercase letter that matches the lowercase letter "u."
지도: 소문자"u"는 첫 번째 열에 있습니다. 행의 네 글자를 보고 소문자 "u"와 일치하는 대문자에 동그라미를 치세요.

u	Y	T	U	Z
u	U	B	N	Y
u	C	Q	U	D
u	J	V	G	U

Classwork

 Name: _____ Date: ___/___/_____ Score: _____

Appendix 22.0

Introduction of the Letter V/v

✓ **Lesson Check Point**

 Directions: Circle the correct letter "v" pair: uppercase and lowercase letters.
지도: 올바른 문자"v" 쌍에 동그라미를 치십시오: 대문자와 소문자.

vW　　　　　Vu　　　　　Cv　　　　　(Vv)　　　　　Wv

 Directions: The uppercase letter "V" is in the first column. Look at the four letters in the row and circle the lowercase letter that matches the uppercase letter "V."
지도: 대문자"V"는 첫 번째 열에 있습니다. 행의 네 글자를 보고 대문자 "V"와 일치하는 소문자에 동그라미를 치십시오.

V	w	(v)	x	y
V	y	w	n	(v)
V	(v)	x	y	u
V	x	z	(v)	w

 Directions: The lowercase letter "v" is in the first column. Look at the four letters in the row and circle the uppercase letter that matches the lowercase letter "v."
지도: 소문자"v"는 첫 번째 열에 있습니다. 행의 네 글자를 보고 소문자 "v"와 일치하는 대문자에 동그라미를 치세요.

v	X	Z	(V)	Y
v	Y	W	X	(V)
v	(V)	Y	N	M
v	W	(V)	X	C

Name: _____ Date:___/___/_____ Score:_____

Appendix 22.0

Letter Recognition V/v

Uppercase and Lowercase Letter

✓ Lesson Check Point

Directions: Read each target word. Read the words in the row and circle the word that begins with a different letter.
지도: 각 대상 단어를 읽으십시오. 행에 있는 단어를 읽고 다른 문자로시작하는 단어에 동그라미를 치십시오.

Target Words				
1. voice	volt	(wool)	vase	verse
2. verb	vest	vow	vogue	(used)
3. vain	(west)	veil	vault	vine
4. view	void	(mouse)	versed	vile
5. vote	vex	voiced	(wig)	vein

Directions: Read the words in the four boxes. Circle two words that start with the uppercase and lowercase letter "v."
지도: 네 개의 상자에 있는 단어를 읽으십시오. 대문자와 소문자"v"로 시작하는 두 단어에 동그라미를 치십시오.

skill	(vouch)
(Vamp)	Wrote

(vague)	(Van)
rose	name

whiz	(valve)
mail	(Vice)

(Vent)	cove
Weep	(verge)

(vane)	(Very)
must	goat

(Visit)	card
(vet)	West

Learn To Read English With Directions In Korean

Classwork

 Name: _____ Date:___/___/_____ Score:_____

Appendix 23.0

Introduction of the Letter W/w

✓ **Lesson Check Point**

 Directions: Circle the correct letter "w" pair: uppercase and lowercase letters.
지도: 올바른 문자"w" 쌍에 동그라미를 치십시오: 대문자와 소문자.

wU   (Ww)   Xw   Vw   Wv

 Directions: The uppercase letter "W" is in the first column. Look at the four letters in the row and circle the lowercase letter that matches the uppercase letter "W."
지도: 대문자"W"는 첫 번째 열에 있습니다. 행의 네 글자를 보고 대문자 "W"와 일치하는 소문자에 동그라미를 치십시오.

W	x	(w)	v	z
W	v	z	(w)	y
W	(w)	y	v	m
W	n	v	y	(w)

 Directions: The lowercase letter "w" is in the first column. Look at the four letters in the row and circle the uppercase letter that matches the lowercase letter "w."
지도: 소문자"w"는 첫 번째 열에 있습니다. 행의 네 글자를 보고 소문자 "w"와 일치하는 대문자에 동그라미를 치세요.

w	V	(W)	Y	M
w	X	Y	V	(W)
w	(W)	V	X	M
w	Y	F	(W)	X

Name: _____ Date: ___/___/_____ Score: _____

Appendix 23.0

Letter Recognition W/w

Uppercase and Lowercase Letter

✓ Lesson Check Point

Directions: Read each target word. Read the words in the row and circle the word that begins with a different letter.
지도: 각 대상 단어를 읽으십시오. 행에 있는 단어를 읽고 다른 문자로 시작하는 단어에 동그라미를 치십시오.

Target Words				
1. wind	west	(vacuum)	whole	waste
2. wrote	(night)	wink	wolf	wish
3. which	wrap	whom	were	(vessel)
4. wept	whale	(card)	whose	wide
5. wash	wrench	watch	word	(zebra)

Directions: Read the words in the four boxes. Circle two words that start with the uppercase and lowercase letter "w."
지도: 네 개의 상자에 있는 단어를 읽으십시오. 대문자와 소문자 "w"로 시작하는 두 단어에 동그라미를 치십시오.

crow	(Work)		(wheat)	nerve		Village	cars
visitor	(wave)		zoom	(Wax)		(wild)	(Wheel)

(will)	x-rays		(Worth)	(when)		corn	(ways)
(Would)	Nile		violet	Never		(Wine)	vintage

Classwork

 Name: _____ Date: ___/___/_____ Score: _____

Appendix 24.0

Introduction of the Letter X/x

✓ **Lesson Check Point**

 Directions: Circle the correct letter "x" pair: uppercase and lowercase letters.
지도: 올바른 문자"x" 쌍에 동그라미를 치십시오: 대문자와 소문자.

Xw xY (xX) Sx Kx

 Directions: The uppercase letter "X" is in the first column. Look at the four letters in the row and circle the lowercase letter that matches the uppercase letter "X."
지도: 대문자"X"는 첫 번째 열에 있습니다. 행의 네 글자를 보고 대문자 "X"와 일치하는 소문자에 동그라미를 치십시오.

X	k	(x)	y	z
X	v	w	(x)	m
X	(x)	z	e	s
X	v	z	h	(x)

 Directions: The lowercase letter "x" is in the first column. Look at the four letters in the row and circle the uppercase letter that matches the lowercase letter "x."
지도: 소문자"x"는 첫 번째 열에 있습니다. 행의 네 글자를 보고 소문자 "x"와 일치하는 대문자에 동그라미를 치세요.

x	K	(X)	Z	M
x	W	K	V	(X)
x	(X)	M	K	Y
x	V	Y	(X)	Z

Name: _____ Date: ___/___/_____ Score: _____

Appendix 24.0

Letter Recognition X/x

Uppercase and Lowercase Letter

✓ Lesson Check Point

Directions: Read each target word. Read the words in the row and circle the word that does not contain a letter "x."
지도: 각 대상 단어를 읽으십시오. 행에 있는 단어를 읽고 문자"x"가 포함되지 않은 단어에 동그라미를 치십시오.

Target Words				
1. fix	wax	excite	(sing)	flax
2. box	taxes	expo	foxes	(cold)
3. flex	ox	(night)	taxi	exalt
4. exam	toxin	axle	sixty	(loving)
5. text	vex	(young)	next	coax

Directions: Read the words in the four boxes. Circle two words that start with the uppercase and lowercase letter "x."
지도: 네 개의 상자에 있는 단어를 읽으십시오. 대문자와 소문자"x"로 시작하는 두 단어에 동그라미를 치십시오.

vogue	(xylems)
(Xanthine)	kid

youth	voiced
(xanthone)	(Xenograft)

kept	(Xanthous)
one	(x-axis)

(xylem)	voiced
(Xerox)	keys

(Xyster)	know
yes	(xylan)

(Xylene)	(xylose)
moose	view

Learn To Read English With Directions In Korean

Classwork

 Name: _____ Date: ___/___/_____ Score: _____

Appendix 25.0

Introduction of the Letter Y/y

✓ **Lesson Check Point**

 Directions: Circle the correct letter "y" pair: uppercase and lowercase letters.
지도: 올바른 문자"y" 쌍에 동그라미를 치십시오: 대문자와 소문자.

Yx   (yY)   Yz   Ky   Vy

 Directions: The uppercase letter "Y" is in the first column. Look at the four letters in the row and circle the lowercase letter that matches the uppercase letter "Y."
지도: 대문자"Y"는 첫 번째 열에 있습니다. 행의 네 글자를 보고 대문자 "Y"와 일치하는 소문자에 동그라미를 치십시오.

Y	v	(y)	b	x
Y	x	z	(y)	u
Y	(y)	x	z	w
Y	x	z	v	(y)

 Directions: The lowercase letter "y" is in the first column. Look at the four letters in the row and circle the uppercase letter that matches the lowercase letter "y."
지도: 소문자"y"는 첫 번째 열에 있습니다. 행의 네 글자를 보고 소문자 "y"와 일치하는 대문자에 동그라미를 치세요.

y	V	X	Z	(Y)
y	(Y)	V	X	Z
y	W	(Y)	X	M
y	U	M	(Y)	X

Name: _____ Date: ___/___/_____ Score: _____

Appendix 25.0

Letter Recognition Y/y

Uppercase and Lowercase Letter

✓ Lesson Check Point

Directions: Read each target word. Read the words in the row and circle the word that begins with a different letter.
지도: 각 대상 단어를 읽으십시오. 행에 있는 단어를 읽고 다른 문자로 시작하는 단어에 동그라미를 치십시오.

Target Words				
1. yield	(grown)	yogurt	yam	yeast
2. yacht	(jeep)	yolk	yucca	yawn
3. yuppie	yodel	young	(quick)	your
4. yellow	yelp	(please)	yummy	yoga
5. yourself	yank	yes	yo-yo	(game)

Directions: Read the words in the four boxes. Circle two words that start with the uppercase and lowercase letter "y."
지도: 네 개의 상자에 있는 단어를 읽으십시오. 대문자와 소문자"y"로 시작하는 두 단어에 동그라미를 치십시오.

gum	jump	(Yarn)	quill	jet	(You)
(yelp)	(Youth)	paint	(yells)	globe	(yaw)

jog	(yak)	(Yet)	(yams)	(yawn)	June
(Year)	grace	judge	glow	(Yeast)	peach

Classwork

 Name: _____ Date: ___/___/_____ Score: _____

Appendix 26.0

Introduction of the Letter Z/z

✓ **Lesson Check Point**

 Directions: Circle the correct letter "z" pair: uppercase and lowercase letters.
지도: 올바른 문자"z" 쌍에 동그라미를 치십시오: 대문자와 소문자.

(zZ)   Nz   Zn   zM   zA

 Directions: The uppercase letter "Z" is in the first column. Look at the four letters in the row and circle the lowercase letter that matches the uppercase letter "Z."
지도: 대문자"Z"는 첫 번째 열에 있습니다. 행의 네 글자를 보고 대문자 "Z"와 일치하는 소문자에 동그라미를 치십시오.

Z	n	x	(z)	t
Z	v	(z)	x	w
Z	m	w	s	(z)
Z	(z)	v	w	n

 Directions: The lowercase letter "z" is in the first column. Look at the four letters in the row and circle the uppercase letter that matches the lowercase letter "z."
지도: 소문자"z"는 첫 번째 열에 있습니다. 행의 네 글자를 보고 소문자 "z"와 일치하는 대문자에 동그라미를 치세요.

z	B	V	(Z)	N
z	W	(Z)	X	U
z	(Z)	S	W	V
z	A	N	X	(Z)

Name: _____ Date: ___/__/____ Score: _____

Appendix 26.0

Letter Recognition Z/z

Uppercase and Lowercase Letter

✓ **Lesson Check Point**

Directions: Read each target word. Read the words in the row and circle the word that begins with a different letter.
지도: 각 대상 단어를 읽으십시오. 행에 있는 단어를 읽고 다른 문자로 시작하는 단어에 동그라미를 치십시오.

Target Words				
1. zebu	zap	zebra	(cage)	zoo
2. zones	(seals)	zany	zeal	zest
3. zip	zing	zero	zinc	(flesh)
4. Zhan	zoom	(moon)	ziti	zonal
5. zest	(sung)	zone	zoos	zebra

Directions: Read the words in the four boxes. Circle two words that start with the uppercase and lowercase letter "z."
지도: 네 개의 상자에 있는 단어를 읽으십시오. 대문자와 소문자 "z"로 시작하는 두 단어에 동그라미를 치십시오.

cents	(Zeta)
(zing)	sea

mix	(zap)
(Zip)	sick

(Zoom)	(zit)
index	wind

(zinc)	remix
(Zipper)	cents

nice	Plant
(ziti)	(Zone)

rest	(Zoo)
eggs	(zoom)

Learn To Read English With Directions In Korean

Classwork

**Your Next Step:
Learn To Read English Vowels With Directions In Korean**

www.ingramcontent.com/pod-product-compliance
Lightning Source LLC
Chambersburg PA
CBHW080800300426
44114CB00020B/2773